PRAISE FOR *CUT ADRIFT*

"In this powerful book, Marianne Cooper weaves together carefully researched data about growing economic insecurity and gripping stories of families coping with these trends. Cooper has written an intimate look into what families are up against and the strategies they use to navigate the challenges they face. *Cut Adrift* provides a compelling examination of the pressing economic issues of our time."

Sheryl Sandberg, COO, Facebook and Founder, LeanIn.org

"*Cut Adrift* is one of the best books I have read in a long time. Cooper's study of families from different social classes shows how worries about financial security penetrate the rhythm of daily life in all of the families (albeit in different ways). The book has impressive ethnographic detail, clarity of the analysis, and originality. My students loved it. Highly recommended!"

Annette Lareau, University of Pennsylvania, President, American Sociological Association

"Talking with moms at soccer matches, accompanying anxious shoppers at the mall, listening to news of a pink slip, Marianne Cooper takes an emotion-sensing stethoscope to the hearts of parents—from richest to poorest—in Silicon Valley, California. In an age of insecurity, Cooper finds that each family assigns a 'designated worrier' to manage anxiety about drawing to—or going over—the financial edge. This is a brilliant book and a must-read."

Arlie Hochschild, author of *The Second Shift, The Outsourced Self,* and *So How's the Family? and Other Essays*

"An important and insightful examination of family life during an economic downturn."

Vicki Smith, University of California, Davis, author of *Crossing the Great Divide: Worker Risk and Opportunity in the New Economy*

"A poignant, powerful story of how families are coping with rampant economic insecurity."

Allison Pugh, University of Virginia, author of *Longing and Belonging: Parents, Children, and Consumer Culture*

The publisher gratefully acknowledges the generous support of Robert J. Nelson and Monica C. Heredia as members of the Literati Circle of the University of California Press Foundation.

Cut Adrift

Cut Adrift

FAMILIES IN INSECURE TIMES

Marianne Cooper

Mariane Cooper (signature)

UNIVERSITY OF CALIFORNIA PRESS

Berkeley   *Los Angeles*   *London*

University of California Press, one of the most distinguished university presses in the United States, enriches lives around the world by advancing scholarship in the humanities, social sciences, and natural sciences. Its activities are supported by the UC Press Foundation and by philanthropic contributions from individuals and institutions. For more information, visit www.ucpress.edu.

University of California Press
Oakland, California

Library of Congress Cataloging-in-Publication Data

Cooper, Marianne.
    Cut adrift / Marianne Cooper.
        p.   cm.
    Includes bibliographical references and index.
    ISBN 978-0-520-27765-6 (cloth, alk. paper) — ISBN 978-0-520-27767-0
(pbk., alk. paper) — ISBN 978-0-520-95845-6 (electronic).
    1. Equality—United States.   2. United States—Social conditions—21st
century.   3. United States—Race relations.   I. Title.
HM821.C676   2014
305.800973'—dc23   2013041571

Manufactured in the United States of America

23   22   21   20   19   18   17   16   15   14
10   9   8   7   6   5   4   3   2   1

In keeping with a commitment to support environmentally responsible and sustainable printing practices, UC Press has printed this book on Natures Natural, a fiber that contains 30% post-consumer waste and meets the minimum requirements of ANSI/NISO Z39.48-1992 (R 1997) (*Permanence of Paper*).

Contents

Preface

Timothy J. Bowers, a sixty-two-year-old man in Ohio, struggled to find a good, stable job after the drug wholesale company for which he made deliveries closed. After a fruitless three-year search, he came up with a plan to get by until he was old enough to receive Social Security. After handing over his apartment keys to his landlady, he told her that he probably would not be back. He then walked a few blocks to a bank, went inside, handed a teller a stickup note, received $80, and then turned the money over to the bank's security guard and waited for the police to arrive and arrest him. At his trial, Bowers explained to the judge that with only minimum-wage jobs available to him, going to jail for three years would "suit me fine" since, upon his release from prison, he would be sixty-six years old and thus old enough to receive his full Social Security benefits.[1] In a *New York Times* article that satirically describes Bowers as "an honest-to-goodness visionary" in the realm of retirement planning, Bowers's attorney, Jeremy W. Dodgion, described Bowers's actions as a sign of the times, stating, "At his age, it was harder and harder to find a job with benefits, [so] he finally said, to hell with it."[2] After three years of barely getting by, of going without health care and sick leave, of worrying about where his next dollar would come from and with his future prospects bleak, Mr. Bowers decided that jail would be preferable to his life of insecurity. At his sentencing hearing a few weeks before his sixty-third birthday, the judge said, "I'm going to give you your birthday present" and proceeded to give Bowers exactly what he wanted: a three-year jail term at a minimum-security prison. As he handed down the decision, the judge said, "It's a pretty sad story when someone feels that's their only alternative."[3]

The upside-down logic of Mr. Bowers's actions illuminates key issues Americans now contend with as they attempt to create security in their lives. Over the past forty years, large-scale economic, employment, and political changes have come together to alter the means and manner by which many Americans build security. Gone are the days when security was achieved through long-term employment at a single company and when devotion to one's employer was rewarded by guarantees of a pension and lifetime health-care benefits. Gone are the days when a typical full-time worker could earn a wage upon which a family could comfortably live. Gone, too, is the assumption that being middle-class means having stability, opportunity, and prosperity. Now Americans are on their own to provide for their retirement, pay for some (or all) of their health care, and figure out how to cover the soaring costs of their children's college education. And they are faced with these tasks amid big increases in the cost of living and great uncertainty in the job market. In a nutshell, since the 1970s the responsibility for managing risk has shifted from the government and employers onto individuals and their families (think of the change from pensions to individual retirement accounts).

The shift in risk affects everyone, including men and women, rich and poor, young and old. As this book will show, however, the relationship that different groups of Americans have to this shift in risk is mediated by another major development: the increase in income and wealth inequality.

For a variety of reasons—from globalization to the rise of the knowledge economy to tax policies—America has pulled apart economically over the last several decades. Increasingly we have become a nation of "haves" and "have-nots." The rich have gotten richer. The middle class have stagnated or fallen behind. The working class have come to look a lot like the working poor. And the ranks of the poor have grown.

So although no one is completely immune to the shift in risk, because of large differences nowadays in terms of how much we earn, how much we can save, and the level of benefits we receive, we live in different risk environments. Consequently, if someone at the top loses her job, she might respond by drawing on her rainy day savings. If someone at the bottom, like Mr. Bowers, loses his job, he might respond by robbing a bank so he can go to jail.

Depending, then, on factors such as their earnings, educational background, or whether or not they have a job with benefits, Americans have responded to the transformations in risk and security in a variety of ways—from making contributions to their 401(k)s, to forgoing health insurance, to saving for their children's educations and going into debt. These responses are in part financial. But, as the case of Mr. Bowers makes clear, these responses have emotional dimensions, too. For what Mr. Bowers sought when he robbed the bank so he could go to jail wasn't simply room and board. What he also sought was emotional relief from his arduous three-year struggle to make ends meet.

It is doubtful that the first time it occurred to Mr. Bowers to go to jail that he immediately embraced this option as the best solution to his problems. Instead, he probably considered a variety of practical strategies and went through several emotional reactions as his situation unfolded. For example, when he was first laid off, he might have felt optimistic about his chances of landing another job. When he didn't find another good job, he probably began to feel anxious. To manage, he likely cut back on his purchases, tried to find part-time jobs, and tried to ignore his uneasiness so he didn't go crazy with worry. He may even have tried to buoy himself up by telling himself that things would get better. As his situation grew worse, he might have started praying to God for help. But maybe God didn't answer. We don't know exactly what Mr. Bowers went through. What we do know is that he eventually came to view going to jail as the best way to get by. In fact, he came to *feel* that a three-year jail sentence would not just be a relief, but that it would be the perfect birthday gift.

This book investigates how families manage in an uncertain world. It examines what we all must deal with, given recent major changes in risk and security, and it explores how fifty families in Silicon Valley, from rich to poor, have addressed these changes. It delves into what these families worry about, how they manage their worry, and how such issues are affected by how much money and education they have and to whom they are married.

By documenting how and why people in different circumstances have come to feel a certain way about their lives and futures, this book tells not just an economic story but a profoundly emotional one as well. For it is people's emotional responses—their feelings of happiness, sadness, anxiety, and dread; their anger toward or appreciation of a spouse during hard times; their equation of jail with a gift—that reveal how they cope with the insecure world that surrounds them.

Acknowledgments

I would like to express my heartfelt appreciation to the many people who have made this book possible.

I must begin by thanking all the families that participated in this study. Despite their work and family responsibilities, the members of these families generously gave me so much of their time and openly shared their thoughts and experiences with me. I am especially grateful to the families with whom I conducted in-depth ethnographic research for allowing me to peer so deeply inside their lives. My hope is that this book sheds light on their struggles.

My deepest thanks go to my advisor, Arlie Russell Hochschild, who chaired my dissertation upon which this book is based. From the start of my project, Arlie embraced it wholeheartedly. She generously spent time helping me refine my ideas and gently pushed me to dig deeper into the emotional realms of inequality and insecurity. She continually encouraged me, especially at times when I felt lost in my data and lost in the writing process, and she always provided wonderful commentary and feedback on my writing.

Arlie retired a few years ago, which gave me the honor of being one of her last students. I am grateful for everything she taught me about the power and the practice of sociology; for giving me a model to aspire to of how to do sociology with courage, creativity, and brilliance; and for showing me how to be a sociologist with compassion and heart.

Many people talked with me at length over a number of years about my project or took the time to provide extensive written feedback. Their analysis and reflections greatly improved this project. In particular, I would like to thank Vicki Smith, Barrie Thorne, Kim Voss, AnnaLee Saxenian, Leslie Bell, Karen Hansen, Anita Ilta Garey, and several anonymous reviewers for their insightful commentary. I would also like to thank Annette Lareau, whose enthusiasm for my project, feedback, and scholarly advice have been invaluable. My friend and colleague Allison Pugh deserves special thanks for reading and commenting upon almost every draft of this book. I am indebted to Allison for her thoughtful analysis, her unwavering encouragement, and her friendship.

Katherine Mooney and Karl Weber provided wonderful editorial assistance, and I am thankful for their guidance. And many thanks to Naomi Schneider at the University of California Press for believing in this book and waiting patiently for it.

I also want to thank C. J. Pascoe, Orit Avishai, and Natalie Boero, my dear friends and colleagues during my days at Berkeley, who sustained me during the many ups and down of graduate school, especially completing my dissertation. Their humor, intelligence, and care got me through both personal and scholarly bumps in the road. I view my friendships with them as one of the biggest gifts of my Berkeley experience.

After leaving Berkeley, I came to the Clayman Institute for Gender Research at Stanford University. I want to thank my colleagues there for creating such a wonderful and collegial environment. I especially want to thank Lori Nishiura Mackenzie and Shelley Correll for their boundless support and encouragement.

I took a break from writing my book to work with Sheryl Sandberg and Nell Scovell on a book called *Lean In*. This experience was transformational in many ways, and it was an honor to work so closely with them on it. From them I learned the importance of embracing one's own voice, of standing firm in one's beliefs, and of using stories to both illustrate difficult truths and move people to action. I benefited from these lessons personally, but they also had a spillover effect on my book, making the final version stronger, more self-assured, and ultimately more interesting. I am grateful to them both for their friendship and for teaching me these lessons.

My friends Erika Vial Monteverdi and Robyn Ryan Packouz, who have been by my side since high school, have stuck with me through too many things to recount here. I thank them for their friendship, love, ability to make me laugh, and continual support.

My sincere thanks go to my oldest and dearest friend, Lisa Martinez Lajous. We met at the age of five and officially became best friends in third grade through the exchange of friendship pins. She is my go-to pal in good times and bad and has always championed my efforts, most recently sending me messages of encouragement during the last intensive round of writing to finish this book. I am so lucky to have a friend like her—one who always has my back, who cheers me up and talks me down, who makes me laugh and gives the best advice.

If not for my family, this book would not have been written. I would like to thank my parents, Ted and Sheila Cooper, for the innumerable ways they have helped me over the years, and in particular for always believing in me and my abilities. I especially thank them for taking such wonderful care of our children and for stepping in and doing whatever needed to be done so that I could finish this book. When our youngest was a baby and I was completely sleep deprived, I needed to turn around a revision of my manuscript. To help me make that happen, my parents took care of our children whenever we needed them to, ran errands for us, and made all of our dinners for months. I could not have completed this book without them and their limitless capacity to care about me and the issues in my life.

I want to give special thanks to my mother, who was my first sociology teacher. She taught me about the power that class, gender, and race have in people's lives and in society at large. These lessons occurred frequently while I was growing up, as when she said to me when I was about ten years old, "Notice in the newspaper that they have a 'business section' but not a 'labor section.' That shapes our perspective on things, doesn't it?"

My mother also taught me the essential elements of interviewing as time and again I observed strangers at the grocery store or on an airplane open up to her and tell her their life stories. This has become a running

joke in my family, and over the years we have tried to figure out an explanation for this unusual phenomenon. "It must be her pheromones," my
dad surmised. But I think that it's actually that she has perfected the art of
listening. I have learned from my mother that people talk when you are
truly listening to them and will answer almost any question if it is asked
from a place of genuine concern. I thank her for teaching me this, since
it has made me a much stronger and more empathetic interviewer and
ethnographer—and a better person.

My biggest thanks go to my husband, Scott Saywell. He has lived with
this project since its inception and has always believed in its importance. In
fact, on several occasions he talked me out of quitting it by convincing me
that it was a story that needed to be told. He has patiently listened to my
unformed thoughts, encouraged me during the hardest moments in the
writing process, and provided comic relief when I needed it. He has also
picked up the slack at home whenever I've needed the extra time to work
on my manuscript. I thank him for the countless ways he has supported
me and my book over the years and for generally giving my life so much
meaning.

Last but not least, I would like to thank my children, Kate (almost five)
and Wesley (two and half), for giving me the final dose of inspiration I
needed to finish this book. I had worked on this book on and off for many
years, but at the end I needed to finalize my manuscript in just a few
months. This required me to work feverishly every day and to miss weekends with my family in order to get it done. One morning, with a pang of
parental guilt, I apologized to Kate that my book was taking me away from
family time. In response my daughter looked me in the eye and said sin-
cerely, "That's okay, Mommy. I have a daddy and a grandma and a grandpa.
You finish your book." The guilt instantly lifted as my own daughter
reminded me of the important goal at hand.

Wesley, too, did his part to rally my spirits. As I was finishing my book
we were reading the children's book *Guess How Much I Love You*, in which
a father and child keep one-upping each other to express their love for
each other. In the final passage of the book, the child says, "I love you right
up to the moon," and in response the father says, "I love you right up to the
moon—and back." After we read this book together many times, Wesley
put his own spin on things. When I told him I loved him, he said, "Back

and the moooon, Mommy. Back and the moooon." There are few things that can buoy one's spirits like your toddler waving goodbye and yelling, "Back and the moon, Mommy," as you drive off to put in another day of writing. So thank you, Kate and Wesley, for being the wind in my sails when I needed it most.

Introduction

On Monday, October 6, 2008, the day we brought our first child home from the hospital, the Dow Jones Industrial Average plunged by as much as 800 points before ending down by 370 points. The Dow closed under 10,000 that day for the first time since 2004. By the end of the week the index had fallen 18 percent as investors started reacting to bad credit news.

I was generally oblivious to these developments. I was physically exhausted from giving birth to our daughter, and all of my attention was focused on caring for our new baby. But my husband was keenly aware. A few weeks earlier his company had received news that the drug trial for their lead product had failed, and in all likelihood the failed trial meant that many people were going to get laid off. Finding a job is often hard, but finding one in the middle of an economic slide of historic proportions could prove almost impossible.

In the midst of the chaos of the stock market crash and the first week of parenthood, I snapped a picture of my husband that captured the central concerns of this book. I took the photo because I thought I was recording a sweet moment—my husband sitting at the computer while cradling our new daughter in his lap. Later, when I finally uploaded the picture

1

from my camera, I realized that I had recorded something else entirely. In the photo, my husband is visibly worried; as he glances up at the camera his eyes are serious and his lips are pressed together. On the computer screen behind him is an image of the S&P 500 falling off a cliff. Nestled in his lap, our daughter is like an exclamation point, fueling the intensity of his concern. What seemed at the time like a cute moment between father and daughter is actually a visual artifact documenting the economic free fall. Unbeknownst to me, I had recorded history through the sharp downward arc of a graph and the worry etched on my husband's face.

Families bear the imprint of the social and economic forces that surround them, whether a crashing stock market that creates a jittery father, a layoff that causes a family to lose their house, an increase in demand for technical skills that raises the stakes for a child to go to college, or a stall in wages that leads parents to have a pessimistic assessment of their children's futures. Cast in this light, issues and problems that seem so personal, like a marital fight about money or a tense parent-child discussion about getting good grades in high school, are actually individual experiences that reflect much larger forces—forces that reside far away from the kitchen tables where these disputes and discussions occur.

The Great Recession has been one of the worst economic downturns in our history. In many ways, however, it is simply the intensification of trends that began back in the 1970s and '80s. Indeed, developments like the hollowing out of the middle class, the decline of good jobs, the lack of access to affordable health care, the drying up of pensions, and financial instability have been on the upswing for the last forty years.

For the most part, sociologists and economists have monitored these trends through examinations of tax records, survey data, bankruptcy filings, and jobs reports. Their analyses have yielded remarkable findings. What scholars have concluded is that at the dawn of the twenty-first century, Americans face almost unprecedented levels of insecurity and economic inequality. By some measures things have not been this bad since the era of the Great Depression. This is a dramatic conclusion, yet somehow its dramatic punch gets lost amid the charts, graphs, and statistical tables that painstakingly illustrate it. To be sure, the numerical calculations are a rather sterile measurement of trends that have such significant personal and societal costs. It is as if, on that day in October 2008, I had only taken a picture of a plunging S&P 500 and I had not also captured the worry on my husband's face. Without both images only half the story is told.

Telling the whole story is important, for underneath the meticulously collected data are real people who experience these trends in their everyday lives. And more and more of them are discovering that they're on their own. In today's insecure world, Americans increasingly have to provide for their own security. They must find new jobs, deal with income fluctuations, purchase their own health insurance, take on debt just to get by, deal with rising costs, fully fund their own retirement, and otherwise make their way in the world. We know that more people are now charged with the responsibility for creating their own security. What is much less understood is how they are dealing with this situation. What are they most concerned about? How are they coping?

Few are immune to the social and economic shock waves that have occurred over the last several decades. Yet the growing divide in our country between the haves and the have-nots suggests that the ways in which we experience and manage our security—what we pay attention to, what obstacles we face, and how we respond both practically and emotionally—should vary enormously from one person and one family to the next. In other words, much of our experience is shaped by our particular location on the graphs or in the statistical tables that document the shock waves and the consequences that they have for different groups of Americans. A full account of these issues thus requires looking not at just one spot on the graph, but at families that are distributed throughout the curve.

To understand how families from across the economic spectrum manage in these uncertain times, I spent two years interviewing and shadowing affluent, middle-class, and poor families in California's Silicon Valley. I looked at the problems they faced, what they felt anxious about, and the coping mechanisms they relied upon, tracing the differences caused by earnings, education, gender, and marital circumstances. In the process I encountered stories of stalwart stoicism, heart-wrenching worry, marital angst, and religious conviction. This book uses these stories to show how families pursue different kinds of strategies to get by in our safety-net-less, go-it-alone age. It documents how people cope with insecurity, how they manage their anxiety, whose job it is to worry, and how social class shapes all of these dynamics, including what is even worth worrying about in the first place. By tracing the strategies families used up and down the class ladder, this book tells the emotional story that goes along with the rise in economic insecurity and economic inequality, and it explores what these differences can tell us about the ways in which Americans may be pulling apart.

.   .   .   .   .

"Laid Off and Left Out: As Old Jobs Die, New
Ones Are Scarce and Not as Good"
Bergen Record, September 14, 2003

"There's No Corporate Ladder to Climb: You're
on Your Own"
Star-Ledger, May 24, 2009

Forty-three-year-old Debbie Clifford sips green tea and settles into the corner of the black leather couch in her family room as she describes her childhood.[1] "I was raised in the Hewlett-Packard family and HP community," she says. "We had the benefits of everything that the company offered, which is pretty substantial if you're raising a family." On the wall behind her is a framed picture of Debbie crossing the finish line of a recent 10K race. Her arms are raised in celebration, her face aglow in triumph—a poignant contrast with Debbie's account of the job losses and economic turmoil she has faced over the last fifteen years.

Debbie lives with her husband, Michael, and their three children in a middle-class neighborhood in Silicon Valley. Though both Debbie and Michael have taken a number of college-level courses, neither has a bachelor's degree. Michael spent many years in manufacturing jobs in the technology industry before deciding to start his own car-washing and detailing business, seeking greater "control" of his livelihood. "If you count on somebody else to take care of you," he says, "it's just not going to happen." At the time I interviewed the Cliffords, they were living mostly on the $130,000 Debbie was expecting to earn that year as an associate in a software sales business. Michael was reinvesting the profits from his business, hoping to jump-start its growth.

Over the years the Cliffords have become accustomed to economic uncertainty. Because of fluctuations and frequent layoffs in the tech industry, their income has been extremely volatile. At times they have had to support themselves, their three children, and Michael's daughter from a previous marriage on just two-thirds of their usual income, which has put them close to the minimum annual income required for a family of their size simply to make ends meet in Silicon Valley.

Silicon Valley is an expensive place to live. Median home prices hover around $600,000, and the median rent for a three-bedroom unit is about $2,000 a month. At the time I interviewed the Cliffords, a family with two working parents and only two children needed to earn $77,069 just to pay for housing, food, child care, and other essential expenses, excluding income set aside for savings of any kind.[2] Thus, with a mortgage to pay and four children to feed, the Cliffords' income volatility often left them in a precarious place financially.

Unlike Debbie's father, a lifelong HP employee, Debbie and Michael have changed jobs and industries frequently, either because of layoffs or voluntary career moves. This new employment reality was highlighted by the career counselors Debbie and her colleagues worked with after one layoff. Debbie recalls, "One of the key things that they told us was, 'It's a new world out here. If you think you're starting with a company and you're going to retire with the company, think twice. Employment has really turned into a situation where you're pretty much on a job project for three to four years, and after that your project's over.'" As a result, Debbie says, "I don't trust any level of my employment. I don't trust that I'll have a career there and stay there and make enough money to satisfy myself, or to satisfy what I need."

Dealing with frequent career ups and downs has been hard on the Cliffords. Tears spring to Debbie's eyes when she describes when her kids were young and she switched to a new career in marketing, hoping for a more stable (though lower) income than she had earned in the volatile technology sales business. "I was changing careers, which really required that I be in the office and learn. So here I was at a time where I needed that flexibility [because I had young children], and I didn't have it. And so it was a huge struggle. And I was paying for day care and I had just taken a huge cut in pay—just a huge struggle. Then just commuting and then learning something that I had no idea what this was. No idea." Wiping the tears from her cheeks with a tissue, Debbie explains how she managed:

> I was very influenced by former President Clinton when all his crap was going on with Monica Lewinsky. 'Cause that was in 1996–98 time frame . . . and I had just changed careers and had taken a dramatic cut in pay. I'm paying a babysitter, and I'm dropping my kids off in the ghetto with this woman who's practically a stranger who turned out to just be the best babysitter . . . but at the time it was very stressful. I just remember thinking, "If this guy [President Clinton] can compartmentalize his issues going on in front of the entire world, I mean your brain is a powerful thing. Put it away, deal with it when you're ready to deal with it, and when you're not, close the door on it . . ." 'Cause it can be done . . .
>
> It's a very conscious decision, I think. But I think it's a matter of training that muscle to do what it's supposed to do, which is "You don't have room for all this shit going on." There's a place for everything, and everything is placed, and [just like] you train your bicep to lift things . . . I think you need to train your brain to handle data in a certain organized fashion . . . Feelings are part of that data. It's information coming in. Where does it belong and when do you react to it? . . . But I was just like compartmentalize [it].

After years of volatility, Debbie and her husband, Michael, have gotten one thing very clear about the "new world" they live in: You can't count on your employer. You can't count on a job being long-term. You can only count on yourself.

To deal with this reality, Michael is starting his own business so he has more "control" over his economic fate. Debbie is trying to do a better job of seeing the writing on the wall before a layoff happens:

> In the technology sales business you're open one day and . . . closed the very next day and you don't see it coming. So I want to try to have a better big-picture view of what is happening and identify those bad situations before they came up rather than just being surprised by them all the time. And I've been surprised by a bunch of them. It's just like, "Okay, I've gotta feel like I'm taking some kind of control here, 'cause this is baloney."

But her desire to be able to compartmentalize as well as Bill Clinton points to another way Debbie is dealing with instability. She is consciously pushing her anxiety away. Like other people I spoke with who were grappling with financial uncertainty, Debbie has learned that submerging her worries and fears can be an effective way of coping with the economic stress she is under.

·   ·   ·   ·   ·

"Education Key to New Economy"
Providence Journal, January 30, 2007

"The Master's as the New Bachelor's"
New York Times, July 22, 2011

"How to Raise a Global Kid"
Daily Beast, July 18, 2011

While the Cliffords are focused on surviving round after round of economic instability, just a few miles away, in an upscale neighborhood in Silicon Valley, the Chopra family is focused on a different but related set of significant changes—the increasing importance of higher education in a more globally connected world. This development is both shaping and gnawing at the Chopra family's security.

Thirteen-year-old Lila Chopra lives with her parents and younger brother in an affluent suburb. When I arrive to interview her, she is sitting at her family's glass dining room table in a black velvet upholstered chair, wearing an oversized gray sweatshirt emblazoned with her junior high school's name and plaid flannel pajama bottoms. Her long black hair is loosely pulled into a bun atop her head.

Playing with a strand of her hair, Lila tells me that she recently signed up for the classes she will take next year as a high school freshman. She says that she chose her courses by using an information sheet that the high school supplied, which explained, "If you want to get into a highly distinguished school [college], these are the classes you need to take each year." Lila adds, "I have ten or eleven copies of the same sheet, of what classes I need to take."

"Why do you have so many copies?" I ask.

She explains matter-of-factly that numerous meetings were held for parents and students about course selection and different colleges' and universities' requirements. She says, "My mom, being my mom, went to every single one . . . She just likes to be really informed and know everything . . . It's just her."

Lila's mother, Ditra, a forty-five-year-old part-time marketing consultant, places great importance on education as one key to thriving in a demanding, globalized economy. "I've been saying for ten years, and I tell my children, too, that you have to get a graduate degree, at least your master's." Ditra herself has an MBA, while her husband, Paavan, who works as a vice president at a technology company, has a Ph.D. in engineering.

For the Chopras, at least, the link between high-level skill sets and high earnings in the new economy has proven to be a solid one. The Chopra family's income is more than $200,000 a year, with Paavan earning most of that. Neither Ditra nor Paavan has ever been laid off. The high pay and steady employment has allowed the Chopras to amass substantial savings, particularly for the education of their children, Lila and Darpan. They expect to pay for both of their children's college and graduate-level educations.

Ditra and Paavan also consider global travel an important part of preparing their children for the future. I ask Ditra what she hopes her children will gain from these trips. "A sense that the world is bigger than [their] zip code," she tells me. "And there's a lot of variety and there's a lot of diversity and a lot of different ways of doing things."

"How does that help them?" I ask.

"I think it's preparing them for life," Ditra responds. "The world is a small place. And for them to be thinking that the world is just this little box that is their life over here is doing them a disservice. They are going to meet and work with people from different parts of the world, and they're going to work in different parts of the world at some point or another."

During one summer visit to India, planned so that Ditra and Paavan could network with business colleagues and the entire family could reconnect with relatives, Ditra arranged for the kids to work at a summer camp in India. "It's not that they needed the money," Ditra says, "but I think they were learning skills about working in different cultures, working in different environments, working with people from different places, and understanding work itself."

To help Lila and Darpan see yet another aspect of globalization—the emergence of a middle class in India—Ditra also took them on a tour of a call center. "It's changing the way the world works," Ditra says, her dark brown eyes growing wide, "and I wanted my kids to see that."

At home, Ditra, along with several other parents from her children's school, developed an enrichment program called Global Eye that is designed to "give the kids an idea of the world beyond their own zip code." Over the last few years, enrollment in the program has grown from thirty students to several hundred.

The message that education is important has not been lost on Lila and Darpan. "I like getting straight A's," Lila says. "Like, if I am given an option, I will do more instead of less or, like, if I have an assignment to write down three quotes from a book, I will do five, just in case or something . . . I can't *not* do a great job on something."

One afternoon I observe the Chopra family at a bone marrow drive Ditra has organized at a local Red Cross blood center to search for a match for a neighbor stricken with leukemia. While Darpan sits at the front table reading *To Kill a Mockingbird* with a bright orange highlighter in his hand, Ditra whirls around the room welcoming donors with cookies and juice and ushering them to available donation stations. After following Ditra around for about forty-five minutes, I sit down next to Darpan to take a break and jot down my notes. "How's your homework coming along?" I ask him.

"Fine, but it's a little confusing," he says, angling the book toward me. Flipping through several pages, I see that Darpan has highlighted practically every sentence.

The Chopras have a level of financial security that the Cliffords can only dream of attaining one day. Yet despite flush bank accounts and vacations to international destinations, the Chopras, too, are uneasy. Their concern hinges on preparing their children for what they see as an increasingly globalized world in which success—even survival—is dependent upon accumulating educational degrees, preferably from top-tier academic institutions.

Noting these large-scale changes, Ditra says, "The path to economic stability is not what used to be considered tried and true. There was a time you went to school, you went to college, you got a job, and you would plod along. That's not true [anymore]." From Ditra's perspective, economic stability now requires "graduate degrees," "entrepreneurship," and familiarity with a global and diverse world. And the critical first step to getting onto this secure path is admittance to a good college or university. As a result, educating their children and making sure they will be qualified for admittance at a top school is a primary focus of the Chopras' lives. Yet it is an endeavor that is primarily worried over and managed by Ditra, who, like the other well-off mothers I spoke with, spends the vast majority of her time and energy on it. Paavan, too, is concerned, but, like the other affluent fathers in my study, he is focused on figuring out how they are going to cover the cost.

Although it is different than dealing with economic upheaval, dealing with positioning one's children in an increasingly competitive and global world creates its own kind of stress. A laser-like focus on children's educational accomplishments involves an intense amount of anxiety that, as we will see, resembles the anxiety Debbie Clifford experiences trying to manage her economic woes.

Yet whereas Debbie addresses her anxiety by trying to push it down, Ditra addresses hers by amping it up—attending all ten-plus meetings about the courses Lila will need to take in high school to attend a selective college. Instead of detaching herself from the process, Ditra fixates upon it, giving her daughter ten copies of the same information sheet, as if giving Lila only one or two copies would fail to communicate the message loudly enough. This fixation on threats to security was common among the affluent families I studied.

.   .   .   .   .

"Boys Lose Ground to Girls in Race to
Finish College"
St. Louis Post-Dispatch, August 10, 2003

"Reliance on Credit Increasing: Rising
Consumer Debt Strains Families"
Lawrence Journal-World, March 16, 2008

"Life Is Harder Now, Some Experts Say: After Paying
the Bills, Middle-Class Pockets Are Emptier"
MSNBC.com, October 16, 2007

Just a twenty-minute drive from the Chopras lives forty-five-year-old Owen Meehan, a married father of three. Unlike the Chopras, the Meehans don't think a lot about globalization and its impact on their children. Their concerns, centering on rising costs and making their dollars stretch, are more similar to those of the Cliffords. And like Debbie Clifford, Owen worries about the economic pressures he faces. However, while Debbie tries to push her anxiety away, Owen outsources his worry to his more educated wife.

"This is how I am," Owen tells me, slicing his hand through the air in a steady horizontal line to indicate his even-keeled nature. "This is the way I've always been described, and this is the way I describe myself. I'm not going to let [things] get to me, and I'm not going to get all jumping-up-and-down happy." His wife, Malinda, is another story, Owen explains, his hand zigzagging through the air:

> She loves to get up-and-down happy over things, but she also has these low points. If it's the family or money or whatever . . . when it's getting down here, watch out! We're not happy and it's obvious. Whereas I am kind of like this in my life [his hand gliding steadily through the air again]. I know what to expect, pretty much. I know where we're going. I know where we've been. I'm okay with it. But she likes to show the emotion and she likes to see it.

Owen's calm demeanor has helped him deal with an uneven career path. After taking a few courses at a local community college, Owen decided to apply his knack for all things mechanical to starting his own business. For most of his working life, Owen ran his own machine shop, manufacturing and fixing parts for construction vehicles such as cement trucks. But several years ago, when business began to slow down and the family's medical insurance premiums shot sky-high, Owen decided to take a full-time job as a technician in a company that produces electronic devices. It pays about $50,000 a year and provides good benefits. But while Owen would like to move up in the company, he feels his opportunities are limited because he doesn't have a college degree. To get by, Owen continues to run his own business, fulfilling orders before and after work. Malinda, who graduated from a state university with a degree in physical therapy, works part-time as a therapist.

Together the Meehans earn $95,000 a year, but they don't feel as though that is much money for a family with three children to live on in the Bay Area. "We live paycheck to paycheck. We don't have a whole lot extra," Malinda tells me. To make ends meet, the Meehans sometimes rely on their credit cards and usually carry a balance of between $3,000 and $5,000. Consequently, money is a frequent source of concern, and sometimes friction, for Owen and Malinda.

Malinda worries more about the family finances, as Owen explains:

> My money [from the business] comes in so sporadically. My check [from work] comes in . . . and it goes right to our [expenses], and that covers X. And now we need to cover everything else. And that [money from the business] comes in every once in a while. My customers pay, I pay out the bills [my business owes], and then I get paid. Sometimes it's great and sometimes it's not. And so a lot of times I wake up and get ready to go to work and I'll say goodbye to Malinda, and it's the third of the month and she'll say, "When is the money coming in? 'Cause I gotta do this, I gotta do this," so she's absolutely the one to do it [worry].

Owen says the reason Malinda manages their finances is because "she's much better at it than I am." "If I were doing it," Owen says, Malinda "would just be on me about it. So it wouldn't change as far as her mind-set goes. It's one of those things where I'd say, 'Yeah, I'll get it done eventually,' and she'd be like, 'I'd like it done now or sooner, because I'm worried about it.' 'Okay, then why don't you do it, because you're going to worry about it anyway and I know that it will get done.'" With Malinda in charge, Owen says, "I know that it's taken care of, so it's just something I don't have to worry about."

Owen feels Malinda worries more about things because "it's her nature" to carry troubles around with her. In comparison, Owen says, "I try not to carry it with me . . . I have to be able to move on. I have to be able to enjoy the kids. I have to be able to go to work with a fresh mind and be able to get things done."

Owen and Malinda's sixteen-year-old daughter, Carly, agrees that Malinda is the family taskmaster. "It's mostly my mom that tells me," Carly says when I ask about college planning. "She'll send me like scholarship stuff on my email, and she'll tell me to go to my counselor and talk to her about scholarships."

It's unlikely the Meehans will be able to send Carly or her two younger siblings to a four-year university unless they can qualify for some kind of financial aid. "My husband is half Mexican," Malinda tells me, "and we will be using that quarter Mexican when they are applying to college for scholarships," she adds with a laugh, her arm wrapped around the shoulder of her son, Matthew, "even if he has green eyes and light skin."

Over the course of Owen Meehan's life, the economic playing field shifted underneath him. For Owen's father, his lack of a college degree did not impede his ability to buy a home and support his family. But forty-four years later, Owen's lack of a degree has had significant consequences. For Owen, it has meant that he must work two jobs to provide his family with a life similar to the one his father was able to provide by working only one. It has also meant that his opportunities to advance at his day job are limited. Working around the clock and always being a little short is stressful. To be free of that pressure, Owen does something that a lot of the other less well-off fathers I spoke with did: he hands his worry over to his extremely competent wife, who, like a growing number of women, is better educated than her husband.[3] With Malinda in charge, things get done. Yet the unequal division of worry between Owen and Malinda reflects how economic changes link up with preexisting inequalities related to education and gender and shape what we do and don't worry about as well as who it is in each family who does the worrying.

SECURITY TRANSFORMATIONS
AND THE INEQUALITY OF SECURITY

Since the 1970s, economic, political, and social trends have transformed the way Americans go about creating security in their lives. Americans can no longer expect to work for the same company their whole career. They can no longer assume that a job will offer health benefits or that a pension will provide for them in their old age. Indeed, Americans are increasingly required to provide for their own security—to fund their own health care, retirement, and the ever-increasing costs of higher education—at the same time they are burdened by increases in the cost of living and an uncertain job market. Yale political scientist Jacob Hacker has described this transformation as the "Great Risk Shift," in which "economic risk has been offloaded by government and corporations onto the increasingly fragile balance sheets of workers and their families."[4]

We now live a new American reality: we are on our own, and it is tougher out there than it used to be. But exactly *how* tough it is depends on where one sits in relation to these transformations. For this shift in risk has been accompanied by an enormous increase in income and wealth inequality. The rich have gotten richer while much of the middle and working classes have stagnated or fallen behind and the ranks of the poor have grown.[5] For example, from 1983 to 2007, the top 20 percent of households accounted for 89 percent of the total growth in wealth, while the bottom 80 percent accounted for just 11 percent.[6] In 2010, the top 20 percent of households in the United States owned almost 90 percent of all privately held wealth. By contrast, the networth of the bottom 40 percent of households was negative.[7]

The shift in risk affects everyone. However, because of the growth in economic inequality, Americans live in vastly different *risk climates* that are shaped by how much they earn, how much they can save, the level of benefits they receive, and their likelihood of experiencing financial hardship.[8] Younger and less-educated workers suffer higher rates of job displacement, while lower-income workers have experienced the largest drop in health insurance coverage and the least growth in retirement benefits.[9] Highly educated professional workers also face a shaky job market, but their benefits have remained more stable. Also, relative to other workers, higher-skilled workers earn more money and have better working conditions.[10] Low-income and middle-class households are more likely to experience financial hardships like bankruptcy or falling behind on payments, and African Americans and Hispanics are more likely to suffer a significant economic loss. In contrast, upper-class households and whites are more shielded from financial trouble.[11] Thus, not only is America highly unequal in terms of income and wealth, it is also unequal in terms of exposure to risk and insecurity.

This layering of inequalities in income, wealth, and risk, one atop the other, leads me to call these disparities in our society the *inequality of security*. It's a serious social and economic problem. Exploring how families grapple with their place within the inequality of security is one of the central themes of this book.

COPING WITH INSECURITY

Hundreds of scholars and researchers have studied the large-scale transformations in security, risk, and inequality and the social forces behind them. I'll summarize their most important findings in the next chapter. Less studied, however, has been the question of how families are responding to these changes. How secure do Americans feel? What do they think about their economic situations and what do they do about them? What problems are they most worried about? How are families managing in such uncertain times?

Even less studied is how a family's place within the inequality of security differentially shapes both what they have to react to and how they respond. In fact, most accounts of the shift in risk and the rise of insecurity are presented in a "top-down" fashion, as if these security transformations affect everyone in the same way and to the same degree.[12] However, the drastic increase in economic inequality and the existence of different risk climates alert us to the variability in how each of us must manage our security. How do the responses of families on different rungs of the inequality-of-security ladder vary depending upon their economic resources and educational attainment?

When I started the research for this book, my plan was to fill this gap in our understanding by exploring the structural and perhaps cultural differences in how a sample of families provided for their own security. Did some families face more insecurity while others faced less? Did some families' skills and resources help them navigate through the new world of risk more easily than other families?

My hypothesis was that the deepening social and economic divisions among Americans would significantly shape a family's level of exposure to insecurity and their ability to plot a steady course. Accordingly, at the start of this project, I imagined that those at the top of the wealth and income ladder would feel great—secure in their jobs, pleased with the luxuries they could afford, happy with the fine schools their children attended, and complacent about the comfortable retirements they planned to enjoy— while those on the lower rungs of the ladder would feel anxious and insecure, worried about their jobs, pressured to stretch their paychecks, resentful of the lower-performing schools their children attended, and despondent over the gloomy futures they foresaw.

As my research unfolded, however, the reality I uncovered was far more complex. I began to suspect that sometimes anxiety was just as palpable at the top of the ladder as it was at the bottom. Thus my initial question, "How secure do Americans feel?," gave way to a series of more probing questions: "What does it take to feel secure?" "How do people define security?" "Where do these definitions come from?" And "What benchmarks and ideologies frame people's understanding of their security—or lack thereof?"

With an ear attuned to the anxiety in people's lives, my narrow focus on structural and cultural differences among the families in my study started to broaden. I began to see that despite their critical importance, these factors didn't fully convey the kind of differences I saw emerging. In the lives of the families I came to know, feelings—anxieties, worries, perceptions of risk, beliefs about responsibility—and the way these feelings were managed also shaped their approach to maintaining and building security.

For example, as the opening vignettes about the Cliffords, the Chopras, and the Meehans reveal, these families contend with the specific pressures bearing down on them—from job layoffs to globalization to credit card debt—in a variety of ways. Debbie Clifford changed careers in search of greater security; Ditra Chopra travels the globe to network with business colleagues and prepare her children for their globalized future; Owen Meehan works two jobs as a way of attaining both the stability of paid employment and the extra income provided by entrepreneurship.

But their stories also show that forging security isn't simply a practical matter of choices regarding work or school; it's also an extraordinarily emotional process. The way Debbie Clifford compartmentalizes her stress, Ditra Chopra fixates on her children's futures, and Owen Meehan "outsources" financial worries to his wife all point to the complex role feelings and emotions play in how families go about creating stability in their lives.

Having attained this insight, when I met a family struggling with debt, I made an effort to examine not only the practical ways in which they coped with the debt but also the steps they took to manage its emotional weight. When I came across a family that meticulously planned for retirement, I examined not only their financial planning approach but also the feelings that gave rise to the need to plan so carefully.

By drawing attention to the feelings involved in people's responses to staving off insecurity, this book captures the interplay between large-scale macroeconomic changes that have increasingly shifted the job of creating and maintaining security onto individuals and the ways in which people are adapting to and coping with these forces. This kind of lens, which pays attention to the back-and-forth among structure, culture, and feeling, enabled me to see that people were *doing security*—they were developing coping strategies, consciously and unconsciously, that helped them deal with the changing nature of inequality and risk in our time. By illuminating how social factors like class position, education, and gender influence our emotional responses, this book lays bare just how deep our economic inequalities seep.

This exploration into both the strategies families employ to handle an economic situation and the emotions interacting with and shaping that strategy extends our understanding about how individuals and families get by in the new economy. In most other sociological examinations, the emotional component is overlooked in favor of documenting economic struggles with particular attention paid to how families with limited means make ends meet in hard times.[13] In the wake of massive economic restructuring, scholars have been especially concerned with the financial situation of those who have lost the most.

However, our understanding of how new inequalities and the shift in risk impact families is incomplete without a comparative understanding of the security strategies families in different socioeconomic boats pursue and the emotional dynamics involved in those strategies. If the goal is to understand inequality and its consequences, then we must study those who have more, not just those who have less. This is ever more the case when the rise in inequality is a result of the top pulling away from everybody else.

Moreover, people are not simply economic actors; they are also emotional actors, whose feelings are heavily influenced by inequality. As epidemiologists Richard Wilkinson and Kate Pickett have shown, where there are great economic disparities, there are also higher levels of physical and mental illness, violence, and social distrust.[14] Thus, inequality must be measured not just by the amount of money in our wallets, but also by the thoughts in our heads and the feelings in our hearts. Consequently, understanding how families are faring requires an investigation that is about more than just the economic conditions they face and the ways in which they acquire, allocate, and manage their financial resources. It also requires understanding how families manage their feelings, anxieties, and emotional burdens, which is inextricably tied to their financial troubles and their economic provisioning. A focus on feelings provides a "buried" yet illuminating perspective on these issues.[15]

DOING SECURITY AND THE EMOTION WORK IT REQUIRES

In conceptualizing families' search for stability and reduced risk as "doing security," and in bringing an emotional lens to my study, I am drawing simultaneously on two distinct sociological frameworks. Sociologists use the concept of "doing" as a way to highlight the extent to which things like gender and social class are socially constructed. With regard to gender, for example, sociologists have shown how individuals are not simply born as men or women but *become* men and women through particular kinds of "doings" such as interactions (opening the door for someone) and practices (wearing cosmetics). In this way, gender is performed and enacted all the time. It is something a person does or says rather than something that a person is—an ongoing activity or a *doing* within daily life.[16] Furthermore, gender is not fixed but fluid. It is continually reconstituted—socially, psychologically, and institutionally.

The concept of "doing security" draws upon this tradition in that it highlights the work (or ongoing activity) involved in the search for (and achievement of) stability and security. In this sense, security—or insecurity—is created, performed, and worked toward in daily life. The notion of doing security reminds us that people are not simply secure or insecure. They "become" secure or insecure in part through social, psychological, and institutional interactions and practices. By viewing security (or insecurity) as partly a social construction, I'm able to illuminate the work—especially the emotion work—that is involved in creating it and performing it. My approach also reveals the degree to which the state of being secure (or insecure) is a deeply subjective one. Who feels secure and who feels insecure is, in many ways, a matter of perception.

My understanding of the role of feelings in the strategies that families develop is also guided by the sociologist Arlie Russell Hochschild's concepts of *emotion work* and *emotion management.* Hochschild's research reveals that people don't simply have feelings. Rather, social factors influence both what people feel as well as what "people think and do about what they feel." In other words, people actively work on and manage their emotions. They monitor, assess, inhibit, evoke, and shape emotions in different ways, often to get their feelings in line with cultural expectations or workplace expectations about how they should feel.[17] Depending on people's sense of what they ought to feel in a given situation, they will "try not to feel guilty," or "try to feel happy," or they will "swallow their pride." In her classic account of emotional labor, Hochschild illustrated how flight attendants must, for example, suppress their anger at a misbehaving passenger, evoke instead an upbeat and pleasant demeanor, and continue to cater to the passenger's needs, all the while smiling.[18]

Emotion work is central to how people do security. For example, Debbie Clifford worked on her feelings when she tried to submerge and compartmentalize her anxiety in order to hold her economic unease at bay. By contrast, Ditra Chopra managed her emotions by focusing incessantly on her concern about her daughter's educational pursuits. As the chapters to come will show, how people manage their feelings tells us a lot about where they sit in relation to macroeconomic change.

In analyzing why those I studied hold certain views about and approaches to their security, I connect the concerns people have and the emotion work they do with their class-based standards and expectations about security. For example, Kate Casper, an upper-class white mother I interviewed, not only expected her three children to attend top colleges, but she also believed that she and her husband were the ones responsible for funding this education. This belief gave rise to her concern about the amount of money they had saved. Despite having about $60,000 saved for their fourteen-year-old, about $45,000 saved for their twelve-year-old, and close to $35,000 saved for their seven-year-old, Kate was worried. "We should have more. I think we need to have a hundred thousand by now . . . If [our oldest child] had to go to college next year, [$60,000] isn't going to do it. Tuition is $25,000 or $30,000 and that's not including expenses . . . so we're behind. In my book, we're behind." Kate's belief about what she and her husband ought to provide their children generates a concern that she must manage.

Tactically speaking, when it comes to standards and expectations about security, if you increase or decrease your threshold for security—what you need to have to feel secure—you inflate or reduce the dynamics of your worry. If Kate Casper instead decided that her children should attend a more affordable community college or that they should be the ones to pay for their own college educations, she would have less to worry about. However, because she held fast to the belief that a part of their parental responsibility was funding their children's higher educations at top-tier universities, Kate and her husband were concerned. Consequently, for the Caspers the $140,000 they have set aside feels like too little. For many of the other families I interviewed, and probably for most Americans, that $140,000 would feel like an enormous amount of money.

As we shall see, the kinds of beliefs people possess about security, whether they tend to round up or round down their security thresholds, and the type of related emotion work they do tell us a lot about their social position, and especially about their place within the inequality of security.

THE SECURITY PROJECT

The key finding of my research is that, as a result of the inequality of security, the security preoccupations, security strategies, and emotional burdens experienced by families in various economic, social, and class tiers are dramatically different. Thus, the families in my study were engaged in widely divergent "security projects."

A security project, broadly defined, is all the economic and emotion work done by a family to create, maintain, and further their particular notion of security. This work may range from crossing national borders in search of higher pay, to cutting hours at work to better address a child's learning disability, to investing in a 401(k) account for retirement, to putting off paying an insurance premium in order to have enough money to pay the electric bill.

Not all aspects of security projects involve intentionality, planning, or even well-advised actions. Some ways of coping, like turning to drugs or alcohol in the face of difficult economic times, can worsen a family's circumstances—yet these, too, can be considered part of their security project. Moreover, since some families have numerous resources to draw upon while others have more limited options, parents may have multiple ways of coping or very few.

Finally, family members may not be in agreement about all aspects of a security project. There may be debate and disagreement about key aspects. For example, husbands and wives can be at odds about where they are going, how they will get there, and who is in charge. In fact, a common source of tension between couples was the security bargains that husbands and wives strike regarding who will be their family's security guard—who it is who will end up taking on the responsibility for worrying about money and security in the first place. A single security project thus may embrace different and even conflicting approaches and coping strategies.

The concept of security projects, then, involves a mix of objective conditions, subjective reactions to and ways of coping with these conditions, deliberate strategies of action, and unwitting coping mechanisms. Security projects are worked on every day, in small and large ways, both consciously and unconsciously. They evolve over time, getting negotiated, renegotiated, refined, and revised as economic and family circumstances change.

All security projects are united by a similar logic—namely, the need to define and attain security for the family and its members. However, a family's position in relation to larger economic forces influences both the objective and subjective dimensions of their security project. These variations are at the heart of my research. For example, middle and low-income families are financially vulnerable to problems like uninsured medical emergencies because of stagnating wages and declines in employer-provided benefits like health care. By contrast, upper-income families whose highly paid jobs provide full benefits are less encumbered by such worries. Also, the security bargains struck by affluent couples in which the husbands were more often their family's security guard looked much different than the bargains struck by less well-off couples in which the wives were usually security guards. Such realities shape the security projects that different families pursue.

What's more, socioeconomic differences among families affect their subjective experiences of security and the design of their security projects. We'll explore how this happens in the chapters to come as we examine security projects among affluent, middle-class, and poor families, each one a different response to the macroeconomic environment surrounding a particular family.

WAYS OF DOING SECURITY

For the typical family, there will be a primary way they go about doing their security. In my study, I discovered four main approaches to security projects, which I describe as *downscaling, upscaling, holding on,* and *turning to God.* Of course, it is hard to know to what extent these patterns can be generalized from a single study that was conducted in one place at one time. Nonetheless, by examining these four approaches in depth, I hope to shed light on important questions about how families do security in insecure times, tracing how the rise in inequality and the shift in risk have played out in the private lives of people impacted by these forces. Here is a brief introduction to each of these four ways of doing security.

Downscaling. During my research, I often left interviews with less well-off families with the sense that I was more concerned about their family's well-being than they were. At times it seemed as if the people I spoke to were trying to convince me—and themselves—that they were doing just fine with fewer material and economic resources and that they really had nothing to worry about.

This attitude of seeming indifference puzzled me until I realized that it reflected a way of managing economic hardships and the deep tensions they provoked. This downscaling of security involves lowering the bar on requirements for security, resigning oneself to living with these reduced levels, and suppressing anxiety when it arises. It's a form of emotion work in which those who are struggling economically submerge certain emotions and bring forth others in order to control their anxiety over difficult or precarious circumstances.

Upscaling. Many of my interviews with affluent families left me with the sense that they were much more concerned about their family's well-being than their objective situation seemed to warrant. The surprising anxieties that I discovered among the rich led me to wonder why privileged families seem to yearn for even more than they already had. Why did they ratchet up what they needed to feel secure, feeling the need for millions of dollars in their retirement accounts as well as savings sufficient to allow their children to attend the world's best colleges and graduate schools?

I call this approach to doing security upscaling. As a result of upscaling, those with the most resources in my study were often plagued by the sense that they didn't *quite* have enough. Gender plays an important role in upscaling: it is generally the men in upper-class families who focus on financial concerns while the women focus on family issues. Nonetheless, both upper-class men and women in my study dealt with their anxieties similarly, mainly by thinking about their concerns, financial or otherwise, incessantly. Ironically, the way they managed their worry was to worry, as if to distill and quantify the exact nature of the problem in order to come up with potential solutions. Paradoxically, however, rather than reducing their fears, this spotlight approach merely heightened their levels of anxiety.

Holding On. Grappling with layoffs, income declines, debt, and insecurity was common among the middle-class, working-class, and poor families I studied. Yet when I interviewed members of these families about how they managed during these rough times, I often got conflicting his and hers accounts. Why, I wondered, were the women in these families expected to be the family's security guards, the "designated worriers" charged with keeping insecurity at bay, while their husbands were comparatively less burdened?

Eventually I found that the process I call holding on—trying to keep a family's security project on track in the face of economic challenges—is a profoundly gendered one. It is the women in middle-class and working-class families who generally do the worry work, figuring out whether there is enough money to pay the bills, afford the after-school activities, and save for retirement. I link holding on to the improving circumstances of better-educated women and the deteriorating circumstances of less-educated men.

Turning to God. Many of the families I interviewed were religious, attending a church or synagogue on a regular basis. However, the interviews in which the church, religion, and faith came up most consistently were with working-class and poor respondents who had dealt with extreme economic difficulties. Social services offered by houses of worship enabled many of these families to survive, while their faith in God and

Table 1 Social Class and Security Strategies			
	Upper income	*Middle income*	*Low income*
Upscaling	✓		
Downscaling		✓	✓
Holding On		✓	✓
Turning to God			✓

their belief that God has a plan provided them with psychic and emotional relief and support. Why, I wondered, was it only these economically vulnerable families that relied so heavily on their churches and their faith to build their security projects? I connect this way of doing security with a growing tendency for government to hand over welfare responsibilities to faith-based organizations. In this book, I'll explore the potential negative consequences of religious institutions playing a central role in providing those in need with social supports.

Table 1 provides an overview of the relationships between social class and the different ways of doing security.

ORGANIZATION OF THE BOOK

Over the years, as I have discussed this project with colleagues and acquaintances, I've often been asked: Why are Americans today forced to do more security? Why has economic inequality increased? Is this problem something new? Chapter 1 answers these questions. It provides a historical overview of the economic, social, and political changes that have occurred over the last several decades to explain why economic inequality has grown and why doing security has taken on more prominence in people's daily lives. This chapter charts the rough waters that families must now navigate. Yet it also explains why some family's boats are sturdier than others.

In chapter 2, I describe my research in more detail. I outline the design of the study, provide demographic details about the families in the study, and discuss some of the unique experiences and dilemmas I encountered while doing the research.

Chapters 3 through 7 provide in-depth case studies that document how families in different socioeconomic groups do security. By placing security projects side by side, the similarities and differences among them are illuminated. Chapter 3 showcases the Delgado family, who engaged in the process of downscaling in order to keep themselves emotionally and psychologically afloat amid great economic difficulties. Chapter 4 explores the process of upscaling through the story of the Mah family, who, despite being among the most affluent group in this country, remained extremely nervous about their circumstances. In chapter 5, I look at the process of holding on through the story of the Calafato family and examine how it is linked to the prominent role women now play in providing for their families. In chapter 6, I examine through the story of the Faleau family the way in which the least well-off families in my study turn to God to make their way. And I explore the potential for coercion that this kind of approach creates.

In chapter 7, I tell the story of Eddie and Chelsea Jenner. I've included their story in this book not because they were representative of the general trends I found, but because of how different their story was. The Jenners reflect the America of old—a country in which a working-class kid was able, through a supportive partnership with his employer, to work his way up into the middle class. Unfortunately, in the new insecurity context, supplying one's own children with a path to the middle class has become an increasingly expensive endeavor. As a result, the Jenners have gone deeply into debt, threatening the middle-class existence they have worked so hard to earn.

This chapter charts Eddie Jenner's achievement of the American dream, his struggle to hold on to that dream for his children, and how he and his wife, Chelsea, are coping with the insecurity this creates. Through the story of the Jenner family we are able to see what security used to look like—and how it could look again.

To learn about what happened to some of the families in my study in the aftermath of the Great Recession, I returned to the field and conducted interviews. The epilogue provides an update on the families profiled in the book.

A NATION DIVIDED

E pluribus unum, "One nation under God," "United we stand"—traditional phrases such as these have been used for generations to evoke a sense that, as a nation, we are all in this together. At one time they may have expressed the way many people actually perceived our country to be. As we'll see, however, those days are disappearing. To a disturbing degree the inequality of security is transforming our country into a collection of countless island-like units, each pledging allegiance to its own highly unequal version of the American dream. This book explores how and why this is happening—and what the deepening problem of inequality of security may mean for our collective future.

1 From Shared Prosperity to the Age of Insecurity

HOW WE GOT HERE

I have pointed out to the Congress that we are seeking to find the way once more to well-known, long-established, but to some degree forgotten ideals and values. We seek the security of the men, women, and children of the nation. That security involves . . . [using] the agencies of government to assist in the establishment of means to provide sound and adequate protection against the vicissitudes of modern life—in other words, social insurance.

Franklin Delano Roosevelt fireside chat, June 28, 1934

Many of our most fundamental systems—the tax code, health coverage, pension plans, worker training—were created for the world of yesterday, not tomorrow. We will transform these systems so that all citizens are equipped, prepared, and thus truly free to make your own choices and pursue your own dream. Another priority for a new term is to build an ownership society, because ownership brings security and dignity and independence. In all these proposals, we seek to provide not just a government program but a path, a path to greater opportunity, more freedom, and more control over your own life.

George W. Bush, acceptance speech at the Republican National Convention, September 2, 2004

Tales of families, particularly middle-class and working-class families, experiencing upheavals and setbacks because of job losses, health-care emergencies, and stagnating wages have become increasingly common. Economic uncertainty has always existed, of course, but the breadth and depth of the problem in twenty-first-century America is alarming. In fact, until relatively recently many people assumed that secure jobs, rising incomes, and upward mobility were an inherent part of American society. Times have changed.

AGE OF SECURITY: THE NEW DEAL ERA

In the broadest historical perspective, today's widespread sense of economic uncertainty is not so much a new phenomenon as a regression to an older state many Americans believed had been safely left behind. Before the Great Depression most jobs in America were precarious: wages were unstable, pensions and health insurance were unheard-of, and labor laws were almost nonexistent.[1] However, in the wake of that economic calamity, a new social ethic emerged that sought to provide Americans with greater security in both good times and bad.[2]

Beginning in the 1930s, the federal government took a more active and formal role in protecting Americans from the "hazards and vicissitudes of life" in modern capitalism.[3] Throughout that decade laws were enacted to govern working hours and establish minimum wage levels. And with the passage of the Social Security Act and the Wagner Act in 1935, Americans gained access to old-age and unemployment insurance and the right to counteract the power of employers through collective bargaining. These kinds of laws dramatically expanded the number of workers with secure jobs, living wages, and robust benefits.

Through large-scale social insurance programs like those grouped under the rubrics of the New Deal (in the 1930s) and the Great Society (in the 1960s), presidents from Franklin D. Roosevelt through Gerald Ford sought to shelter Americans from economic ups and downs by expanding programs like unemployment insurance and disability benefits and by providing health insurance through Medicare and Medicaid to the elderly and the poor. Many private employers, spurred on by a powerful labor movement, also came to embrace the collectivist approach put in motion by the New Deal; they offered workers good wages and health, disability, and pension benefits as a way of rewarding them for their hard work (and as a way of fending off more intrusive government intervention in the private labor market).[4]

Over time, an unspoken agreement was struck among government, labor, and big business that shaped a hybrid public/private system for providing security and prosperity to tens of millions of Americans.[5] From the 1930s through the 1970s, the government took responsibility for tempering the effects of the business cycle through economic policies based on the theories of the twentieth-century British economist John Maynard Keynes, coordinating national monetary policy and fiscal policies to minimize the depth and duration of recessions. It also helped train young people for jobs (through public support for colleges and universities, subsidized student loans, and scholarship programs) and helped stimulate mass consumption by supplying subsidies for housing and funds to develop a national highway system. Yet the government was careful not to go too far, abstaining from centralized planning or meddling in corporate decision making. For their part, workers tacitly agreed to minimize labor unrest in return for promises by companies to provide stable employment, good benefits, and wage increases that reflected workers' fair share of the profits gained through rising productivity.

Although this three-way social contract among government, employers, and workers varied in its effectiveness and excluded many women and minorities, it nevertheless enabled several generations of Americans to prosper. Countless statistics tell the story. Here are just a few: From 1950 to 1970, the yearly income of the median worker more than doubled, and those at the bottom of the earnings distribution saw their earnings increase even more.[6] Family income increased by 56 percent between World War II and the mid-1960s.[7] There was an upgrading of the entire employment structure in the 1960s, with strong employment growth in middle- and high-wage jobs and only modest expansion in low-wage jobs.[8] From the mid-1940s to the late 1960s, America became a more equal society as family income inequality decreased by 7.5 percent.[9] Pension and health-care coverage were on the rise.[10] At the peak of this system, in the late 1970s, private pensions covered 40 million people—49 percent of private wage and salary workers—while private health-care coverage reached more than 80 percent of Americans.[11] Affordable housing became more available and home ownership almost doubled, growing from 17 to 33 million.[12] Thanks to government initiatives like the G.I. Bill (1944) and the Higher Education Act (1965), 2.3 million veterans went to college and the number of low-income students attending universities nearly doubled between 1965 and 1971.[13]

Collectively, these forces helped to create a large and thriving middle class whose growing wealth stimulated decades of unprecedented economic expansion. President John F. Kennedy's words "a rising tide lifts all the boats" summarized the experience of hundreds of millions of Americans, whose gains during the New Deal and after World War II made economic optimism seem inevitable and permanent.[14]

FROM THE 1970S TO TODAY: STAGNATION, INEQUALITY, INSECURITY

At first almost imperceptibly, then with growing force, the economic tides began to shift away from growth, security, and shared prosperity for Americans in the 1970s.[15] Lurking behind the bad news were potent transformations that would gradually alter the dream of universal progress that Americans had come to consider their birthright.

Once again, the numbers map the trends. In the early 1970s, median earnings began to stall; by the 1990s, a considerable number of workers were earning less than their counterparts had decades earlier. By 1996, real wages for the workers at the bottom had fallen about 13 percent, and real wages for workers in the middle had fallen by close to 10 percent.[16]

Men, especially those with less education, have been particularly affected. Between 1969 and 2009, men's median annual earnings decreased by 14 percent. Among men with only a high school diploma, median annual earnings declined even more, falling by 47 percent over the same period. Other troubling developments have been the decline in the number of men working full-time and a rise in the number of men with no formal labor-market earnings at all. Between 1960 and 2009 the share of men working full-time decreased from 83 percent to 66 percent and the share of men with no formal labor-market earnings increased from 6 percent to 18 percent.[17]

Women have fared better. Spurred on by the women's movement, a desire to work, and the financial needs of their families, women have poured into the labor force over the last fifty years. Given how low women's wages were several decades ago and how many women are now working, women's earnings have dramatically increased, rising 56 percent (for the median full-time female worker) since the early 1960s. However, women's wages, too, have recently plateaued. Since 2001, median earnings for women have mostly stagnated.[18]

When we look at individual male and female workers over time, the numbers are somewhat bleak. From a household perspective, however, economic well-being looks a bit better. Between 1975 and 2009, the median wages for two-parent families increased by 23 percent. However, this increase has been fueled by parents, mostly mothers, working more hours, not by rising wages. On average the typical two-parent family now works 26 percent longer or seven hundred more hours per year than the typical two-parent family did in 1975.[19] If women had stayed home, middle-class incomes would have grown by only about a quarter as much as they did between 1979 and 2000, while low-income families would have seen a significant decrease in real income.[20] The consecutive recessions of 2001 and late 2007/2008 have put downward pressure on family household incomes. Since 2007, median family household income has declined by 8.4 percent. In real terms, median family household income has returned to 1996 levels.[21]

Another troubling sign that began to emerge in the 1970s is the failure of most families to realize economic gains from rising productivity. Although median family income and productivity grew in tandem at 2 to 3 percent a year in the immediate post–World War II years, from 1973 to 2005 median family income grew at less than one-third the rate of increases in productivity.[22] Thus, even though American workers are producing more goods and services per hour, they have not been rewarded for it. Instead, most of the gains from increased productivity have gone to executive compensation and corporate profits.[23]

With the top receiving most of the gains in both income and wealth, economic inequality has risen drastically. During the 1980s—the worst decade by this measure—workers earning the least saw their wages decline by 14 percent, workers earning the most saw their wages increase by 8 percent, and the wages of workers in the middle remained flat, reflecting a widening income gap from the top to the bottom of the scale.[24]

Since the 1990s, a different pattern has emerged, with inequality growing between the highest earners and those in the middle while it decreases between earners in the middle and those at the bottom.[25] Inequality has thus increased because the incomes of the highest-earning Americans have outstripped those of both the middle class and the poor.[26]

Overall, from 1976 to 2005, the growth of post-tax income among the poorest households was just 6 percent, while among middle-income households it was 21 percent (less than 1 percent a year). In comparison, the post-tax income among the top fifth of households grew by 80 percent.[27]

Furthermore, recent evidence finds that the increase in wage inequality is becoming more concentrated at the top. The wage gap between those with graduate degrees and those with only college degrees has grown more than the gap between those with college degrees and those with only high school diplomas.[28]

Wealth inequality has grown even faster than income inequality. In the beginning of the 1960s, the wealthiest fifth of all U.S. households held 125 times more wealth than the median wealth holder. By 2004, the ratio had increased to 190 to 1.[29] From 1984 to 2004, the top 20 percent of households received 89 percent of the total growth in wealth, while the bottom 80 percent received just 11 percent.[30] By 2010, median wealth in the United States reached its lowest point since 1969. In that year (2010), the top fifth of households held 88.9 percent of all wealth, households in the middle held 12 percent, and households at the bottom had a negative net worth—they owed 0.9 percent of all wealth.[31]

Taken together, the rise in both income inequality and wealth inequality since the postwar years has led some to conclude that the United States has not seen such high levels of inequality since just before the Great Depression.[32] Among all the industrialized countries in the world, the United States is now one of the most unequal.[33]

Other developments loom darkly over the economic status of American families, starting with work insecurity. Studies have found a decrease in employment stability, especially for men.[34] For example, the average job tenure for men working in the private sector at age fifty has declined from 13.5 years in the 1973–83 period to 11.3 years in the 1996–2008 period.[35] Job losses often result in long-lasting economic setbacks. Research shows that today's displaced workers can suffer from prolonged periods of unemployment and that once they find new jobs, their earnings are often substantially lower than their previous earnings.[36] A 2013 survey of more than a thousand American workers found that among those who had gotten a job after being laid off during the recession, 54 percent earned less in their new jobs.[37]

Other research has found that economic volatility has risen even faster than inequality. By 2003, the rate of income instability (as measured by drops in income) was three times greater than in the early 1970s.[38] To be sure, the number of Americans experiencing economic difficulties without having sufficient financial resources to weather the storm has steadily increased, from 14.3 percent in 1986, to 18.8 percent in the early 2000s, to 20.5 percent during the Great Recession.[39] Furthermore, when family income drops, it now drops much further than it did in the past. In the early 1970s, the usual loss was around 25 percent of a family's previous income; by the late 1990s the loss had grown to 40 percent.[40] A report released by the Rockefeller Foundation estimated that in 2009 the level of economic insecurity was greater than at any other time in the last twenty-five years, with about one in five Americans experiencing a decrease in household income of 25 percent or more.[41] With only about half of Americans equipped with savings to cover living expenses for three months, the increase in economic volatility puts many families on the edge of insolvency.[42]

Other signs of economic insecurity have risen as well. The number of filings for personal bankruptcy grew from around 300,000 in 1981 to about 1.5 million in 2004 and 2 million in 2005. The latter figure reflected a rush of people filing before a new bankruptcy law went into effect that made filing for chapter 7 bankruptcies harder and more expensive.[43] Because of the tougher bankruptcy legislation, the number of people filing fell drastically. Despite these more restrictive rules, the subsequent economic downturn nonetheless led to another uptick in filings. After dipping to 775,000 in 2007, there were more than 1.5 million personal bankruptcy filings in 2010 and about 1.2 million in 2012.[44] And experts believe that even these numbers are artificially low, since many who would like to file cannot afford the legal costs involved.[45]

The housing market reflects similar trends. Foreclosure rates tripled from the early 1970s to the early 2000s and have skyrocketed in recent years because of the subprime mortgage crisis.[46] From 2007 to 2011 there were more than 4 million foreclosures nationwide.[47] A 2012 report from the Center for Responsible Lending noted that an average of five hundred families in California have lost their homes every day since the beginning of the Great Recession.[48]

Finally, levels of indebtedness have reached record highs in the United States. In 2004, debt held by households was equal to 80 percent of GDP, up from 50 percent in 1980.[49] For almost every group of households in the United States, the ratio of mortgage debt to income has doubled since 1989, and for many the ratio of total debt to income has also more than doubled.[50] The median value of debt held by American families increased sharply between 1989 and 2007, rising from $24,000 to $67,300.[51] The percentage of American households reporting debt payments that exceed 40 percent of their income grew from 10 percent in 1989 to about 14 percent in 2010.[52] In 2007, 46 percent of American families carried a balance on their credit card, with the average balance having increased by 30 percent from 2004 to $7,300.[53] By 2010, as access to credit tightened, fewer families carried credit card debt (39 percent), and the average balance had fallen a bit to $7,100.[54]

These higher levels of debt are linked with rising costs. Housing leads the way. Karen Dynan, a researcher with the Brookings Institution, argues that much of the increase in aggregate household debt, from about 0.6 times personal income during the 1960s through the mid-1980s to close to 1.2 times personal income in recent years, can be linked to bigger mortgages taken out in response to rising home prices.[55] Since 1975, the proportion of middle-class Americans who might be considered "house poor" because they spend more than 40 percent of their earnings on housing has quadrupled.[56] Many families seeking to send their children to good schools have had to spend a larger proportion of their income to afford increasingly expensive homes in coveted public school districts.

Health-care costs are on the rise, too. Between 2000 and 2007, the average annual premium for job-based family health coverage rose more than 90 percent (from $6,351 to $12,106). The average worker's share of this family premium rose from $1,656 to $3,281, an increase of more than

98 percent.[57] By 2012, average annual family health insurance premiums rose to $15,745, and families were responsible for 28 percent of the cost, or about $4,409.[58]

The cost of education continues to soar. In the late 1970s, the average tuition cost for a state college was just over $1,900; by 2007–2008 it had risen to $6,185 (in constant dollars).[59] By 2008, about two-thirds of college graduates took on debt to finance their educations. Upon graduating, they owed on average about $20,000 if they attended a public university and close to $28,000 if they attended a nonprofit private university.[60] In 2010, almost one in five U.S. households held student loan debt, a share that more than doubled since 1989.[61]

In addition to the high costs of housing, health care, and education, families with young children also have large child-care bills. In almost half the states in this country, the cost to send a four-year-old to day care exceeds 10 percent of the median income for a two-parent family. In 2011, the average annual cost for an infant to attend a center-based child-care program cost more than a year's tuition and fees at public universities in thirty-five states.[62]

Similar statistics could be cited for several more pages, but the pattern is clear—and very troubling. From the 1970s to today, income stagnation, growing inequality, increasing economic instability, soaring debt, and rising costs have steadily eroded the well-being of American families.

BEHIND THE REVERSAL OF FORTUNE

It is clear that American families have been struggling in recent decades. Less obvious are the forces that are responsible for this reversal of fortune. However, a significant body of research now points to a confluence of economic and social trends that many scholars agree have played a crucial role in the rise of financial insecurity.

The Rise of the Service Economy

Since the 1970s, work in the United States has undergone a dramatic transformation—a regression from the New Deal quest for stability and security to a state in which work is precarious. In the words of sociologist Arne L. Kalleberg, work has become more "uncertain, unpredictable, and risky from the point of view of the worker."[63]

One reason for the rise of precarious work is the wholesale restructuring of the American economy from one based on manufacturing to one based on services. After World War II the manufacturing sector comprised 40 percent of the labor force; by 2005, that share had fallen to only 12 percent. The service sector now makes up about 80 percent of the jobs in the United States.[64] Durable manufacturing jobs (autoworker, machinist, chemical engineer) offering higher wages and good benefits have been replaced by service sector jobs (store clerk, cashier, home health-care aide) that pay less, offer few or no benefits, and are more insecure.[65]

Moreover, while the manufacturing sector tends to create good jobs at every employment level, the service sector tends to create a relatively small number of high-skill, high-paying jobs (in fields like finance, consulting, and medicine) along with a large number of low-skill, low-paid jobs (in retailing, child care, and hospitality). The result is that secure, semiskilled middle-income jobs like those that once fueled the rapid expansion of the American middle class are increasingly hard to find.[66]

The Impact of Globalization

Beginning in the mid- to late 1970s, U.S. firms began to face dramatically increased competition from around the world. To compete, American companies sought to lower labor costs, in part by outsourcing work to lower-wage countries. Technological advances aided this outsourcing process, as the growth in electronic tools for communication and information management meant that goods, services, and people could be coordinated and controlled from anywhere around the globe, enabling businesses to more easily move their operations to exploit cheap labor sources abroad.[67]

Perhaps the most far-reaching effect of globalization has been a renegotiation of the unwritten social contract between American employers and employees. Managers now demand greater flexibility to quickly adapt and survive in an increasingly competitive global marketplace. In this context, the traditional employment relationship, in which work is steady and full-time, workers are rarely fired except for incompetence, working conditions are generally predictable and fair (often defined by union-negotiated contracts), and good employees can expect to climb a lifetime career ladder in the service of one employer, has come to seem unrealistic and onerous to business leaders. Today that traditional arrangement has largely disappeared, replaced by nonstandard, part-time, contract, and contingent work, generally offering reduced wages and scanty benefits.[68] Mass layoffs are no longer an option of last resort but rather a key restructuring strategy used to increase short-term profits by reducing labor costs in both good times and bad.

The Decline of Unions

In this new environment, unions are struggling. Although manufacturing workers have a long history of labor organizing, service sector workers such as restaurant and retail employees do not, making it harder for service employee unions to grow. Moreover, globalization, technological changes, and the spread of flexible work arrangements have combined to enable employers to make an end run around unions by moving jobs to countries or parts of the United States where anti-union attitudes and laws predominate. As a consequence of these developments, union membership has steadily declined. In 1954, at the peak of union membership, 28 percent of employed workers were in unions.[69] By 1983, only 20 percent of workers were union members. In 2012, union membership reached a historical low, with membership comprising only 11 percent of American workers. Among full-time workers, the median weekly earnings for union members is $943, while among nonunion workers the median weekly earnings is $742.[70] The decline of unions has severely curtailed and diminished workers' ability to collectively bargain to maintain high wages and good benefits, indirectly fueling a steady decline in the value of the minimum wage.[71] Moreover, the decline of unions has eroded a broader moral commitment to fair pay, which even nonunion workers previously benefited from.[72]

Together, the rise of the service economy, globalization, the decline of unions, and the erosion of the old work contract between employers and employees have created a precarious work environment for more and more Americans. Between the 1980s and 2004, more than 30 million full-time workers lost their jobs involuntarily.[73] And during the Great Recession of 2008–2009, another 8.9 million jobs were lost.[74] In the past few years, long-term unemployment has reached levels not seen since the government began monitoring rates of joblessness after World War II.[75]

Risk Shifts to the Individual

Over the last several decades, both government policy and private sector labor relations have evolved to reduce the sharing of the economic risks involved in managing lives, caring for families, and safeguarding futures. Instead, individual Americans are increasingly being asked to plan for and guarantee their own educations, health care, and retirements. If today's families want a safety net to catch them when they fall, they need to weave their own.

Underlying this shift in risk is neoliberal political ideology, often identified with leaders like Ronald Reagan and Margaret Thatcher, which holds that people will work harder and make better decisions if they must defend themselves against the vicissitudes of life.[76] Neoliberal doctrine views dependence in a negative light (arguing that "coddling" by government undermines individual initiative) and actually celebrates risk and uncertainty as sources of self-reliance. In this new paradigm, the individual is encouraged to gain greater control over his or her life by making personal risk-management choices within the free market (and living with the consequences of any misjudgments). In this "ownership society," individuals must learn to be secure with insecurity; the goal is to amass security on our own rather than look to government help or collective action as sources of support.

With the rise of neoliberalism, the ethic of sharing risk among workers, employers, and the federal government that emerged after the New Deal was replaced by an aggressively free-market approach that pushed deregulation and privatization in order to minimize the role of government in economic life. At the same time, responsibility for social welfare has steadily devolved from the federal government to states, localities, and even the private sector. The push toward privatizing social services reached a new level when President George W. Bush, through his establishment of the office of faith-based organizations, sought to formally create public-private partnerships in which welfare provision would increasingly be supplied not by the government but by religious organizations. The result of this devolution of social services has been the replacement of a relatively stable, consistent system of safety-net programs with a patchwork of state, local, and private programs, all of which scramble to find funding.

Though many Americans may be unfamiliar with the risk shift story, the results are widely known. From 1980 to 2004, the number of workers covered by a traditional defined-benefit retirement pension decreased from 60 percent to 11 percent. In contrast, the number of workers covered by a defined-contribution retirement benefit like a 401(k) plan, in which the worker is fully responsible for saving and managing his or her savings, grew from 17 percent in 1980 to 61 percent in 2004.[77]

Traditional employer-provided health-care coverage began to erode as well. From 1979 to 2004, coverage dropped from 69 percent to 55.9 percent.[78] In 2010, 49 million Americans were uninsured, an increase of close to 13 million people since 2000.[79] For workers who continue to receive coverage, their share of the costs has increased drastically. A survey conducted by the Employee Benefit Research Institute found that to cover medical costs, 45 percent have decreased their contributions to other savings, 35 percent have had difficulty paying other bills, and 24 percent have had difficulty paying for basic necessities.[80]

The Affordable Care Act, passed in 2010 and upheld by the Supreme Court in 2012, will greatly expand affordable health care. As a result of the legislation, it is estimated that by 2019, 29 million Americans will gain health insurance coverage. However, an equal number will still be uninsured.[81] And the number of uninsured may rise depending on how many states opt out of expanding Medicaid eligibility. Currently twenty states will not participate in the Medicaid expansion.[82] Analysis of states that won't expand Medicaid has found that, as a result, about 5.3 million people will earn too much under their state's Medicaid eligibility level to qualify but will earn too little to be eligible for tax credits that help offset the cost of insurance.[83] Of the top ten least-insured metropolitan areas in the United States, seven are in states that will not expand Medicaid eligibility.[84]

When it comes to aid for higher education, federal funding has grown, but that aid has mostly come in the form of loans rather than grants. Over the last decade, grants have made up between 22 and 28 percent of federal aid for education, while loans have made up between 61 and 70 percent.[85] Moreover, even though there has been a 15 percent increase in the number of low-income students who receive a Pell Grant, the maximum award these students can receive now covers only about a third of the costs of a college education, as compared to around three-quarters in the 1970s.[86]

The high price of a college degree is linked with a significant decline in the number of low- and moderate-income students who enroll in and graduate from college. Between 1992 and 2004, the percentage of low-income students enrolled in a four-year college decreased from 54 to 40 percent and the percentage of middle-income students decreased from 59 to 53 percent.[87] For low-income children, the college completion rate has increased by only 4 percentage points between the generation born in the early 1960s and the generation born in the early 1980s. In contrast, among high-income children the college graduation rate increased 18 percentage points between generations.[88] If education is the ladder by which less-advantaged Americans can hope to rise to the middle class and beyond, the rungs of that ladder are increasingly out of reach—yet another way in which the traditional system of shared social responsibility has been gradually dismantled over the past forty years.

FEELING INSECURE

With instability and uncertainty figuring prominently in people's lives, it is important to ask if these social and economic trends are reflected in the way Americans feel. Do Americans feel more insecure? Have they become more worried? This question turns out to be a difficult one to answer.

The first obstacle to figuring out the answer is that we lack rich, long-term survey data that would enable us to tease out an in-depth answer. As a recent Rockefeller Foundation report noted, efforts to assess and measure people's sense of security are rare. And the surveys we do have focus almost exclusively on job loss, which is just one risk among many that needs to be explored.[89]

A second obstacle to measuring perceptions of security and insecurity across the decades is whether or not, over time, people continue to judge and evaluate their situations by the same criteria. In other words, can we assume that year in and year out people use the same yardstick to measure whether or not they are having a good or bad year? If assessments and meanings change over time and surveys don't capture these subjective changes, then it's not clear what our assessments are really measuring.

Analysis by Richard Curtin, the director of the Survey of Consumers at the University of Michigan, addresses the subjective nature of evaluation in his analysis of changes in the standards by which consumers have judged the economy over the last fifty years. For example, during the 1960s people had high expectations and were very confident about the government's ability to control the economy and keep things on track. Such optimism about rising affluence ran into a brick wall during the economic shocks of the 1970s and early 1980s. Initially, dissatisfaction ensued as people continued to hold on to the economic aspirations from the past. By the mid-1980s, however, after repeated economic setbacks, consumers lowered their expectations about achievable growth rates and became more tolerant of high inflation and high unemployment. By the early 1990s, fears about job security grew as Americans became skeptical about the government's ability to use economic policy to prevent downturns.

At this point expectations were so diminished that it took one of the longest economic expansions in U.S. history to reset high levels of optimism. Fueled by the dot-com boom, aspirations soared. In 2000, consumer confidence hit a new peak. With expectations high, consumers in the early 2000s cited high unemployment as an issue even though it was only around 6 percent, half as much as it had been in the early 1980s.[90] The optimism of the late 1990s soon gave way to pessimism because of the successive recessions of 2001 and late 2007. In fact, between January 2007 and mid-2008, the Index of Consumer Sentiment fell by 42 percent, the greatest percentage decline compared to any other recession.[91]

By mapping out historical shifts in consumers' assessments of the economy, Curtin illustrates how "the same level of economic performance, say in terms of the inflation or unemployment rate, can be evaluated quite differently depending on what was thought to be the expected standard." Moreover, changes in standards of evaluation usually occur very slowly and therefore can be difficult to detect.[92] And since different groups of Americans have fared differently as a result of macroeconomic changes, it stands to reason that some Americans may have altered their standards and expectations sooner than others, and some may have altered their aspirations more significantly, and perhaps more permanently. In all likelihood, for example, those employed in the waning manufacturing sector, like autoworkers, had to let go of their expectations for a secure economic life long before and to a much larger degree than have college-educated Americans employed in the expanding service sector.

With this in mind, when sociologists Katherine Newman and Elisabeth Jacobs looked at survey data from the late 1970s to just before the Great Recession that examined people's economic perceptions, they found something interesting. Their analysis revealed that, despite a few peaks and valleys, overall trends during this period suggest that Americans came to see themselves as more secure and in better financial shape, with about the same likelihood of losing their job. As we might expect, their analysis found that those with the lowest incomes and least education expressed the most vulnerability to employment insecurity and financial hardship, while those with higher incomes and more education expressed lower levels of concern.

Yet, despite their lower levels of concern overall, Americans with higher earnings, bachelor's degrees, and managerial jobs have nonetheless exhibited the biggest increase in worry. Over the last thirty years, the proportions of college graduates and managers who said that they are likely to lose their jobs next year and the proportions who said they did worse financially this year than last year have gone up. The rise in concern about job security and financial stability among this group reflects new realities. During this period, the rate of job loss for the most educated went up faster than the rate of job loss for less-educated Americans. And when these workers lost their jobs and found new ones, the new jobs often didn't pay as much. By 2001, workers with a bachelor's degree experienced about a 23 percent drop in their earnings after losing a job.[93] Such trends stand at odds with a long-standing belief among Americans with college degrees that their skills and credentials will translate into a solid footing. If discontent emerges when there is a gap between expectations and outcomes, then it would make sense for concern to increase more among the group that still thought it was well positioned to maintain a good, secure life. When this kind of an expectation smacks into job loss and downward mobility, people will start to worry.

For Americans with less education and lower earnings, it is very possible that worry as measured by feelings about job insecurity and financial hardship did not increase as much over a sustained period because they altered their expectations sooner and more permanently than did better-off Americans. As Newman and Jacobs point out, when those at the bottom lose a job, there is not as far to fall. For such families, their economic situation doesn't change much from year to year; it's always bad. Alternatively, other families may have taken on debt in order to hold on to their standards for security. The lack of a consistent and steep increase in worry among less well-off Americans thus does not necessarily signal that they feel more secure than they used to feel. To be sure, it could actually mean that they have gotten used to having less or gotten used to the high levels of debt required for them to hold on to traditional conceptions of security amid declining fortunes. What is also likely going on is that people's frame of reference for what security even means has undergone a transformation. Finally, it could also be the case that our standard measures for these issues (concern about job security and whether or not we are worse off this year than last) don't allow us to accurately assess people's feelings.

We do not have the kind of comprehensive longitudinal survey data that would enable us to detect subjective changes in Americans' views about what constitutes security and insecurity and whether such definitions shape trends in worry and concern over time. But other measures point to increases in insecure feelings among Americans. For example, even before the Great Recession started, about half of those surveyed worried somewhat about their economic security, with one-quarter "very" or "fairly" worried. By 2009, just over half of those surveyed were now "very" or "fairly" worried.[94] A Pew Research survey done in 2011 found that only 56 percent of those polled felt that they were better off financially than their own parents were when they were the same age, which is the lowest percentage since the question was first asked in 1981, when 69 percent said they felt better off.[95] In 2012, the General Social Survey (GSS) found that less than 55 percent of Americans agreed that "people like me and my family have a good chance of improving our standard of living," the lowest reported level since 1987. That same year, the GSS also found that a record number of Americans (8.4 percent) identified themselves as "lower class," which is the highest percentage reported in the forty years that the GSS has asked this question.[96]

And we may be seeing changes in the definition of the American dream. The American dream has long been equated with moving up the class ladder and owning a home, but recent surveys have noted shifts away from such notions. When Joel Benenson, chief pollster for President Obama, examined voters' thoughts about economic security and the American dream in 2011, he found something new. His polling discovered that middle-class Americans were more concerned about keeping what they have than they were with getting more.[97] Another 2011 survey found the same thing. When asked which is more important to them, 85 percent of those surveyed said "financial stability" and only 13 percent said "moving up the income ladder."[98] In 2007, a survey found that owning a home defined the American dream for 35 percent of those surveyed.[99] By 2013, the top two definitions of the American dream were "retiring with financial security" (28 percent) and "being debt free" (23 percent). Only 18 percent of those surveyed defined the American dream as owning a home.[100]

As the economy experienced wide-reaching transformations, meanings and feelings have likely changed along with it. A *National Journal* article noted how even the definition of being middle class has undergone adjustment, especially in light of the rise of contract workers or "permatemps," those who may make a good wage but receive no benefits and can expect no job security. Capturing this adjustment, the article asks, "If they make a decent income, are permatemps middle class? Not by the standards of the past. But by the diminished redefinition, maybe they are: earning a middle-class living—for the moment."[101]

Amid these shifting economic tides and morphing definitions, many have lost their way. While old beliefs such as that hard work will lead to security and prosperity have fallen by the wayside, it's unclear to many Americans what new truths lay in their stead. As President Obama's pollster Joel Benenson discovered, this lack of direction causes a great deal of unease. "One of the big sources of concern for the people we talked with," Benenson said, "was that they didn't recognize any new rules in this environment. All of the rules they had learned about how you succeed, how you get ahead—those rules no longer apply, and they didn't feel there was a set of new rules."[102] These kinds of examinations suggest that in the age of insecurity, Americans are not just trying to weather an economic storm, but they are also feeling their way through the dark.

THE AGE OF INSECURITY

In the throes of the Great Depression, Americans decided that there had to be a better way to organize government and society, one that would allow individuals and families to enjoy greater stability and security. This philosophical shift from "rugged individualism" to "united we stand, divided we fall" paved the way for the New Deal, the Great Society, and the forging of an unwritten but pervasive social contract between employers and employees that rested on mutual loyalties and protections. The government invested in its citizens, employers invested in their employees, and individuals worked hard to make the most of those investments. As a result, in the decades immediately following World War II, prosperity reigned, inequality decreased, and a large and thriving middle class was born.

Beginning in the 1970s, this system began to unravel. Large-scale changes from globalization and the rise of the service economy to a philosophical shift toward free-market ideology and a celebration of risk changed the landscape of security in America. Against this backdrop, the government curtailed its investments in and protections of its citizens, and employers rewrote the social contract to increase their own flexibility and demand greater risk bearing by workers. Individuals continued to work hard, but instead of getting ahead, more Americans struggled harder and harder just to get by.

Insecurity now defines our world. The secure society has become the "risk society."[103] The belief that we are all in this together has been replaced with the assumption that we are each on our own.[104] Cut adrift, Americans are struggling to forge security in an insecure age.

How are people coping with this new and often frightening reality? And how do the emerging strategies and psychological adaptations for managing insecurity vary from one social and economic group to another? These are the questions I will turn to next.

2 Forging Security in an Insecure Age

THE STUDY

It was my desire to understand how families were responding to the powerful forces described in chapter 1 that led me to be in the living rooms and lives of fifty families, from rich to poor, in Silicon Valley to explore how they forge security in an insecure age. For my project I conducted just over a hundred interviews with members of fifty diverse families from across the economic spectrum. I also conducted in-depth ethnographic research with five of these families. The intensive data collection period lasted for about two years, from the summer of 2005 to the summer of 2007, right before the economic downturn. Over the next few years I stayed in limited contact with the families with whom I conducted ethnographic fieldwork, touching base every now and then. Between 2012 and 2013 I went back into the field and formally interviewed a number of the families profiled in the book to get an update on their lives and situations in the wake of the Great Recession.

HOW IT ALL BEGAN: THE UNEVEN PLAYING FIELD
BEGINS IN LITTLE LEAGUE

In early June of 2005 I met Laura Delgado, whose story I profile in chapter 3, at the big-box store where she worked as a cashier. I'd been thinking about launching my research into insecurity for some time, but I hadn't actually begun the work. In an impressive feat of procrastination, I'd convinced myself that before I started this project I really needed to organize my office. After my office was organized, I decided that I really needed to organize my closet . . . and then the kitchen pantry. In the midst of these tasks, I decided I needed more plastic bins to store the books and clothes I was organizing. And that brought me to the check-out counter where Laura Delgado rang up my purchases.

The two of us began talking about the different kinds of plastic bins, which sizes worked best for which types of storage, and how expensive the bins were. As we talked, Laura checked to make sure I had the lids that matched the bins I'd chosen, remarking on how many people picked the wrong lids and were annoyed that they had to return to the store.

As Laura scanned my purchases, it occurred to me that I should ask her if I could interview her for my project. "She seems nice," I thought—nice enough that she probably wouldn't turn me down, or at least would let me down gently. And just as important, the fact that I knew Laura worked in retail solved a problem I'd been wrestling with: how to figure out the income level of prospective interviewees so I could sample families by their level of earnings. (It isn't the kind of question you normally ask a stranger.) So with nothing left to organize at home, I decided that I just needed to start the project, and I asked Laura if I could interview her.

"Sure," she said, and I interviewed her that very week. During Laura's interview I learned about the difficult economic times that she and her family had experienced over the last year and was surprised by her positive attitude. I remember wondering whether that would be a common finding in my interviews or if it was something unique to Laura.

Toward the end of the interview Laura mentioned that her life was about to get even busier since her son, Dylan, would be participating in an all-star Little League tournament. Dylan's neighborhood team would play against other all-star teams from across Silicon Valley, which meant that in the coming weeks Laura would be going to a lot of baseball games. Sensing an opportunity to meet more families I might interview, I asked if I could come along to one of Dylan's games.

"Sure," Laura responded again.

So a week later, on a hot June evening, I found myself sitting in the bleachers next to Laura watching her son, Dylan, play for the Easterns, a team of the best ball players from the Delgados' working-class hometown.

The game did not go well. Within a few minutes the opposing team had scored six runs, three of them on home runs. On the field, the Easterns looked like the Bad News Bears—making wild throws, muffing ground balls, dropping pop-ups, and running into one another.

At first Laura and the other parents tried to be encouraging, shouting, "It's okay!" "Shake it off!" "You can do this—you just have to believe it!" and "Start working together, boys." But as the mistakes mounted, the parents' mood began to sour and they started to sigh or groan loudly after each mistake. After Dylan failed to complete a seemingly easy play, Laura yelled in a voice thick with annoyance, "If your foot had been on the bag, that would have been an out!"

Focused as I was on Dylan and Laura, I hadn't given much thought to the opposing team until one of their players hit a foul ball into the parking lot where most of his team's cars were parked. "Uh-oh," Laura remarked. "There are some *nice* cars in that parking lot!" Sure enough, I followed her gaze and spotted a collection of BMWs, Mercedes, and high-end SUVs.

"What team are they playing," I asked Laura.

"Woodlyn," she said.

My sociological senses lit up. Woodlyn is one of the most affluent cities in Silicon Valley. I suddenly realized that the game on the field that day was a microcosm of my entire study.

Once I had made the connection the evidence was hard to miss. The Woodlyn parents drove very nice cars, wore expensive clothes, and brought their pure-bred golden retrievers with them to the game. The Eastern parents drove older cars with more than a few dings and dents, dressed casually, and brought their mutts with them.

The fathers of Woodlyn were out in force, though some had arrived a little late to the game, hurriedly walking from their cars to the bleachers while doffing suit jackets, unbuttoning dress shirts, and rolling up their sleeves. As each Woodlyn boy got up to bat, his father would come up to the fence and stand behind him—encouraging, coaching, commiserating, or congratulating him before and after each swing. By comparison, there were only a handful of fathers on the Eastern side, and only one approached the fence while his son was up at bat.

If the Eastern team played like the Bad News Bears, the Woodlyn team played like a well-oiled machine, despite the fact that the boys, drawn from several different teams in Woodlyn, hadn't played together before. The three Woodlyn fathers who coached the team were armed with Excel spreadsheets that they used to confirm batting orders and defensive positions. For their part, the Woodlyn boys took the game very seriously, exhibiting little emotion no matter what happened on the field, good or bad.

The two coaches for the Eastern team, neither of whom had a son on the team (both coached simply because they liked it), were more low-key, consulting handwritten notes about the batting order and seeming confused at times ("Is Dylan supposed to be at first or third?"). Throughout the game the umpires frequently had to remind the Eastern coaches about the rules (no more than three substitutes) and guidelines (if you want your batters announced, you need to give the announcer a list of their names). The Woodlyn coaches apparently needed no such guidance.

As the game grew more and more lopsided, some of the Eastern boys began to get frustrated. Finally, Eduardo, the Easterns' first baseman, flung his glove angrily to the ground and then sat down on first base. When one of the Eastern coaches picked up Eduardo's glove and handed it back to him, he threw it to the ground again. Appealing to the umpire, the Eastern coach said, "Can you kick him out of the game, or at least reprimand him?"

The umpire said, "Come on, son, let's play ball!"

Reluctantly, Eduardo picked up his glove and stood near first base, but he never put his glove back on.

In the end, Woodlyn defeated Eastern 13 to 3. The score might seem surprising, since both were all-star teams made up of the best players in their neighborhood leagues. However, I later learned that many of the Woodlyn players received regular one-on-one training from personal baseball coaches, many of them former professionals who charged between $100 and $200 an hour.

Suddenly the one-sided score no longer seemed quite so surprising.

RECRUITING FAMILIES

On our way home from the game, I stared out the cracked window of Laura's aging minivan and wondered what life would look like if I were driving home in a gleaming SUV with one of the Woodlyn families. That's when it dawned on me that I could use these Little League tournaments as a way to identify families from a range of communities representing widely varying income levels. With a sense of relief, I realized I'd stumbled upon the initial recruitment strategy for my study.

Over the next few weeks I attended Little League games around Silicon Valley in an effort to find families to participate in my study. I sat in the stands, talked with people nearby, and explained why I was there. I told people I was interested in how families in different economic groups and income levels are faring in the wake of changes brought about by the new economy, and that I wanted to explore their experience of making a living and raising a family in Silicon Valley. This is the same "sales pitch" I used throughout my subsequent recruiting efforts. After the game, I would ask people for an interview. I was frequently turned down, but I was able to recruit at least one family at most games. In the end, I recruited twelve families at baseball games.

Next, I recruited three more families by posting a flyer about my project at an economically mixed high school and then passing out the flyer at the high school's graduation. Some of my experiences during these recruiting efforts were revealing in themselves. For example, at the graduation ceremony, after I handed my flyer to an affluent-seeming white woman who was walking past me, she suddenly stopped, turned around, and walked back to me.

"So you are a student at Berkeley?" she asked.

"Yes," I said, explaining that I was a Ph.D. student.

"Are a lot of the students at Berkeley really driven . . . really stressed?" she asked.

"Um, yes," I said, wondering where this conversation was going. "I've taught a lot of students. They work very hard and are under a lot of pressure."

"My son is going to Berkeley next year," the woman said, with real worry visible on her face. "He lacks discipline. He's going to have to get a lot more organized. He's just relied on his intelligence so far. He's going to have to work *a lot* harder."

I was a bit taken aback that she was sharing her concerns with me, a stranger—and at her son's graduation no less. "Well," I said, trying to assuage her worries, "if he had a strong enough record to get into Berkeley, he will probably be okay."

"We'll see," she said, real uncertainty in her voice, and she went on her way.

Later that day I wrote in my field notes, "What was *that* about?" This woman, who should have been having a wonderful day, enjoying the fact that her son was graduating from high school and going off to one of the best universities in the country, was instead weighed down with anxiety. I wondered if any other parents attending the graduation felt the same way or if such worries were unique to this woman. For a long time afterward my thoughts returned to this woman as I tried to figure out why, on such a happy day, she was unhappy with her son.

I rounded out my sample through other recruiting methods, including referrals from participating families to their friends, neighbors, and colleagues. I also recruited people I met while spending time with other families—for example, when I encountered a likely candidate during a community concert in the park. Toward the end of the project I located interviewees from specific income levels through my own social networks. The fifty families I recruited for this study are not intended to be a representative sample in any way. Rather, they were selected to provide a range of viewpoints and subjective understandings.

In this book I have changed all the names and identifying characteristics of the research participants to preserve their confidentiality. I have also added in fictional details, combined aspects of different families, and in some cases merged stories to further protect the privacy of those in the study without unduly altering my findings. These techniques enable researchers to illustrate their conclusions while still protecting individual identities.

What motivated people to help me with my research? I'm sure the reasons varied, but I got the sense that most people agreed to participate simply because they wanted to help a student. For example, when I asked one upper-class father to participate, he said, "Sure, I know it can be hard to get people to do these things." In other words, they were just being nice.

As for me, I hated recruiting people for my study. I hated walking up to people I didn't know, introducing myself, describing my research project, and then dealing with their reactions. I quickly realized that recruiting subjects is a kind of sales job—and as with any sales job, it involves plenty of rejection, which is an unpleasant experience at best. So I am very grateful to the fifty Silicon Valley families that generously agreed to share their time and stories with me.

FAMILY DEMOGRAPHICS

Because I wanted to understand how economic position shapes the experience of security, I chose to prioritize social class over race or ethnicity when recruiting my research subjects. Race and ethnicity are clearly important issues, but it would have been difficult to limit my subjects to just one or two ethnic or racial categories. For example, of the twelve families I initially recruited through the Little League tournament, five were interracial families, five were white, and two were Hispanic. In my sample as a whole, twelve families were interracial, twenty-four were white, seven were Hispanic, three were Asian, two were African American, one was Pacific Islander, and one was Native American—a reflection of the considerable racial diversity that exists in California and in Silicon Valley more generally.

Although I focused on social class rather than race or ethnicity, determining which social class someone belongs to is not always straightforward. To be sure, methods for determining an individual's class position are hotly debated, even among social scientists. Though I generally define class differences among my respondents in terms of income, the groups also differed according to other measures, such as level of education and occupational type. For the purposes of this study, I view education, occupation, and income as the main determinants of a family's social class. I refer to the group of sixteen families with the highest incomes and highest levels of education as upper class, the eighteen families with at least one parent with a college degree, some college, or vocational training as middle class to lower middle class, and the eight families in which neither parent had any college or vocational training as working class. I classified two of the single mothers as middle class and the remaining six single mothers as working class.

Among upper-class families, the most common work-family pattern was a full-time working father and a stay-at-home mother. This pattern changed for middle- and working-class families. For these families, the most common pattern was for both parents to work full-time. Among the eight single mothers, seven worked full-time and one worked part-time and went to school at night.[1]

Typical jobs held by those in the upper-class sample were technology executive, financial analyst, and engineer. Typical positions held by those in the middle-class sample were physical therapist, middle manager, and construction worker. Typical jobs held by those in the working-class sample were house painter, security guard, and administrative assistant.

The incomes of the families who participated in this study ranged from as low as $21,000 to as high as several million dollars a year. Given this broad range and the numerous educational and employment differences among these families, it is difficult to put them into tidy boxes in terms of these variables. To provide some benchmarks, however, table 2 illustrates important educational and income groupings.[2] For the sixteen families in this study in which both parents had at least a college degree, the median annual income was $250,000. This group is highly educated, with all parents possessing a college degree and almost three fourths of them also holding graduate degrees. For the eighteen families in which at least one parent had a college degree, some college, or other vocational training, the median family income was $119,500. For the eight families in which neither parent had any college or training, and in a few cases not even a high school diploma, the median family income was $72,500. In the eight single-mother families, the median income was $45,500, with one of these mothers possessing a college degree and one other having some college experience.

These median incomes may strike you as high, but the cost of living in Silicon Valley is also quite high. A 2007 report found that to pay for basic living expenses (housing, food, child care, etc.), a single-parent family with two children would need to earn about $65,000 annually and a two-working-parent family with two children would need to earn $77,000 annually.[3] By 2010 the required income had increased to about $72,000

Table 2   Annual Income Distribution by Family Education Level

Group	Upper income	Middle income	Low income	Single mother
N = 50	16	18	8	8
Education	Both parents have at least undergraduate degrees	One parent has at least some college education or vocational training	Neither parent has any college education or vocational training	Varied
Median income	$250,000	$119,500	$72,500	$45,500
Minimum income	$177,000	$70,000	$35,000	$21,000
Maximum income	$11,000,000	$180,000	$92,000	$65,000

for a single-parent family and close to $83,000 for a two-working-parent family.[4]

THE SETTING: SILICON VALLEY

I'm not the first sociologist to study how families make their way in Silicon Valley. In the 1980s, Judith Stacey conducted an ethnography of several working-class families living there.[5] In her book Stacey raised concerns about trends in the emerging "new economy" that cast an ominous shadow over the families she came to know. As Stacey predicted, changes in work, particularly the increased demand for people with advanced education and technical skills and the decrease in the number of well-paying jobs for those with less education, have reduced opportunities for middle- and low-income families.

Twenty years later, these changes continue to hit people hard in Silicon Valley. Between 2000 and 2010, real median household income decreased by 19 percent. Over this same period, the number of households on the bottom half of the class ladder grew rapidly, with the most growth occurring in households earning the least. The share of households that earn between $10,000 and $34,999 rose by almost 40 percent, and the share of households that earn under $10,000 more than doubled. In contrast, the percentage of households with higher middle incomes (those earning between $50,000 and $199,000) declined from 62 percent of all households to 55 percent. At the top, the number of households earning $200,000 or more increased slightly, by .5 percent. These changes signal the emergence of what some call the "Victorian gown economy," where income distribution is shaped like a Victorian gown—small at the top, cinched in the middle, and "ballooning out" at the bottom.[6]

Given that Silicon Valley is such an unequal and insecure place, it provides the ideal setting in which to study the inequality of security. Its economy, labor market, and population include many of the factors scholars point to as causes of the rise in inequality and the shift in risk: a large service sector, flexible working arrangements, extensive use of contingent labor, high demand for technical skills, and economic markets heavily impacted by globalization (in the form of both international competition and an immigrant workforce). This exaggeration of key features of the new economy creates the right context in which to study how families in different economic positions do security.

Furthermore, it is also a place where national trends are often magnified. For example, those in the Valley with a bachelor's degree earn two and a half times what those with only a high school education earn. This is the largest wage gap in the nation. While median household income in the United States dropped by about 5 percent in the 2000s, it dropped by 19 percent in the Valley. And while many Americans are now spending a greater share of their income on housing, those in the Valley are spending even more because of the high cost of housing there. Just since 2000, Valley homeowners are spending 43 percent more on housing and renters are paying 20 percent more on rent.[7]

In many ways, such magnified trends make Silicon Valley unique and therefore not reflective of what life is like in other parts of the country. Yet in order to understand how high-level trends are playing out in people's everyday lives, it is helpful to examine an extreme case. In an extreme case, trends and social dynamics can be more visible and thus easier to spot and document.

PHASE ONE: THE INTERVIEWS

I ended up with forty-two two-parent families and eight single-parent families. Most of the two-parent families included married heterosexual partners. However, one family consisted of divorced parents who lived in apartment buildings next door to each other, one family included a common-law husband and wife, and one married couple was separated. Since the interviews were conducted, two other married couples have separated that I know of. I attempted to interview two people per family in the two-parent families and one person per family in the single-parent households. For five of the two-parent families I was able to do only a single interview due to a lack of interest by other family members or a lack of English fluency.

In a few cases I thought it would be helpful to get information from people outside the immediate family. For example, in one family in which the parents were separated and in two single-mother families, I did additional interviews with extended kin (for example, a daughter-in-law) in order to get more insight about what happened to them and why. In one case, with the Faleau family, whom I profile in chapter 6, I also interviewed someone from their church to learn more about the educational scholarships their children received.

Usually I interviewed both the mother and father in two-parent households, the mother in the single-parent households, and one or more children if the family had a teenager. The interviews took place at either cafes or participants' homes and workplaces. I conducted a total of 103 interviews.[8]

I followed a semistructured, open-ended interview guide that covered a range of topics related to security, including the interviewee's work and economic history and his or her thoughts about what security and insecurity look like. I tried to learn about the obstacles that had shaped their lives, the things they worried about, their concerns for their children, the methods they used to manage their worries, and if and how they shared their worries with a partner if they had one. What gradually emerged from the interviews was the concept of a "security project," or the program by which a particular individual or family "does security" in a world where insecurity is rampant. I increasingly found myself focusing each interview on the challenge of defining that family's security project and comparing it with those of other families situated in both similar and different ways.

However, because I interviewed people from such different walks of life, interviews veered in different directions. When I interviewed someone deep in debt, we spent a lot of time on that topic. Where did the debt come from? How did they manage it? For others, a very different topic might dominate, such as retirement planning, a child's college application process, not having medical insurance, or something else. While making sure to touch on a number of preplanned issues, I also trusted that important themes I hadn't anticipated would bubble to the surface during the interviews, and when that happened I followed the conversation where it naturally led.

As countless researchers, social service workers, and journalists have discovered, establishing rapport at the start of an interview is a crucial challenge. And like most of those professionals, I found that it took time and experimentation for me to develop a method that usually worked for me.

The approach I settled on was to start each interview with the same question, something like, "Can you tell me about your background: where you were born, what kind of family you grew up in, and how you got from there to here?" And then I would chuckle and add an ironic remark like, "Just a little question." Most of my interviewees would respond in kind; they'd laugh, too, and say something like, "Have you got a day or two? It's a long story."

I liked this opening gambit for two reasons. First, I needed to have this kind of rich biographical information to understand the person's life story, including the social class they were raised in, their early family life, and the factors that shaped their later experiences. Second, the question is an easy one to answer, so it helped to put those who were nervous or uncomfortable at ease. I sensed a bit of anxiety among some of the poor and working-class people I interviewed in particular. "I've never done this before," one low-income mother admitted sheepishly before I turned my recorder on. Inviting someone to talk about where they were born and the family they grew up in seemed to help them to relax.

In some cases, achieving rapport took patience. One middle-income mother who had been outgoing and friendly while we watched her son's Little League game seemed quite standoffish when we met at a Starbucks for the interview. She started the conversation by asking, "I don't have to tell you my income, do I?"

"No," I said, "you don't have to answer anything you don't want to." This seemed to appease her, but the interview got off to a rocky start. She answered the questions very briefly and seemed on guard. However, as the conversation about her childhood and her family continued, she finally began to relax, speaking with increasing depth about her life, thoughts, and feelings. She spoke with particular poignancy about how her parents had never pushed her to go to college and how she had come to regret not going.

At the end of the interview I thanked her for her story and mentioned that it was sometimes difficult to recruit families. She said, "People might be worried about the college thing."

I said, "Meaning like they haven't been to college?"

"Yes." She nodded. "They hear you are writing your thesis or whatever, and they might be worried that they wouldn't have anything to say."

Suddenly the underlying cause of her initial reticence became clear. After hearing this feedback, I began telling people before I interviewed them that there were no "right" answers to my questions and that I was just interested in their personal thoughts and experiences, whatever they might be.

At the other end of the class ladder, some upper-class interviewees were uncomfortable disclosing their financial information. One upper-class father whose wife I'd previously interviewed started our conversation by crossing his arms sternly and saying, "I'm not going to talk about my income, how much I make."

"That's fine," I said, explaining that he didn't have to answer any question he didn't want to. Based on his body language, I expected a short, unhelpful interview. But asking probing questions about his background, his family, and the choices he had made about his education and career seemed to work like magic. Twenty minutes into the interview he got up from the kitchen table, pulled a beer out of the refrigerator, took a big gulp, and began explaining how his relationship with his parents had impacted his life. Two beers later—much to my surprise—he had answered all of my questions, talked at length about his financial situation, and expressed deep interest in my study overall.

As the work progressed I came to discover that an interview is often an emotional journey, both for the interviewer and for the interviewee. Many people cried at some point, especially when we talked about a difficult childhood, troubled times in their lives, worries about their children, or painful romantic relationships. I would try to be comforting, offering a Kleenex and saying something like, "Wow, that must have been really hard." Sometimes I got emotional myself; in some cases, the interviewee wasn't the only person to shed a few tears.

In the end, most people said they enjoyed being interviewed. I received many comments such as, "Thank you. It was great to talk about that." After I interviewed one middle-class mother who had recently been laid off from her job, she said, "Thank you! That was like therapy." Another time, after one upper-class father poured out his worries to me, his wife walked me to the door, put an arm around my shoulder, and said, "I feel like I should pay you."

After each interview I immediately went home and wrote up field notes in which I summarized the interview, noting both the answers given and the tone and body language that accompanied the words. I wrote these field notes in a stream-of-consciousness style, recording anything that came to mind—a description of the person's house or clothes, comments that puzzled me, and observations about how this interview reminded me of another—or struck me as dramatically different. These wide-ranging reflections later proved invaluable in helping me sift through the huge amount of data I collected over my two years of fieldwork.

PHASE TWO: THE FIELDWORK

As my interviews progressed and a number of specific themes started to emerge, I began doing in-depth ethnographic fieldwork with a few families that seemed to represent the trends I was uncovering. This involved observing, hanging out with, and tagging along with families for a three- to five-hour stretch as they went about their daily lives. I might join a family for an evening and have dinner with them, attend a soccer match and lunch, or drive around with parents as they picked their children up from school. This ethnographic work allowed me to observe families as they went about creating security in their lives and gave me the opportunity to get to know their personal histories in much greater detail.[9]

Like interviewing, performing fieldwork is a skill that takes time, practice, and experience. My first attempt was disappointing. An upper-class family had agreed to allow me to follow them around and signed consent forms defining our agreement (the usual protocol for such arrangements). In hindsight, however, the understanding between us was too informal. The family implicitly retained control over when and where I would spend time with them, and although they were open to having me join them when they were out and about, they were less open to having me around when it was just the four of them at home. As time went on I came to feel as though my calls were viewed as intrusive. I remained an outsider, walled off in some subtle but distinct fashion from the real life of the family. In the end, the observations and insights I gleaned from my fieldwork with them were about what life was like, in a general sense, at the top. This knowledge was valuable but not sufficiently detailed enough to support an in-depth case study. This is why there is no chapter about this family in this book.

My first bungled attempt at in-depth fieldwork taught me an important lesson. I subsequently decided to pay the families who agreed to let me conduct research with them in order to create a more formal, mutually binding contract between us. All of the families I approached to ask if I could observe them in this way agreed to be studied in depth. I conducted the fieldwork one family at a time, and in return for allowing me to observe them, I paid each participating family $200 using funds from a fellowship grant. Now when I called to arrange a visit, I felt less like an intruder—after all, we had a deal, and the family was being recompensed for any nuisance my presence might cause. In the end, I spent about thirty to forty hours with each family, since I tended to continue conducting fieldwork as long as I felt I was learning something new. I've remained in contact with many of the families, talking to and seeing them occasionally so that I can keep abreast of their lives. I also conducted more limited fieldwork with four other families for periods of two to three hours, for which they were not paid.

Some ethnographers ask those they study to treat them like "the family dog," as a continual, unobtrusive presence that they generally ignore as they conduct their daily lives.[10] I sometimes took this approach, trying to settle into the background and just observe what unfolded. Other times I took a more active role, talking with family members about their favorite contestants on *American Idol*, helping out with cooking, and offering my two cents about which outfit looked best. And sometimes I actively probed to better understand what I was observing, asking follow-up questions to elicit more detail, background, and context. Not asking these probing questions would have left me with an incomplete picture.

When I tell people about my research work, many ask whether the families ever really let down their guard or whether they instead censored themselves, giving me only a sanitized view of their lives. In my first few visits with families, I did get the sense that they were on their best behavior. But over time, as they got to know me and understand what my visits would be like, they definitely let me backstage, sharing emotions in an apparently spontaneous, unself-conscious fashion. Like reality TV stars, people seemed to forget that the cameras were rolling after a while.

Doing in-depth ethnographic fieldwork of this nature is both fascinating and exhausting. It is fascinating to be permitted such an intimate glimpse into people's lives, but it is exhausting to be continually on the lookout for insights and clues into people's thoughts and behaviors, knowing that every word, action, and gesture may be significant. After several hours with all my sociological senses tuned to high, I would come home mentally amped up but physically drained.

Then I had to tackle writing my field notes, working from the scribbled notes I'd jotted down while with the family. Writing up these notes in greater detail and with more coherence generally took several hours. I tried to summarize the events I'd witnessed, usually in chronological order, and to capture the conversations (including both the words spoken and the tones used). I would then reflect more generally on the events that had transpired to see how they compared to those I had observed with other families.

I'm not sure exactly what the families I studied this way thought I was doing. Of course they knew they were being watched, even (in some sense) evaluated, as suggested by the comment one mother made to her children, "You know, guys, Marianne is taking notes, so if you want to change something you've said, say it now." Another time, when I was out walking with a family in their neighborhood, the father said to me jokingly, "Hey,

Marianne, a registered sex offender lives over there . . . I let the kids play in front of his house all the time!" He added, "I'm just kidding." He knew I was analyzing him and his family, but this comment suggested I might be focused on his parenting, which of course was not my main concern.

Whatever they thought I was doing, over time they became increasingly eager to share their lives with me. When I arrived at a family's house, I would often be greeted with smiles, hugs, and updates on things that had occurred between visits: "Tell Marianne about the talent show you were in," or "Show Marianne our holiday card." When I went out with the families to church or school events, I was introduced as "a friend."

Often I became a kind of confidante to specific members of the family, who used me as a sounding board to vent about their frustrations with their spouses, kids, or jobs. Gina Calafato (chapter 5), for example, shared with me how difficult her job was and how much stress she was under, and Laeta Faleau (chapter 6) whispered to me that she had some concerns about her son's girlfriend. On a lighter note, Paul Mah (chapter 4) once said to me, "Of course, no one asks me what I want," after his wife and children had spent five minutes discussing where the family would go to dinner without soliciting his opinion. Occasionally I even felt I was being called upon to be a kind of arbiter. For example, one spouse might venture a criticism of the other, then turn to me to ask, "Don't you think so, Marianne?"

These emotional entanglements were tricky for me to navigate. In general, I tried not to give my opinion. I tried to keep a poker face and neither confirm or deny what people were saying about other family members. Sometimes this meant I had to play dumb. When one father asked me directly whether he and his wife had answered questions similarly during their interviews, I said, "You know, I've done so many interviews, I can't really remember anymore." In reality, the main reason I was at their house was precisely because my interviews with them couldn't have been more different, and I wanted to probe the reasons for the discrepancies.

I found being with these families to be both easy and extremely difficult. On a personal level, I genuinely liked everyone I ended up doing research with. They were all nice people who generously opened up their worlds to me, and I enjoyed learning more about their histories and their lives. Many times when I got home from fieldwork and my husband asked about my day, I would say, "It was fun."

But it was painful to be around when families were struggling with financial, career, and psychological burdens, as I hope you will see when you read the chapters that follow. Life in today's America is extraordinarily difficult for countless families at virtually every rung on the ladder of wealth, income, and class. I experienced this reality firsthand throughout my research, and one of the central purposes of this book is to make it vivid and tangible for readers.

DETECTIVE WORK

Being a qualitative researcher is, in many ways, like being a detective.[11] Like a detective, you arrive on the scene where something has happened. You interview witnesses, gather clues, and inspect the crime scene, studying events from one angle and then from another. After hours of fieldwork, you sit by yourself in a room and think. You feel lost—again and again. You follow up with key witnesses, hoping they will provide you with a big break. You look at all the evidence over and over. Something keeps gnawing at you. You keep searching. And then one day in the shower, or out for a jog, or in conversation with a friend, the answer dawns on you. The penny drops. The mystery is solved.

When I started my research, I focused my attention mainly on the question of the degree to which families were exposed to insecurity. In the new risk-based society, which families were sinking and which were swimming? Most of my thinking at this time was centered around the social, economic, and cultural capital differences among Americans and the way in which these differences help to define winners and losers.[12] But as I worked through the interview and fieldwork data, I had a nagging feeling that I was missing something important. It took a long time before the notion of "doing security" dawned on me along with the central role that emotions play in it.

Once I gained this perspective, I went back and reread my interviews and field notes through a lens that finally felt in focus. And I found that these new insights seemed obvious, as if they had been shouting out for my attention from the beginning. In fact, two of my first research experiences—my initial interview with Laura Delgado, in which she seemed so positive in the face of economic hardship, and my confusing conversation at the high school graduation with the upper-class mother who was racked with worry about her Berkeley-bound son—now struck me as vivid, unmistakable case studies of the downscaling and upscaling of security. With each case brilliantly illustrating how people at different levels on the class scale develop varying mechanisms for coping with the anxiety generated by an insecure world. Once I discovered that people were doing security, I could see the bread crumbs that wove a clear path through all of my data, from the first interview I conducted to the very last.

How could I have missed these insights, which now appeared so obvious? For a researcher, it's terribly frustrating that it takes so long to figure out what your data is telling you, because it inevitably means that you feel as if you have left a lot on the table. Today I find the early interviews I conducted for this project almost unbearable to listen to. There are so many follow-up questions I should have asked, so much more I could have learned. When I shared these feelings with a colleague, she said with a sigh, "Welcome to qualitative interviewing."

3 Downscaling for Survival

LAURA DELGADO

You know, having nothing isn't always a bad thing.

Laura Delgado

It's a cold, windy November afternoon. Forty-four-year-old Laura Delgado is sitting in the stands at a local elementary school's baseball diamond, watching the baseball game of her ten-year-old son, Dylan. She is wearing gray sweat-pants, a bright orange San Francisco Giants sweatshirt, and a black baseball cap pulled down low so that it covers her closely cropped dark hair. Laura's fourteen-year-old daughter, Hayley, and her sixteen-year-old daughter, Megan, are standing off to the side, talking with friends from the neighborhood. Laura is mostly engrossed in the game, yelling supportive comments as Dylan takes his turn at bat: "You'll get it next time," "Keep your eye on it." But from time to time she glances over at Hayley and Megan. Occasionally she motions for them to come and watch their brother's game with her. Hayley and Megan shake their heads no, preferring to stay with their friends. In response, Laura shrugs and returns her attention to the field.

Being there for her kids, as she is for Dylan on this chilly November day, defines Laura's life. In their current economic circumstances, it's the only security she can offer them.

At first glance she blends into the crowd of other adults surrounding her, cheering after a good play and scowling after a bad call. But a closer look reveals that all is not okay in Laura's world. For one thing, her sweatpants are worn very thin, particularly in the knee, because she wears the same clothes nearly every day. Laura buys clothes for herself so infrequently that she can remember the last time: "Last year I only bought three pairs of sweatpants from Costco, and they cost $6 each." More tellingly, her front teeth are mottled with brown, a sign that she hasn't been able to afford a visit to the dentist in many years. Her ability to go without is something Laura has relied upon in her effort to eke out an existence, especially after her husband, Vince, from whom she is now separated, was unemployed for about twelve months. Yet money has always been tight for the Delgados, even before her husband's long-term unemployment.

I got more insight into how tough Laura has it when I met her younger brother, Matt, at a Little League baseball game early in my research. "She's studying me," Laura told Matt when she introduced us. "Why, are you studying losers?" Matt asked in a sibling's sardonic style. We all laughed. He then turned to Laura and said, "So she heard your tale of woe and thought she'd study it?" Laura quickly responded, "I guess so," then immediately turned to coordinating after-the-game transportation plans for the family.

Even though I had explained to Laura that I was studying how families like hers coped with financial setbacks, she seemed to prefer to think that I was studying her as an example of an involved parent. Consequently, she typically began our conversations by telling me about her kids' activities and how she had been driving around like a typical overscheduled middle-class parent. She would talk about the ways her life imitated that of other middle-class parents, such as attending the upcoming back-to-school night or the Little League playoffs. Only later would she set aside this rosy version of her life and reveal the way her life was, in truth, an imitation of middle-class existence, lived on the very edge of poverty. This ability to emphasize one interpretation over the other proved to be a key coping mechanism for Laura.

Laura grew up in a middle-class suburban neighborhood in Silicon Valley among blocks and blocks of 1950s-style ranch houses. She lived with her parents and two siblings in a four-bedroom, two-bath house. While standing inside that house and looking at the flowering plum tree in the backyard, it's hard to imagine the events that could lead someone to fall so far so fast. But Laura's story vividly illustrates the experience of many people in a changing economy and an insecure world.

Since getting married and starting a family, Laura Delgado's security project has centered on dealing with one derailing event after another. To cope, she has worked on her emotions in order to adapt to and survive a difficult life. Her story is a stark illustration of the security strategy I call downscaling, a way of paring down the criteria for security, pushing away anxiety, and evoking an attitude of optimism and acceptance even when things are bad—and getting worse.

LAURA'S EARLY YEARS

To see just how much Laura's family had lost in a single generation, I would occasionally ask her how her current life differed from her childhood years (when her name was Laura Samson). When I asked this question, she often contrasted her own unstable marriage with her parents' stable relationship. Rarely did she mention economic matters. But one evening I got a better look at these differences when Laura went out to the garage and came back with two leather-bound photo albums under one arm. "Remember," Laura said, "when you asked me how my life is different now than when I was growing up . . . Well, I was thinking about it, and I thought I should get these pictures out and show you what growing up was like for me." She sat down on the couch next to me and opened one of the albums, saying, "This is the kind of life I had."

The albums are filled with page after page of pictures of the Samson family's trips: visiting friends in Georgia, seeing the sites in Washington, D.C., and touring the Statue of Liberty. Smiling broadly, Laura pointed to a picture of the family posing in front of their luggage at the airport in 1976. Laura, her sister, and her mother were wearing dresses and her brother and father were in matching navy blue suits. "This is when you still had to dress up to get on the plane," Laura laughed. As she continued to turn the pages, pictures of a happy high school career flitted by: Laura in her cheerleader's outfit, Laura with her high school band, Laura cuddling with friends at her sixteenth birthday slumber party, Laura triumphantly tossing her graduation cap in the air. The album concluded with pages of pictures documenting a high school trip to Europe.

Laura thoroughly enjoyed her high school experience at the private school she and her younger brother attended "on the other side of tracks" from where the family lived in a school district with lower-performing schools. Laura talks about her high school years in glowing terms. But she also notes the sacrifices it entailed. To come up with the annual tuition, her dad supplemented his full-time work as a firefighter by joining the National Guard, working rotating weekends, and her mom took a part-time job as an administrative aide at city hall. "I had a comfortable life growing up," Laura says. "My parents talk about it like we didn't have enough money, but I never felt it. It was very stable." Laura's mother, Gloria Samson, confirms this memory of a mostly happy, stable childhood where money was occasionally tight. "If we didn't have the money, we just didn't spend it," she says.

During my research with the Delgado family I had the chance to talk with Laura's parents. William and Gloria were both in their early seventies, enjoying retirement and living on the decent pensions they received. Yet at the time of our interview, most of Gloria's monthly pension check— and then some—was going to help support Laura and her children in the wake of Laura's separation from her husband.

Twenty-five years after Laura was a teenager, she is no longer recognizable as the smiling, effervescent girl in the blue and white cheerleader uniform. Now in her mid-forties, Laura still smiles, but she doesn't seem to do so as effortlessly as she did when the photos from her childhood were taken. Rather, Laura has learned to work on her feelings to make herself feel happy, to make herself feel as if everything is okay, even when it is not.

BETTER TIMES: LIFE ON KEARNEY STREET

After Laura graduated from high school, she attended an affordable state university, where she majored in psychology. Toward the end of her college career, she met Vince at a bar. From the beginning, Vince had personal problems. Laura describes him as "directionless" at that point in his life. But by the time they decided to marry, Laura had assumed— mistakenly—that most of his problems were under control: "When I met him he was working as a bartender and drinking and doing cocaine. He got off the cocaine, but I guess the drinking never left him."

However, the early years of their marriage seemed happy. Laura worked for an organization that helped girls who were struggling with psychological and emotional problems—work she found demanding but rewarding—and Vince had moved on from bartending to construction-related work and had begun to focus on plumbing. Laura looked forward to being a mother and was delighted when she got pregnant with their first child.

A studio portrait of Laura with her one-year-old daughter Megan on her lap hangs in a hallway in Laura's parents' house. Laura's hair is long and flowing, her eyes agleam with life and happiness. "This picture was taken in 1989," her mom recalls. "That's when things were a little better for them." Laura, too, remembers this time fondly, saying, "That was the most stable part of our marriage, the years that I worked."

After having Megan, Laura decided to stay home. "I didn't want my kids to end up like that," she says, referring to the troubled girls she worked with. She also felt that working wasn't practical because day-care costs would have exceeded what she earned in the nonprofit world. But it appears that Vince was ambivalent about Laura's decision. Laura's mother, Gloria, puts it this way: "Vince's whole philosophy was—she went to college, she graduated, she should have a job that helps pay for the things that they want. And that was a big disappointment to him because she didn't do that."

To earn some extra money, Laura worked part-time selling cosmetics door-to-door and at house parties at night or when the kids were at school, a job she had started in college because of its flexibility. Laura did well selling cosmetics; she earned several hundred dollars a month and even managed a few other people. But her priority was her family, and she spent the rest of her time volunteering at her children's schools because she wanted them to know that school was important.

Unfortunately, I was never able to interview Vince and get his side of the story. We scheduled an interview that he canceled on short notice, and he never returned any of my subsequent calls. However, I did observe Vince at various events and talked to him socially at a Little League picnic I attended with Laura and her children. He was drunk at the picnic, wobbling back and forth and slurring his speech a bit as he asked about my project. We never got a chance, however, to talk about his life and circumstances.

According to Laura and her parents, though, during this early period in the Delgados' marriage Vince kept his drinking in check. Nonetheless, his employment opportunities were limited because he had only a high school diploma at a time when the economy was changing and better opportunities were largely reserved for those with more education or technical skills. So money was always tight, and the Delgados occasionally had to turn to Laura's parents for help. Fortunately, they had found an affordable two-bedroom, single-bath house to rent on Kearney Street, in the working-class neighborhood where Vince was raised, about twenty minutes away from Laura's parents. Although Laura did not like the drug dealing and violence in the community, she liked the layout of the house and knew they were getting a good deal at only $740 a month. Laura felt lucky that she could stay at home with the kids, and she and Vince settled into a mostly stable life.

In the mid-1990s, when Laura was thirty-five years old, Vince took a job with a company that didn't offer health insurance. Like others with only a high school education, Vince was on the front lines of the shift in risk. The Delgado family couldn't afford to pay for health insurance on their own, and Laura believes they earned too much to qualify for a government-sponsored program. Laura says that even if they had qualified, she would have felt uncomfortable relying on government aid: "I'm not sure how I would have felt doing something like that."

Sadly, the worst happened. Laura had a seizure while driving and crashed her car into a parked car and suffered severe internal injuries. Fortunately, her kids were not with her at the time, and no one else was injured, but she spent about a week in the intensive care unit. Between the hospital stay and follow-up therapy, the bill totaled $50,000, not to mention the additional debt they amassed on their credit cards to make ends meet during the ordeal. The hospital declared the Delgados "medically indigent" and waived half the bill. But for a family barely making ends meet to begin with, the $25,000 debt was a heavy burden.

A few years later, things appeared to be looking up for them. Vince gained entry into a plumbers' union. His wages rose dramatically; after an apprenticeship and several years of work, he began to earn as much as $80,000 a year. Though union dues and health and retirement contributions ate into his take-home pay, the family was doing better than ever financially.

During this time Vince pressed Laura about his long-standing desire to leave the high-priced Bay Area. If they moved away, he reasoned, they might be able to afford to buy a house of their own. But Laura resisted, and the disagreement turned into a long-running battle. Laura recalls Vince asking, "Why don't we move somewhere else and own a house?" In response, she would point to the overriding importance of family:

> [I would say], because an earthquake can take a house down, fire can take a house down. You can lose it for not being able to make the payments. But having four living grandparents for my children, having all of their aunts and uncles except one live locally so they have all these cousins that they get to see regularly, which I make happen because I was raised that way . . . it's a gift. And my in-laws live two blocks from where the kids went to elementary school. So there were times when the kids could walk there to go see them. And I like that we're that close to them and they can go see them any time they want. My in-laws live in the same house where my husband grew up so they have roots in that. My parents live in the same house where I grew up, so my kids have roots in that.

Years later, when I was talking with Laura again about why she had never left the Bay Area, she pointed to another reason. Recalling a conversation with her parents in which they brought up Vince's desire to move away, she remembers telling them,

> "One, I'm not going to uproot my kids. And two, why would I want to be in a strange place where I have no family and no support system if my husband decides to leave?" And it was the first time my parents had heard me say that. My mother looked at me with a shocked face and I said, "It could happen." And so that was the first inkling that they had that maybe things were worse than they thought.

From Laura's words, as well as her decision to stay in the Bay Area, it is clear that she has always prioritized family over material things. Yet her tendency to downscale, to circumscribe more and more narrowly what she and the kids needed to be secure, to be rooted, intensified as the family's financial situation declined. And in the end, ironically, the change that Laura sought to insulate her kids from came anyway—right through the front door.

HITTING ROCK BOTTOM

For a time Vince's rising wages provided the family with overall financial stability and great benefits, despite their large medical debt. However, after the dot-com bust and the economic downturn, events conspired to undermine the Delgados' financial and then their emotional security.

Vince's union job worked on a rotation basis. After he completed a job, his name would be placed at the bottom of a list of plumbers available for work. Jobs were doled out according to placement on the list, meaning that the waiting time between jobs depended on overall demand. In the late 1990s, when the economy was booming, business was so good that Vince's waiting time was often as little as a few days. However, as the economy declined and jobs dried up, Vince's waiting time stretched first to two or three weeks, then to a month at a time. Things worsened, and Vince ended up being out of work for close to twelve months total, with one stretch lasting long enough to threaten the Delgados' ability to maintain their health insurance. (According to union rules, if a member is out of work for six months straight, his health benefits are terminated.) Vince did his best to get work, even listing his name with unions outside the Bay Area, but the whole state was experiencing a downturn and he could find no other work.

Meanwhile, the elderly woman who owned the house that the Delgados rented died. Her heirs decided to sell it, planning to split the profits. The Delgados tried to figure out a way to buy the house, which was priced at $500,000.

Laura asked her parents to contribute half the down payment and then co-own the house with Laura and Vince. William and Gloria, however, balked at the idea. They simply didn't want to be landlords in their retirement, especially to Laura and Vince, since, even with Vince's better wages, the couple often struggled financially. William and Gloria also believed that Laura and Vince had caused some of their own problems by overspending on things they really couldn't afford, such as dinners out.

Laura agrees with her parents. "We should have been saving when we were living on Kearney Street, with our rent low like that; but I took Vince's lead—he was the one earning all the money, [and he spent it]. We should have been saving instead of living on the high life."

"Living on the high life"? That's a matter of perspective. From my conversations with Laura, I gather that much of their spending went for household appliances, going out to eat, buying a new car they needed, and daily expenses during Vince's periods of unemployment. In any case, the debt they ran up on their credit cards, combined with the car loan and the outstanding medical bills, meant that the Delgados' debt approached $45,000. With Vince out of work and their good housing deal about to disappear, the Delgados were on the financial edge.

In the middle of all of this, they moved from the Kearney Street house they had called home for nine years into a two-bedroom apartment in the same city. Their rent more than doubled, rising from $740 to $1,800 a month. The significantly higher rent, combined with Vince's unemployment, financially squeezed the family. Things were so difficult that a couple of times Laura's parents covered their rent. Relying on her family when necessary had long been part of Laura's tacit security strategy. But the Delgado family now faced financial pressures they had never experienced before, and things began to buckle under the strain.

It's well established that financial distress has a negative impact on both marital quality and family life.[1] In the Delgados' case, the hard times led to a heavy increase in Vince's drinking. Laura feels that Vince drank more because "he had a lot more opportunity to drink," but she also thinks his drinking was related to depression over his unemployment. If true, this wouldn't be surprising: sociologist Lillian Rubin's research among working-class families has found that men's drinking often intensifies after job loss.[2] Vince's drinking, then, may have been an emotional response, a way to numb his negative feelings about the economic and employment problems he faced.

Vince apparently agreed. Even though he had often described Laura's psychological perspective on problems as "psychobabble," when she began to express feelings of depression after the move, Vince told her he felt the same way. But whatever the cause of Vince's drinking, it worsened the Delgado family's problems. Though Vince was a functioning alcoholic (in the sense that he could drink at night and get up and go to work in the morning), he was not a happy drunk, and he would often come home in a bad mood. Laura says that at times he was violent toward her and that the children were afraid of him; in her words, "the kids would just go to their room and shut the door to get away from him." Ultimately, the Delgados were asked to vacate the apartment they rented because of Vince's drinking. Laura explains, "We were asked to leave because of the noise—because Vince would come home and be drunk and start yelling, and then he would swear up and down in the morning that he didn't remember."

Laura's life was in a downward spiral. After fighting with Vince at night, she would get up in the morning to work part-time as a cashier at a local big-box store to earn some desperately needed extra income. Even though the job was "below [her] educational qualifications," she took it because she wasn't sure what her other options were after being out of the workforce for fourteen years. She felt she could work only part-time since her three kids needed to be picked up at school and taken to their various sporting activities.

The Delgados found a cheaper place to live, but the change of scenery didn't alter the family's trajectory. Laura and Vince continued to fight, especially after Vince decided to buy a new truck, an act Laura views as a selfish attempt to rejuvenate his masculinity, which had been bruised by their economic setbacks. She talks about it sarcastically: "When he was really depressed about not being employed, what did he do? He went out and bought a truck. I mean, c'mon, a truck, with oversized wheels . . . that we couldn't afford—that says masculinity." Work is often central to the achievement of masculinity.[3] Thus, it could be the case that Vince's unemployment undermined his sense of self, both as a husband and as a father. Buying the truck may have been an attempt to make himself feel better because by driving it, he might have felt more like a man.

The chain of events touched off by a souring economy did not leave the Delgado children unscathed. The first and most serious victim of the "emotional waterfall" cascading over the family was their eldest child, Megan.[4]

One fall day Laura came home from work and had a bad feeling, "sort of mother's intuition." In the bathroom she found Megan lying on the floor, groggy and incoherent. On the counter was a bottle of sleeping pills that Laura had occasionally used. Megan was conscious and responsive, but Laura decided to take her to the emergency room anyway, even though she knew that doing so might cause the hospital to call Child Protective Services (CPS). "But I didn't care," Laura said, "because I knew I needed to do what was best for my daughter."

Megan was assessed by the emergency room doctors and her stomach was pumped. Several hours later Megan was evaluated by a psychiatrist who said that she needed to receive intensive therapy that would require her to see a specialist three times a week for several months. After four months of therapy, Megan seemed to be doing better, though she continued to see her therapist on a regular basis. Laura participated in the recommended family counseling, but she complains that Vince went only twice. Vince, it seems, began to disengage from the difficulties in his life by retreating from his family.

When Laura told me the story of Megan's breakdown, she did not mention the family strife surrounding the events. Rather, she said, "There were a couple things that set it off, but one was that Megan had gone to see a movie, and in that movie there's a character that takes sleeping pills." Laura's father, William, offered a different interpretation: "Now there's a prime example of what the fighting between Vince and Laura and Vince's drinking will do to you." William also believes that the economic stress the family was suffering played a role in the breakdown, in part because Vince's father had told Megan she should "go and get a job" to help out her parents.

When I asked Megan about why she had resorted to taking sleeping pills, she put the blame squarely on her father: "It was mostly him, because he was like an alcoholic and he would be stupid. It was mostly because of him." CPS concurred with Megan's assessment. Laura recalls that CPS interviewed all the children after the incident and determined that Megan's problems were related to Vince's drinking. In Laura's account, CPS decreed that Vince either needed to stop drinking or leave the house, "so he decided to leave." Vince moved into a room he rented from a friend, further removing himself from his family, and Laura and the kids began a new life on their own.

On their own, life was not much better. In fact, when I interviewed Megan almost nine months after she had taken the sleeping pills and seven months after Vince's departure, she confided to me that she still occasionally thinks about hurting herself, "but not like I used to." Megan explained that she was still in a lot of pain. She said, "Talking doesn't really do anything for me, though. I'll talk about it and get it off my chest, but, like, it's still going to be there, it doesn't really do anything. Nothing really does anything. Talking takes it away for a little, but then when you come back, it's always going to be here." Megan remains quite angry with her father. On her cell phone, her dad's phone number is listed under "unimportant person."

I don't have firsthand knowledge of what life was like when Vince and Laura were together, but life inside the Delgado household after the separation was quite hard. Numerous studies have found that women's standard of living declines between 13 percent and 35 percent after the first year of divorce, while men's standard of living goes up 11 to 13 percent.[5] In Laura's case, since she worked only part-time and for low wages ($9.50 an hour), her income dropped drastically, even after she increased her work hours as much as she could. The lack of funds was a constant problem for the family, as illustrated by offhand remarks Laura made to me, such as references to "one of the times the phone was disconnected" and supposedly optimistic comments like, "I think things are okay. I don't think they're going to shut anything off." Laura relied (once again) on help from her parents until her divorce settlement was finalized, at which point Vince would be forced to pay her child support and alimony.

When my research began, I expected to find Laura visibly weighed down by the burden of her debt and the financial distress she lived with. Instead, she often seemed to be doing fine. Only occasionally did I see her get really upset, and even then her unease was fleeting. This finding was repeated in interviews with others of limited means when they would tell me things were fine, that they were okay because they could get by with very little. At first this led me to take Laura's version of reality at face value: maybe things weren't as bad as I thought. However, the more time I spent with the Delgados, the more I realized what was really going on. It wasn't that Laura (or other interviewees) didn't feel the financial strain she was under. Instead, she had developed techniques to manage her anxiety, ways of masking or managing the brutal reality she faced.

This downscaling of security is a form of emotion work or emotion management, a concept introduced by sociologist Arlie Russell Hochschild. As Hochschild has shown, people work on their feelings; they monitor, inhibit, evoke, and shape emotions in different ways so that their feelings are in line with what they think they should feel or what they want to feel.[6] In a similar vein, the downscaling of security involves working to transform feelings of insecurity into feelings of security, an emotional adaptation that makes life and its problems more bearable and manageable.

Scholars have studied a number of kinds of emotional transitions, including changing embarrassment to anger, contentment to happiness, shame to pride, and guilt to innocence.[7] But as sociologists Kathryn Lively and David Heise point out, certain emotions are closer together than others, which allows for easier transitions between them, while other emotions are more distant, making the transition between them more difficult to achieve.[8] I would argue that security and insecurity, comfort and fear, are distant emotional states, which means that enormous work is needed to transition from one state to the other. In Laura Delgado's case, she relied on several techniques to make herself feel secure even though she faced extreme insecurity over the years.

THE DOWNSCALING OF LAURA'S SECURITY

Laura always expected to have the kind of stable middle-class life she experienced growing up. On several occasions she made comments such as, "I got married with the intention of staying together forever. I expected that we would have kids, watch them grow up, and then be together to watch our grandkids" and "That's one thing I thought I would have done by now, own my own house." To reduce the tension between the life she thought she would have and the one she actually had, Laura downscaled. The main mechanisms involved in this process were lowering the bar on her requirements for security; embracing the power of positive thinking; and worrying only about today, not tomorrow. Together these strategies allowed Laura to better cope with her painfully insecure reality.

Lowering the Security Bar

One of the primary ways Laura downscaled was to alter her feelings about security so that they aligned with the types of security she could actually provide for her family. Whereas the affluent people in my study upscaled their definitions of security to include living in the best school districts, sending their children to the best colleges, and saving millions of dollars for retirement (as I will discuss in the next chapter), Laura downscaled security to mean nothing more than being close to family and being present for her children.

One of the ways Laura shifted her focus to family was by deemphasizing the importance of material things, as she did in her fights with Vince about leaving the Bay Area when she stressed that living near family gave her children roots and a sense of security that money couldn't buy.[9] In our interviews Laura continually emphasized the importance of family and minimized the value of material things, arguing that extended kin provided more security than money ever could. For example, when she told me about her younger sister moving to Washington for more affordable housing, she said, only half-jokingly, "She deserted us." She also often made comments such as, "It annoys me when people want things more than they want to spend time with people" and "I don't really care that much about material things or possessions. I guess I just wasn't raised by people who thought those things were important."

To underscore to her children that family comes first, Laura relied on her own family history. She told me:

> The other night, I was watching TV with the kids and it was about the people who survived Hurricane Katrina in New Orleans, and I said to them, "See they are just happy to be alive. At that point, all the stuff you have just doesn't matter, because surviving and being with your family, that's all there is." And I learned that from my grandmother, who was a single mother of four kids who came out to California by herself after her husband died, and she had nothing. She worked hard her whole life, and when she was old she lived with her daughter and got a small amount of money from Social Security. But she would give the grandkids little amounts of money, and she would say, "Here's a little bit of Gran to take with you." You know, having nothing isn't always a bad thing.

Laura's downscaling strategy was mirrored by other economically disadvantaged interviewees in my study. Twenty-one-year-old Molly Farmer, a single mother, told me she feels secure as long as she has a roof over her baby's head and has something to eat. Jenny French, a forty-year-old administrative assistant, told me, "I've been broke my whole life, and so it's like, if I'm broke, it doesn't scare me, it doesn't bother me." Jenny said that she didn't need many material possessions to feel secure and that she feels fine "as long as I have a few bucks in my pocket and my car is running." Laura possessed a similar definition, telling me at various times that her view of security was "having a roof over my head, having enough food to eat, and having clothes to wear."

This doesn't mean that those with less don't suffer anxiety about their economic status. Describing a time when she was burdened by tax debt and she was too sick to work, Jenny explained, "We [were] barely living, eating. We couldn't afford anything. We couldn't afford clothing, nothing . . . We were basically just paying our rent, and we did have food . . . it was just like bare necessities. And there were times that I would just pray about it." At trying times like these, Jenny mastered her anxiety and generated a sense of security by focusing on the basics. And even today, with Jenny's economic situation improving to the point that she has more savings than she has ever had, she retains a pared-down notion of security in which "all we really need is like food, clothing, and shelter."

There are several ways to analyze Jenny's downscaled conception of security. On the one hand, it reflects a kind of resiliency and fortitude that has likely emerged from her repeated need to get by on very little in difficult times. On the other hand, minimizing her threshold for security provided a ready-made emotional coping mechanism that helps cushion the psychic impact of any financial blow—a kind of emotional armor against the feeling of insecurity. Thus even as Jenny strives to improve her family's circumstances, she simultaneously protects herself by holding in reserve a scaled-back definition of security that provides a way to emotionally weather life's ups and downs.

Although interviewees like Laura, Molly, and Jenny seemed to readily embrace downscaled notions of security, others seemed to accept the reality of their situations more reluctantly. For example, Marshall Casey, who had recently returned to teaching after being laid off from a technology project management job, described his financial situation as "living one step ahead of the red line. [He laughs.] It's not a good feeling." He added, "We'd like to have a nice buffer to where you don't have to worry about it . . . 'cause we've got kids that are going to be needing to go to college here pretty soon. And I don't know how we're going to manage that. We haven't really done much preparation for that either." When I asked Marshall about saving for retirement, he said, "Well, I mean, it doesn't look like I'm ever going to be able to retire."

Owen Meehan, an electronics technician, offered a similar comment about retirement: "I tell people, 'I've only got a couple more lifetimes to work before I have enough to retire.'" Unlike many of the upper-class interviewees in my study who have an ever-present concern about retirement, Marshall and Owen seem to have a more fatalistic, if realistic, viewpoint. Rather than worrying incessantly, wallowing in frustration, or questioning the fairness of the system, they seem resigned to the new economic reality that without pensions, many will never save enough to retire. In this, of course, they're not alone. A survey of middle-income Americans found that 37 percent think they will never retire and will work until they are too sick or die.[10] Another survey by the Center for Retirement Research found that 53 percent of households sampled will be unable to maintain their standard of living in retirement.[11] In a world like this, Marshall and Owen's sense of resignation is an understandable coping mechanism, quelling any unhappy feelings they may have about their situation.

As for Laura Delgado, as long as everything was okay at home, she feels that her security project is on track. She repeatedly emphasized that the basis of her security was her children's well-being, not her financial well-being. In her mind she and her children are "poor by choice" because she chooses to spend time with them rather than working more. It was only when things were not good on the home front that she expressed a lot of unease. "I don't mind that Vince breaks his promises to me," she says, "but when he breaks his promises to the kids, that gets me angry." One time Vince had promised to take their son, Dylan, shopping to celebrate his graduation from sixth grade. When Vince failed to show, Dylan began to cry and lay down on the couch with his head in Laura's lap. In response, Laura's family-centered security project kicked into action: "So I took him shopping for graduation and just used money that I was going to use to pay a bill. It's not like I don't have other bills I haven't paid."

While part of Laura's response to her situation was to cushion the emotional and financial blows for her children, Vince's response to economic crisis seems to be to drink and avoid the family so as not to be reminded of its collapse. Ignoring his children was something new for Vince, and it seems linked to the difficult financial situation the family now faced. Upon hearing about the graduation incident, their next-door neighbor noted the change in Vince's behavior, saying, "Wow, Vince has really changed. He used to come around here more to see the kids, and now I never see him." Laura agreed. "He checked out of our family a while ago," alluding to the fact that at one point, in better times, he had been checked in. Vince's retreat from his family leaves Laura with the additional task of protecting her children from their sadness and disappointment about their father's abandonment of them. Re-emphasizing the importance of family and minimizing that of material things is a crucial element in her protective strategy.

The Power of Positive Thinking.

During my final visit with the Delgados during the intensive phase of my research with them, I explained to Laura that I felt I had enough information to tell their story. Laura responded with a smile, saying, "That's because I talk too much." Then, with a more serious expression, she said, "And I don't prevaricate at all. I tell it like it is . . . and it's like when things get this bad, it's like okay, this is where we are, here it is."

Laura's words struck me as a poignant blend of truth and half-truth. On the one hand, Laura did "tell it like it is"; she was open about her family's painful situation. On the other hand, however, she actively tried to suppress the dark reality of her situation through the power of positive thinking. Such an approach led her to search for silver linings and redeeming features, even in the most dire straits, to maintain a deep sense of gratitude for what she did have, and to actively avoid negative thoughts because of their potential to do her in. Laura thus didn't lie about her situation, but she continually interpreted her reality so that it had a rosier hue.

One way she spun reality was to focus selectively on particular aspects or versions of events in order to depict a more encouraging view of life. When discussing her lack of retirement savings, Laura downplayed its importance, saying, "But it's okay. I told my kids I really don't foresee myself not working anyway. I don't really think that when I'm in my sixties or seventies I'm going to want to sit and do nothing." She later added, "I tell my kids, 'I will probably work until I die.' I think I would work a little even if I didn't need to, because it keeps you active."

Laura also downplayed the enormous differences between her life growing up and that of her children, focusing solely on the contrast between an intact family and a divided one and ignoring the economic differences. "We don't have a whole lot of disposable income," she once told me, "which in a lot of ways I don't think is so bad. I don't think it hurts my children to hear the word 'no.' It doesn't hurt them to know that we can't afford everything that we want, that a little bit of working for something isn't a bad thing." Later she expanded upon these sentiments by comparing her children's situation to the one she faced when she went to a private high school: "When I got to high school, I realized in comparison to some of the kids there that my family was not well-off. My friends had lots of things that I didn't, and my parents had to work hard to put me through school there."

These remarks might make it sound as though the Delgado children are simply living without luxuries like the latest video game or a cool pair of sneakers. In reality, however, they often lack basic necessities such as heat in their home. Yet Laura's insistence that her children's lives resembled her own childhood survived even this discrepancy. One winter afternoon Laura told me, "I'm not turning on the heat because I can't afford it. I haven't paid the electric bill in two months. But my parents taught me to turn off the heat at night, because if you are under the covers then everything should be fine. It's kind of cute, because in the morning the kids and I will be in the living room cuddled up in our sleeping bags." Laura's repackaging renders invisible the symbols of insecurity in her life (the lack of heat) and replaces them with symbols of security (family bonding).

Another time Laura put a positive spin on her children's economic behavior, saying, "My kids have become very good at bargain hunting. At the grocery store, they saw that Hot Pockets were on sale there for $2 each, which is basically a dollar a pocket." Explaining the children's behavior as "bargain hunting" is one way of looking at it, but the children themselves often expressed real concern about whether they could afford to eat. Laura told me that once, when the bill at the grocery store totaled $78, Dylan had said to her, "You're spending money we don't have," to which Laura replied, "You're right, but we need food." Calling the kids' shopping strategy "bargain hunting" put an innocuous gloss over a sad reality, which was that the children were trying to stretch the family's money in order to survive.

Perhaps the ultimate tactic that Laura uses to reinterpret the grim truth of her situation is simply to assert that the family's problems are temporary. One time she drew an analogy between her own situation and the difficulties of life in the 1930s: "You might think that, given how I was raised, that I would be really upset about the way my life is now, but I'm not . . . My parents were Depression-era babies; they watched their money and weren't overly indulgent." Here Laura repackages her poor financial state as simple penny pinching and belt tightening, just as she imagines her parents and grandparents did during the Great Depression. This interpretation supplies Laura with the view that her situation is temporary, something that saving and skimping will enable her to overcome.

Another time Laura told me, "I tell the kids, 'We'll get all this stuff worked out and then get back to taking trips again.'" Prior to their financial downturn, the Delgados had enjoyed taking trips to Disneyland and to family reunions in Napa Valley. It is hard to envision the change in circumstances that will make such travels possible again, but part of Laura's security project is to envision a brighter future, even in the face of much evidence to the contrary. Laura seemed to edit the reality of her life and worked on her emotions to turn lemons into lemonade. In doing so, she suppressed anxiety, concern, and fear and evoked a sense that things were not so bad; their situation was just short-term anyway.

Another aspect of Laura's positive thinking strategy was to highlight the things she is grateful for as a way to bury negative thoughts and experiences. One afternoon at the Delgados' house, I witnessed Laura's response to a call from a bill collector. The family generally relied on their answering machine to screen incoming calls; as Laura explained, "I don't answer the phone because there are just days when I really can't deal with the bill collectors." But on this occasion, Laura was expecting a call from Megan, so she picked up the phone after the second ring and heard, to her chagrin, the voice of a bill collector. I listened as Laura tried to explain why she wasn't making payments on the outstanding bill:

> I get paid on February third next, but I don't know how much I'll have to pay this bill because I can't even pay my rent . . . My paycheck will be for about $400 and my husband doesn't give me enough money as it is. I'm doing the best I can. I don't have $50 to give you. I spent over $70 on groceries the other day, and that is going to have to last me to the end of the month.

Holding the phone away from her mouth, Laura said to me, "I get tired of going through this, but there isn't anything I can do." Returning to the conversation, Laura added,

> Look, my entire paycheck is $400. I only work part-time because I've got three kids. I survive by whatever my husband gives me and what I make. We're playing catch-up with everybody. And what really gets me is that this card is not in my name, it's in my husband's name. I'm a responsible person, and I do the best that I can to pay my bills.

After finally agreeing to send the creditor some money, Laura hung up the phone. Given the circumstances—the browbeating call, Laura's understandable exasperation, her painful economic situation, and the potential embarrassment of my witnessing the phone call—I expected her to be very upset and perhaps to start crying. Instead, she sank heavily into the couch and said, "I just try to focus on the good things in my life—the kids and Maggie [their dog]." She petted the dog's head and smiled at her. In a matter-of-fact tone she explained that she was trying to work out some deals with other credit card companies. She then got up to change out of her store uniform. That was the extent of her reaction.

Other interviewees in my study use similar repression strategies to quickly banish the negative reality of their lives by focusing on what they are thankful for. Jeff Kenney, an injured construction worker, whose uninsured medical bills forced him to declare bankruptcy, told me, "I don't have a pot to piss in. I won't lie to you. Not a thing. I barely made my rent this month." But then he added, as if to push away the reality of his financial plight, "It's all good, too. Everything happens for a reason. I'm a firm believer in that. By the grace of God I'm still here today . . . As far as I'm concerned, I'm blessed with a beautiful kid, and I live in California, and I have a great family and friends."

This repression work is also clearly illustrated in Katie Monroe's description of how she deals with the fact that, at fifty years old, she has zero retirement savings:

> It burns a hole in my heart when I think about it . . . I'm fifty . . . and I have nothing to fall back on. I can get up some days, and I could think about that and fall into like this big depression, but I can't allow myself to do that. I'm glad every month that goes by that I was able to pay the rent; I was able to

pay the bills and I still have more money in the bank than I have ever had. At this stage of the game ... whatever is gonna happen is gonna happen. [She sighs.] I can't drive myself nuts thinking about it ... The way I look at it is I'm in the best place that I've been in a long time ... but I can't put more pressures on myself right now because there's some days where I just feel like I'm gonna snap anyway. I'm running around and doing things and not getting any help from the kids.

Katie's words reveal how she consciously works on her feelings. She suppresses her fear about her lack of savings and focuses instead on something more positive, which is her improved ability to keep up with her bills. It is only by burying her anxieties about retirement and calling forth her sense of accomplishment about paying her bills that she is able to feel she is in control.

Other people I spoke with repress bad news by limiting their exposure to it. A few interviewees, for example, stopped opening their mail in order to avoid having to face the stress of unpaid bills. As one working-class mother explained, "There have been times when I haven't opened up the mail for like three months because I just know it's nothing good in there. Now probably if I paid [the bills] every couple weeks, I'd figure out where I'm at. [But] I've learned not to look every day. It just makes me crazy." Describing how his wife reacted to their mounting bills, Marshall Casey told me, "She just didn't even want to think about it, so she just ignored the problem, ignored the bills, put them in a box and hid them under the bed. And the next thing you know you've got people knocking on your door wondering where [the money is]." In these examples, interviewees were not necessarily trying to focus on the positive. Instead, they were trying to protect themselves from getting dragged under by mounting debts.

Over time I came to realize that Laura employed the power of positive thinking all the time. Almost every time I talked to her, although she might start by commenting about something that was wrong, she would always finish with a more upbeat remark. For example, one time she said, "I guess in [my life] it's been one horrible thing after the next ... I'm pretty positive, though. I put the good things in front of me and try to focus on them." Another time she said, "Life can throw you curves. It's how you cope with those curves that counts ... I think my life is good, I'm blessed. You've gotta keep a positive attitude. I tell my kids, don't whine or complain. Don't throw yourself a pity party."

Finally, Laura banished negative thoughts and cultivated a positive outlook by comparing her situation to that of others, such as a friend who had lost a young child to cancer. Laura would say, "I'm for the most part happy with my life. It's kind of amazing. The last year has been horrible in a lot of ways, but I'm still like, 'Hey, it could be worse.' I have a friend who buried her child at eight. So that's a good reminder that, 'Hey, mine are sixteen, fourteen, and ten and they're all healthy. They're all reasonably happy. They're all here, so you know.'" On other occasions Laura compared herself to others who had no family they could rely on for support and to a family member who was paralyzed as a result of a car accident. By comparing herself to others in more dire circumstances, Laura underscores the blessings in her life, which makes her feel better.

Other interviewees in pressing financial circumstances used the same tactic. After expressing concern about not having enough money to save for retirement or help her older children out, Maria Townsend, a fifty-year-old administrative assistant, said, "Hey, I am a hell of a lot better off than a lot of people, and so in that respect I am happy." Jeff Kenney, the injured construction worker, said, "I'm grateful as hell. I'll go hand a homeless guy twenty bucks and just remember I'm lucky to have everything I have."

For Laura, "focus on the positive" became a kind of self-help mantra that she told herself, her kids, and me over and over again. However, the unending need to generate that positive energy sometimes revealed the darker truth that Laura was trying to cover up. Laura once said to me, "I don't know how I've gotten through the hardships of the last two years. I've got all this stuff to get done and no one else to do it. I've just got to plow through it." Another day, in an almost confessional tone, she told me that because of all her bills, "I've been walking around with my chest constricted, like I'm going to have a heart attack." Yet just as these words left her mouth, she quickly added, "But I feel like things are getting better, since I've paid off one card and only have $900 to go on another one."

To deal with her difficult reality, Laura tried not to dwell on the problems in her life that reflected the economic volatility, personal indebtedness, and individualized risk of the economy. Rather, she actively worked to ignore her anxiety and stress by cultivating a positive outlook and an appreciation for all she had. As Barbara Ehrenreich has pointed out, this kind of positive thinking provides an "apology for the crueler aspects of the market economy."[12] In Laura's case such an approach enabled her to live with the bleak realities she faced—to view her situation in more tolerable terms, as a life she could accept, a life she could manage.

Worrying About Today, Not Tomorrow

A final strategy used by many of the less well-off people I interviewed was to take things one day at a time, to focus on the here and now rather than an overwhelming future. As Laura often said, "It's like I don't have time to worry about it, so I just don't. If it's happening today, I worry about it. If it's not happening today, I can't worry about it." Or, as Jeff Kenney said, "I live week to week, dollar to dollar."

Past disappointments help to explain the appeal of this coping mechanism. As one father put it, "It seems that when I plan, things don't ever fall into place, so I think I stopped planning for things." Molly Farmer, a young single mother, told me,

> [I had] a lot of dreams that just weren't going to become a reality that I just set my heart on. I had a plan to become a veterinarian. I had a plan to become a basketball player. I set my heart on that and it falls apart. Things out of your control can just blow it for you . . . I don't set my heart on it anymore . . . So not having to plan has kind of been the best route for me. I don't get disappointed, and I get excited over the little things.

Maria Townsend put it this way: "So I have kind of learned . . . and that's kind of like a pessimist way to put it, but you know, I don't set this major goal because in the back of my head I am thinking, 'You know, you will probably not get there.' Let's just get from day to day, you know. And see, that's kind of where I am." Similarly, Laura Delgado said she didn't plan because "there was always something that was a priority right then. I was so busy with babies and did volunteer work at the school . . . But there was always some crisis happening or something else going on, and now I realize I was living the life of someone married to an alcoholic. I have read about it before, and now I realize that was me. I was living that."

When people's circumstances are constantly shifting such that they have little control over what happens in their lives, it becomes hard to map out the future and execute long-range goals. Indeed, in this context, the combination of income instability and income scarcity makes the exercise of long-term planning not only pointless but painful.[13] To cope with this hard reality, people with few resources often rely on an emotional plan, which is *not* to plan very far into the future.

INTENSIVE DOWNSCALING

For most people, the need to downscale probably ebbs and flows over time as circumstances change. It is likely that downscaling is cyclical in nature, bubbling up when this kind of coping is necessary. In Laura Delgado's case, however, the difficult straits she was in during the in-depth phase of my research appeared to require a high degree of downscaling.

Indeed, although I've presented the downscaling strategies Laura used as analytically distinct, in her daily life she often relied on multiple techniques at the same time. For example, about a year after I had completed my in-depth research with the Delgados, I called Laura to see how things were going. No one answered, and the answering machine did not pick up. It took several days of calling for me to get through to Laura. When we finally connected, I asked what was wrong with her answering machine. Laura replied, "They turned the electricity off. I'm getting paid tomorrow, and I'll go down and pay it, so it's not that bad." She went on to use several of her coping techniques to explain how she and the kids were managing:

> I'm trying to make a game out of it with the kids. We use candles at night, like we're camping. But I tell the kids, I have to make choices, and they needed things like yearbooks, school pictures, sports pictures, and you can't redo those things. Bills I can go back and redo . . . I told the kids that people have lived without electricity before. It's not a necessity. TV is not a necessity. They already know cable isn't a necessity . . . I tell the kids I have choices to make and some of my choices have been hard, or dumb, and some of the choices I've made have consequences we don't enjoy, but it's about what is a priority . . . so we're doing our own earthquake drill. How we can handle it

and how we can survive . . . It's all in how you look at things. Dylan and Hayley are going along with it. Megan is complaining a lot, but she always complains.

Instead of interpreting the electricity being turned off as a negative event, Laura turns it into a game, an "earthquake drill." She pares down what her family needs (electricity isn't a necessity) so she can continue to feel secure in the face of real insecurity. This interpretation of reality confirms that she is still okay because her family is still together and her kids still have the trappings of middle-class life (yearbooks, school photos) even if, financially speaking, they are not living a middle-class life. She bucks herself up by cultivating an optimistic interpretation ("It's all in how you look at things"). Finally, rather than viewing hardship as destabilizing, she'd rather bring her family along with her into the more innocuous, even fun, version of her life. For the most part, her two younger children comply, although her older daughter resists.

Faced with Laura's bleak situation, some people might cope by praying to God and believing that God has a plan for them. Others might have a mental breakdown, turn to drugs or alcohol, or pin their hopes on a new romantic relationship. Instead, Laura embraces the power of positive thinking. She develops an outlook that filters out bad news and highlights good news.

Perhaps as an escape, perhaps as a way to maintain her optimism about the future, Laura avidly reads romance novels. On one occasion when I accompanied her to the library, she checked out a stack of six romance novels. A self-described "voracious reader," Laura is also a voracious consumer of fantasy, of stories that reinforce her belief that painful events can be overcome, that fairy tales do come true. Years later, when I asked Laura why she likes to read romance novels, she said, "I don't know. I guess maybe it's the happy ending . . . They're very formulaic, they're very predictable . . . And maybe my life is just so [she sighs] . . . that a lot of the time that's kinda how I get through."

But Laura's parents don't buy into the fantasy. From their perspective, Laura is in denial. When I interviewed them, her father, William, sounded exasperated, saying, "She's not dealing with reality . . . You know everything is okay with her when it's not okay. She's gonna have to wake up and say, 'Okay, things aren't good. Things are terrible. The kids are suffering, I'm suffering.' . . . And she's not doing that. She's just like, 'Everything's fine.'" Her mother, Gloria, agrees, saying, "She's in a place that she thinks, you know, Vince is coming back and everything's going to be fine, and it's not." I disagree with Laura's mother on this point—I didn't get the sense that Laura thought Vince was coming back—but I share their belief that Laura viewed her life through rose-colored lenses.

Laura's parents also strongly disagreed with her vision of the future. Contesting Laura's belief that she would be able to work "until the day I die," William said, "those kids are going to have to support her when she's old." And Gloria disagreed with Laura's estimate that she could pay off her bills in "five to six years if it's managed well." Gloria said, "Well, it's going to take her forty years to get it covered. That's not working. We told [Laura and Vince] that maybe they should have gone through bankruptcy."

Laura and Vince fought about whether to declare bankruptcy. Vince wanted to take that step, but Laura was strongly against it. From her perspective, the debt they faced was a result of the choices they had made, and in Laura's worldview, "if you play, you pay." Apparently discounting the fact that much of their debt was due to an uninsured medical condition and unemployment, Laura was determined to pay back what she felt they rightly owed. Her focus on the individual causes of her situation as opposed to its structural causes ultimately compounded the problem, making it harder for the Delgados to get out of the hole they were in.

Laura likely inherited this ethic of individual responsibility from her parents. In my interview with them, William and Gloria placed the blame squarely on Vince and Laura's shoulders, discounting external explanations that largely accounted for their debt. "Both of them have always been spenders," Laura's father said with a judgmental tone.

While William and Gloria viewed Vince and Laura as a cautionary tale, they saw their son, Matt, a divorced father of two children, as an exemplary tale. William described Matt in glowing terms: "He's Mr. Coupon man. He's got the first nickel he ever made." Like Laura, Matt went to a local state university. Unlike Laura, however, he was never uninsured during a medical emergency and never dealt with long-term unemployment. Matt may indeed have managed his money better than Laura did, but he also avoided the structural constraints that impeded Laura and Vince.

This difference, however, is invisible to Laura and her parents. And in the end, Laura's parents have a pessimistic view of Laura's future. In fact, her father said, "Things could change, but right now I have no vision of a light at the end of the tunnel." When Laura's parents walked me to the door at the conclusion of our interview, Laura's mom said, "Let us know if you can think of anything that will help Laura."

A lot of things come to mind when thinking about how to improve life for Laura and for millions of other people like her: widely available, affordable health care, which is something the Affordable Care Act will help provide for more people (though millions will remain uninsured); decent unemployment benefits; subsidized child care; well-paying jobs; secure pensions; and affordable housing, to name just a few. Yet with few of these policies realistically on the horizon, I share the pessimism of Laura's parents about her future. According to our newly rewritten social contract, people are now supposed to bear the responsibility and the risk for attaining their own security. But when the social goods that would help them achieve this goal are in short supply, then we need to understand how they manage this contradiction.

For Laura Delgado and for many others I interviewed, the key to getting by is a security project built around the strategy of downscaling: paring down thresholds for security, embracing the power of positive thinking, and worrying about today rather than tomorrow. This kind of security project enables those facing hard times to be resilient in the face of tremendous difficulty. Like a kind of emotional life jacket, downscaling keeps people's heads just above water as they fight the economic tides that are carrying them out to sea.

4 The Upscaling of Security at the Top

BROOKE AND PAUL MAH

It's Halloween night and Brooke Mah and her two children, twelve-year-old Jacob and ten-year-old Alec, are warming themselves near the fire pit a neighbor has set up in his driveway. Jacob is dressed like a monster and Alec is dressed like a scarecrow, with long pieces of hay streaming from his costume. Brooke and her neighbor are chatting, but Brooke is focused more on keeping Alec away from the fire, even pushing him back at one point and exclaiming, "Alec, your costume could easily catch fire—*stay back!*"

Brooke remains on high alert as her children trick-or-treat around the neighborhood. For example, if Jacob and Alec try to cross the street before Brooke has checked both ways for traffic, she yells "Stop!" in a panicked tone.

Brooke's concern about her children's safety is apparent not only on Halloween. One time she told me, "I'm always saying, 'Don't run, the pavement is wet!'" The need to protect the children from threats has even prompted Brooke to seriously consider remodeling their home. Driving home from one of Alec's baseball games, Brooke explained that if they added an office area adjacent to the kitchen she could better monitor her children when they are online.

The Mahs are a prosperous family, with access to material goods that Laura Delgado and her children can only dream about. Yet Brooke and Paul worry a lot, particularly about their children and their financial plans.[1] This paradox was mirrored among the other upper-class families in my study: they did not seem to feel completely secure despite their high level of financial security. In fact, the heightened level of worry I expected to find among the disadvantaged was often just as prevalent among those with the most resources, the best opportunities, and the greatest prospects. The palpable presence of anxiety among the best off in my study reflects their tendency to upscale their approach to security. Rather than paring down their needs, focusing on the positive and minimizing the negative, and employing the other strategies associated with downscaling, those who upscale increase their notions of what they require to feel secure, focus on perceived negatives more than positives, attune themselves to the future, and seek to perfect the world around them. This approach to doing security, including the way affluent families divide security work between husbands and wives, reveals these families' take on the inequality of security and its future. Their stories show how the continual ratcheting up of needs and the quest for perfection often left members of this group feeling as if they have come up short despite their often impressive achievements.

THE MAHS' SECURITY

At forty-eight years old, Brooke Gibson Mah is a petite blond woman whose hazel eyes are in constant, almost frenetic motion behind her tortoise shell glasses. To siphon off some of her extra energy, Brooke wakes up each morning at 5:00 and runs for close to an hour, getting back home before the rest of her family awakens. By contrast, Paul Mah, also forty-eight and a third-generation Chinese American, is more laid back, given to sitting on the couch, feet up on the coffee table, hands clasped casually behind his head. While Brooke is so electric that her presence could never be missed, Paul is so low-key that you might forget he's there.

Brooke and Paul Mah live with their children in a prosperous Silicon Valley neighborhood in a home worth approximately $2 million. Despite the high price tag, it's a modest house, a 2,500-square-foot four-bedroom, two-and-a-half-bath ranch-style home nestled behind a meticulously kept rose-filled English garden. Thanks to a recent kitchen remodel, the house has an up-to-date feel; the kitchen sports stainless-steel appliances, a breakfast bar, and granite countertops.

Like most of the home-owning participants in my study, the Mahs could not afford to buy their own house at today's prices. Fortunately, they got into the real estate game before the market took off, and, with help from Brooke's parents, they bought their house for $500,000 fifteen years ago, a few years after they were married. Although childless at the time, they selected the neighborhood "because of the schools' reputation," a reputation that was confirmed, Paul explains, by the high housing prices and the schools' excellent standardized test scores. The schools have remained first-rate, with test scores on statewide exams placing the school district at the front of the pack every year.

Education has always been a high priority in this family—so high that after a neighbor told Brooke that in order to get into certain desirable preschools she would need to apply right after their first child was born, Brooke filled out the application and sent it in the week after she gave birth to Jacob.

Like many other upper-class parents in my study, Brooke and Paul both attended elite private universities for their undergraduate education. They met while attending a top business school, where each earned an MBA. Today Paul is a vice president at a start-up technology company, earning more than $200,000 per year. When their children were little, Brooke worked part-time in marketing for several technology companies, but for the past five years she has been a stay-at-home mom, and she currently spends a lot of time volunteering at her children's schools.

From a security perspective, what is notable about the Mahs' history is the absence of destabilizing events like those that Laura Delgado experienced: long-term unemployment, income decline, and uninsured medical emergencies. Although the Mahs and the other upper-class families I studied occasionally experience a layoff or a health problem, they encounter them less often than other families. Furthermore, the derailing potential inherent in destabilizing events is reduced by four elements of upper-class families' security positioning: their high incomes, in-demand skills, stable benefits, and social networks. These elements have provided the Mah family with a tremendous amount of security.

Having earned top-flight educational credentials and amassed a continuous work history of twenty years in finance and marketing for technology companies, Paul Mah clearly has business and technical skills that are in high demand. Yet Paul's work history is also a function of his social network, including business school classmates and former colleagues, which has supplied him over the years with numerous opportunities. Paul explains,

> From '82 [when I graduated from business school] till 2000, all the jobs that I ended up taking or being recruited into were all pretty much through the network of folks either I went to business school with or worked with over the course of that time. So it really wasn't until my current job [that] I took a job purely based off a headhunter connection, not knowing anybody. So for twenty-odd years it was all through the network.

Paul's security positioning is thus strengthened by the business network that keeps him in the loop about work opportunities. These jobs offer Paul high pay and excellent benefits in return for his valuable skills, enabling him to amass substantial savings and deal with a serious chronic health problem (diabetes) without suffering economic dislocation.

Paul's resources—his skill set, network, and savings—came together to protect him and his family from potential life disruption when he was laid off after a reorganization at a start-up he worked for. Being out of work for two months with just two weeks' severance pay was worrisome for Paul, but his security positioning proved to be a great buffer:

> Was it uncomfortable? Yes. It was the first time I didn't have to get up in the morning and go to work in twenty-some-odd years, but it wasn't like I was going to retire. At the same time, we had enough cash where if I needed to go a year without working, we could do that. So I started networking pretty aggressively at that point—trying to see what else was out there. I started writing a couple of business plans with some friends of mine and did this, that, and the other thing. But then I ran into a guy I used to work with who was starting up a company and needed a marketing guy, so it worked out.

Brooke shares Paul's perception that the family is fundamentally secure, and was so even during his stretch of unemployment: "I guess we haven't really been in a situation where we felt like we were on a decline that we might not be able to pick up from." Most American families would find a two-month lapse in income difficult, even devastating. As John Valencia, a middle-class father in my study, said, "Everyone is two weeks away from being broke." But the Mah family's multiple protections against risk meant that the loss of income was just a blip on their radar screen and never determined what food was put on the dinner table or cut into other things like saving to send their children to college.

The divergent security trajectories of the Mahs and most of the other families in my study are linked to the rapid rise of income and wealth inequality, driven by the fact that the earnings and assets of those at the top have outpaced those of everyone else.[2] A less widely recognized factor is the way changes in work have benefited those at the top and hurt those at the bottom. As sociologists Neil Fligstein and Taek-Jin Shin have found, changes in employment relations mean that less-skilled workers are "systematically being treated worse."[3] The result is that job insecurity, which has increased among all Americans, has increased more substantially for those at the bottom, who have also experienced greater reductions in workplace benefits, a combination of effects that Fligstein and Shin describe as the "bifurcation of work" between higher- and lower-skilled workers

For families like the Mahs who have good jobs, robust benefits, ample savings, and access to top-notch public schools, what is there to be worried about? What is left to strive for? What my research with upper-class families revealed is that their anxieties and concerns represent a response to their understanding of how the world is changing around them, from the increasing importance of education in the knowledge economy to the need for individuals to fund their own retirements. Indeed, people like the Mahs have a particularly acute awareness of these changes and think about them a lot, almost as if they are hearing emergency news bulletins on a radio frequency that other families simply don't receive. Ironically, this heightened level of awareness does not bring them much, if any, reassurance. Instead, their understanding of the rising inequality of security and the shifting of risk simply fuels their anxiety and encourages them to increase the scale of their security projects.

Two related concerns dominate the lives of the upper-income families in my study: securing both their children's futures and their own financial futures. Although parents in other social classes are largely content with how their children are doing socially and academically, saying things like "They're good kids" and "I like what I see," it was rare for upper-income parents to be content. They often indicated that there was something wrong or that their children were a bit off track. Moreover, while families with fewer resources often try to ignore or suppress their financial concerns, upper-class families, particularly fathers, think about their finances more frequently and in greater detail, feeling the need to achieve ever greater levels of financial success. Accordingly, the security benchmarks upper-income families feel the need to achieve are much higher than they are for other families, and they are continually rising, always a bit out of reach. Consequently, even when an objective observer might think that everything is going well, these families talk about problems and shortcomings that need to be addressed. This never-resolved anxiety about goalposts that are constantly receding is at the heart of the security strategy I call upscaling.

SECURING JACOB AND ALEC'S FUTURES

Growing up, Brooke Mah "couldn't wait to be a mother and have kids." Yet she put off motherhood in order to focus on a career in business. She had her first child, Jacob, in her mid-thirties, followed almost three years later by Alec. When her children were young, Brooke worked part-time so she would have her afternoons free with them. However, after her children began elementary school, she began to worry about their academic and social lives and felt the need to dedicate more of her time to helping them. So, as Paul explains, Brooke decided to stop working altogether to "make sure this whole education thing sorted itself out." This meant that Brooke became focused on fostering her children's educational and social development. She explains, "I'm trying to give them the tools to reach their fullest potential. I want them to be maximizing their skills and developing ethics that will help them learn later on, with their job or whatever. And I get frustrated when things are undermining that. I'm not okay with anything less than what's possible. When there are clear solutions, I want those solutions implemented." Paul, too, viewed Brooke's efforts as helping their children "fulfill their potential," saying that anything less would be "like a waste of a natural resource." Like the highly educated parents in sociologist Annette Lareau's study of child rearing, the Mahs viewed their children as projects to be developed.[4]

Brooke takes this responsibility very seriously, making sure to keep up with a host of educational issues that she feels could impact her children. In the past few years she had signed up with numerous educational and political groups to receive email updates on subjects ranging from the status of public school funding to developments in approaches to educational curricula. She sets aside time, on a regular basis, to read through these emails to keep herself informed.

Though Brooke told me that she didn't have the time to spearhead any specific school-related initiatives herself, she helped at her children's schools a lot. She assisted a group of parents who organized an auction at Jacob's school to raise money for field trips. She volunteered to help a committee of teachers and parents charged with helping select new textbooks. She made phone calls to encourage voters to help pass a bond measure to support music, language, and technology programs in the local public schools. With a sigh, she said, "I probably spend several hundred hours a year on this stuff."

Though these efforts were a huge time commitment, Brooke didn't mind. She liked being at the school on an almost daily basis, having access to behind-the-scenes information, and knowing whom to contact to learn more about a specific issue. For example, she was friends with a mother who had been involved in collecting the data that confirmed that in comparison to similar school districts in other parts of the country, the schools Brooke's children attended devoted fewer resources to music, language, and technology classes. Brooke asked her friend to send her the report and took the time to read it "because of my sense of wanting to know everything," Brooke said, "to have the big picture. I mean, I'm a very detail-oriented person."

After reading the report, Brooke was concerned about the impact that the lack of such programs would have on her children. "It's debatable whether money buys a good education," Brooke said, "but certainly cutting classes and opportunities limits things [for them]." Pointing out that her children's school had fewer technology classes than did other schools, Brooke said, "That's embarrassing. I mean, we're in Silicon Valley." But the differences in language education troubled her even more: "In Greenwich, Connecticut, those kids take language [starting] from the third grade. They will have an advantage over my kids on the advanced placement test [in high school]." In the race for security in an increasingly competitive world, Brooke is worried that her children are already behind.

JACOB AND ALEC'S PROBLEMS

The passage of the bond measure that guaranteed funding for music, language, and technology classes did not seem to assuage Brooke's worries about her children's futures. When I began my in-depth research with the Mah family nearly two years later, Brooke still had specific concerns about each of her children. Jacob's troubles centered on his social skills (or perceived lack thereof), and Brooke feared that his writing skills were subpar. As for Alec, Brooke and Paul worried that he was not being sufficiently challenged in science and math and fretted about how to position him to apply for private junior high school. The Mahs' security project centered on addressing these issues—on achieving what might appear to other families as "perfection" in their children's lives.

Like his mom, thirteen-year-old Jacob has a small frame. He has long dark brown hair that hangs to his ears and often covers his face. He is also shy, barely raising his eyes to meet mine when I visit. Jacob's introversion has been a concern of his parents for some time. As Brooke explains, "In the last few years at school he had a couple friends, but in the early years during lunch he would just sit by himself and read. It was so painful." Brooke believes that Jacob's shyness stems in part from his problem with stuttering. After working with speech therapists he has greatly improved, but at times he is still hesitant to talk, particularly in class. Instead of talking with friends, Jacob retreats into reading. "Jacob devours books," Brooke says. "He reads everything. His idea of a great vacation would be to have a pile of books this high and just read through them." Though Brooke and Paul are pleased that Jacob is a good reader, they worry that his shyness and his tendency to hide behind books will hinder him later in his life. Brooke says, "If it were up to him, he would stay home and read a book on a Saturday night, but that won't help him navigate through life."

Because of Jacob's quiet disposition, the Mahs had concerns about sending him to the public junior high school, where they feared he might get lost in the crowd. Noting that the public high school in their area is very good, the Mahs decided that a smaller, more directive private junior high school would provide Jacob with the foundation (the "sea legs," in Paul's words) that he would need to return to the public school system later. The Mahs paid close to $20,000 a year for Jacob to attend private school.

To Brooke's delight, Jacob's social skills seemed to improve after only a semester at the private school. He made several friends and had a very full social calendar. His stuttering had diminished until it was almost nonexistent. But Brooke's happiness about these developments soon gave way to concern that Jacob was confining himself to just one social clique. Since Jacob preferred reading over being very active, she worried he was not making friends with the high-energy boys who spent their time during recess running around. She began asking Jacob about the different groups of boys in his grade, where these groups sat at lunch, and whether they ever interacted with one another. Brooke even organized a pizza party one weekend and invited all the boys in Jacob's class in an attempt to reduce any real or perceived social barriers.

Brooke was also encouraged to hear from Jacob's advisor that he was actively participating in his Spanish class, which Brooke attributed to his attending a small school. She said, "With only forty kids [for the teacher] to get to know and deal with, I can say to the teacher, 'Don't respect my son's reserved nature.' At a bigger school, you can't really do that." Whatever the reason for Jacob's progress, Brooke was delighted. "I just couldn't believe it, my son raising his hand and talking in class!" she said, though she quickly added, "Wouldn't it be great if it were in math?"

While Jacob was doing well in most subjects, they had concerns about his writing abilities—a concern compounded by their dissatisfaction with Jacob's English teacher:

> I mean, when I was touring the school and talking with the principal, I explained that writing was the most important subject to me because I felt that Jacob had had mediocre teaching for the past two years. And the school assured me that they had a strong program, but this teacher seems really bad to me. Jacob showed me his writing assignment and he got a perfect

score, but the first sentence was incomplete, there was no verb, and he didn't circle misspelled words. So I've called the teacher and the principal because I want to meet with them before break so they can stew on it over break and come up with a way to address it.

Brooke sighed and added with a tone of resignation, "Well, maybe nothing is perfect."

But Brooke, like other upper-income parents, seems perpetually dissatisfied. Jacob is more verbal in Spanish class? Great—but why not in math class? Jacob is making new friends at school? Wonderful—but why isn't he friends with a broader group of boys? Jacob is doing well in several classes? Fine—but what's the matter with English? It's as if Brooke is incapable of feeling that things are on track.

This is quite a contrast with the downscaling Laura Delgado, who focuses on the positives and blocks out the negatives. Paul attributes this tendency to emphasize problems to Brooke's personality: "Brooke is proactive, organized, she does a lot of worst-case-scenario thinking; [it's her] personality. That's just her orientation." But most of the upper-class parents I studied exhibit this type of thinking. For example, several whose children earn straight A's in school describe their kids as not "intellectually curious enough" or "too lazy to reach [their] maximum potential" or lacking in "passion." Emily Horvath Colson, a lawyer, has a daughter, Melanie, who takes a lot of advanced placement classes, hopes to attend an Ivy League college, and has the grades to do so. But Emily told me, "I was a little disappointed because Melanie was invited to be part of a leadership group and she declined to do that, 'cause she was a little bit worried about being overscheduled. And so I have to admit that I was disappointed that she was looking at the limits of her abilities rather than at the opportunity to have something that would look good [for college applications]. I have to admit that I was disappointed about that—that she was being realistic." Measured against these inflated notions of what "being on track" means, most children in upper-class families don't measure up.

Paul and Brooke's younger child, Alec, is an inquisitive ten-year-old, given to furrowing his brow as he watches the goings-on in his ant colony. Since he and Jacob are allowed to watch only three hours of TV a week, he entertains himself by practicing baseball in their backyard and reading comic books. Alec is also the most playful and lighthearted of the Mah clan, and apparently the only one who pushes back against the familial quest for perfection.

Alec is an exceptional athlete, earning a spot on his city's all-star baseball team for the last two years. He is also a very strong student, particularly in science and math, and he performs very well on standardized tests. But in the last few years Alec has found his science and math classes boring, which Brooke and Paul blame on the tendency of public school teachers to focus on students in the middle, disregarding those with higher or lower levels of proficiency. Brooke says, "Alec has quite an aptitude for [science and math], and he didn't like it because it was boring. And it seemed that if you go on that continuum, that would be unfortunate. Who knows what he'd do with his life, but it would be an unfortunate thing for him to turn off to subjects that he finds the easiest of the subjects that he works on." With Alec's love of baseball growing and his interest in science and math waning, Brooke started to worry that sports would overtake academics in Alec's life. The quest to prevent Alec from losing interest in his studies became another focal point of the Mahs' security project.

To address the situation, Brooke signed Alec up for an after-school math group at a local community center. She explained, "I wanted him to have an opportunity to do math together [with other kids], like logic games, where they're excited about math and math is fun. And once a week they did that, and it was great. So again, it was to counter my son's perception that math is boring." Brooke also pushed for other interventions. Brooke knew of a few other parents who wanted to create a specialized class at Alec's school where students with special aptitude could do science. Brooke got involved with this group and attended several meetings with the principal to help make their case, but their efforts went nowhere. The principal said the school didn't have the staff to devote to such a program. Despite the goodwill Brooke had with school because she volunteered so frequently, she began to sense that her pushing for the class was creating ill will. Her sense was confirmed when one of Alec's teachers told Brooke in a snippy tone that the principal described the group of parents pushing for the specialized curriculum as "having an agenda" and "being overly demanding."

Alec wasn't pleased with the special program either, especially after he went to a demo of the proposed class and discovered that the science experiments were less sophisticated than the ones he had done at summer camp the previous summer. With the school digging in its heels and Alec still not challenged, Brooke relented and gave up pushing the special program.

Brooke's inability to fix Alec's issue with his science and math education is painful for her. Sitting in a chair, shoulders hunched, watching Paul and the children splash around in the pool at their local community center, Brooke appears almost broken. "I don't have an ally at the school with whom I can advocate for my son," she laments, adding, "I'm desperate for a solution here, without compromising our values."

This failure drove Brooke to consider some unusual solutions. After telling me that she had examined all the schools in the area and researched each one's fifth-grade math curriculum, she said, "I'm just not happy with my options; they are all parallel moves. I'm now thinking about going overseas." She explained that she had researched programs in India and Singapore and was thinking about moving the whole family for six months to let Alec finish out the year overseas. "It would be a great experience for the kids to live in another culture, make friends with kids from other countries, get immersed in a language," Brooke said.

Stopped at a red light on the way home from swimming, Brooke turned to face the children in the backseat. "India might be an interesting experience," she told them. "But what would we eat there? Do you think all Indian food is spicy?"

Alec responded by pushing back against Brooke's attempt to solve his science and math problem. "Let's not go to India and not eat the food," he said, his expression fixed and grim.

After learning that Paul would be unable to telecommute to work for such a long period, Brooke dropped the idea of going overseas. Instead, she began to focus on positioning Alec to get into the best possible private junior high school the following year. Brooke met with another mother from Jacob's school who taught her some special tricks for the process, such as submitting more than one recommendation (though only one is requested) and having other families speak highly of the applicant (though support from other families supposedly does not matter). Brooke pursued both of these tips, saying, "We've got to start meeting people and making connections."

Brooke also focused on making sure that Alec was sufficiently prepared for his violin recital. Her plan was to send a recording of his performance along with the rest of his school application, hoping that his performance would help set him apart from the other applicants. Alec is a dedicated violinist who dutifully sets the oven timer every afternoon to time his practice. As the date of the recital approached, however, Alec began to push back against his parents' anxiety regarding his performance.

One Saturday evening, Brooke, Paul, and Jacob sat in the family room, where they listened as Alec practiced in the living room. But it was impossible for Brooke and Paul to merely listen. Soon after Alec began playing, Paul went into the living room and told Alec, "Slow down a bit, don't play so fast." (Having studied violin himself when he was young, Paul was usually the one who advised Alec about his playing.) Paul returned to the living room and started talking with Brooke about where they should go out to dinner that night, but as Alec kept playing, both Brooke and Paul heard mistakes and winced in response.

"What is he doing?" Brooke exclaimed.

"It's okay," Paul responded. "He's just doing his own thing, playing the song his way."

"Alec has to be perfect . . . perfect," Brooke said, making the "okay" sign with her fingers. "He shouldn't play through his mistakes. You should make him start over."

Paul glanced at me as if to say, "My wife is being a little over-the-top here," then said to her, "Okay, but why do I have to be the go-between?"

"Because you're the one who took violin," Brooke insisted. Hesitantly, Paul returned to the living room to deliver the message while Brooke remarked, "I'm *not* being unreasonable. You don't *sit there* during the lessons!"

Through the wall we heard Paul tell Alec, "You need to play more slowly." As if to back Paul up, Brooke yelled, "Alec, you're playing too fast, you're relying on your motor memory and not thinking about the notes, about where your fingers should be placed. You need to play the piece the way the composer wrote the notes to be played . . . it isn't supposed to be improv."

Annoyed, Alec yelled back, "Mom, the song is *supposed* to be played fast," illustrating his point by setting the metronome first to a slow tempo, then to a fast one.

"Okay," Brooke replied, "but you need to play it perfectly, Alec." The debate continued through the rest of Alec's practice session until the oven timer finally rang.

Over dinner Alec was quiet, appearing somewhat annoyed at his parents. On the way home, Jacob opened a different debate, begging his mom for more TV and computer time when they got home. Brooke held firm. "No, you've already been on the computer a lot today, and you'll have your time tomorrow. It's not going anywhere. It's not too hard to wait until tomorrow, right?"

Jacob smiled in response, impressed that his mother had stuck by her guns, then remarked to everyone in the car, "I don't think I'm ever going to be a better parent than my mother."

Brooke asked, "Well, am I better than my mother?"

Jacob enthusiastically answered, *"Yes!"*

"So you will, too. You'll be better than me."

"It's difficult raising me now," Jacob observed.

"You're not difficult," Brooke responded. "I mean, all kids are difficult, but parents like that. That's part of being a parent is raising your kid and teaching them to have certain values, to help them develop to be a certain kind of person, to not be spoiled."

Finally Alec chimed in from the backseat. "You shouldn't try to make us perfect." He stared out the window, aggressively chewing on his fingernails.

After a moment of silence, Paul asked, "We shouldn't try to make you more perfect than you already are?"

Alec responded by silently shaking his head, "No." Paul observed the gesture in the rearview mirror but said nothing.

Finally Jacob broke the silence. "You don't want us to be spoiled," he commented thoughtfully, as if mulling over what that meant.

Alec said, "If I'm spoiled, then my friends are moldy cheese with a mouse eating it." Everyone laughed.

Brooke said, "Well, spoiled isn't the right word, but you guys have a lot more than other people. You get three meals a day."

Alec said, "Even poor kids get that."

Brooke said, "That's not true. Poor people don't get three meals a day, a bedroom of their own. I mean, let's look at it this way . . . One might ask, 'Why should I spend any of my money on my kids?'"

There was a short pause and then Alec angrily said, "If you feel that way, then you shouldn't have had kids."

Brooke smiled as if to soften the tone of the conversation. "From my perspective, we spend *all* of our money on you guys."

Jacob agreed. "If you guys didn't have kids, you'd be millionaires."

Paul got back into the conversation at this point, also seeming to want to shift emotional gears: "Yes, but there's more to life than money."

In the silence that followed, Alec's anger and annoyance were palpable, while Brooke and Paul seemed perplexed and confused. Finally Brooke said, "You know, guys, Marianne is taking notes, so if you want to change something you've said, say it now."

More silence followed. Alec, for one, was not changing his story.

THE ORIGIN OF UPSCALING

Most parents in my study, no matter their social class, worried about their children and wanted them to do well in school. However, the middle-class and working-class families I interviewed set more modest benchmarks for evaluating how well their children were doing. As long as the children tried their best and their teachers spoke highly of them, these parents appeared happy. One father, Manuel Lopez, explained, "I have never had any complaints about them. And when I go to open house, there's always compliments . . . we have no problems."

By contrast, the upper-class families I studied tended to dwell on the "troubles" experienced by their children and even seemed to search for problems to worry about. For example, Nadia Parsons Chow, a stay-at-home upper-class mom, told me, "I have a little notebook that whenever Camilla makes a comment that is concerning to me where I'm like, 'Wow, what would that mean?' I date it and I write it down . . . so if I ever need to refer back to it . . . I can go, 'Oh yeah, that was in fourth grade.'" If middle- and working-class parents' level of concern for their children registered about a five on a scale of one to ten, upper-class parents' concern seemed to consistently register at a nine or ten. Where, I wondered, did these upscaled expectations and this heightened level of anxiety come from?

Scholars who study contemporary parenting strategies among the professional, educated classes have suggested that such child-rearing logics may be linked to parental concerns regarding a changing economic climate in which their children's abilities to reproduce their privileged-class position appear uncertain.[5] My study substantiates these suggestions, finding that it was precisely upper-class parents' broader concerns regarding macroeconomic changes that both fueled their anxiety about how well their children would turn out and intensified their expectations of their children.

Indeed, early in my research I noticed that upper-class parents were finely attuned to changes taking place in the world around them. One afternoon, after interviewing Amy Newman, an upper-class mother, I ran into her husband, technology executive Rob Newman, and stopped to discuss my project with him. The words "economic differences among families" had barely left my lips when Rob launched into a description of how he felt the U.S. economy was evolving. He described a talk he had heard by a Department of Labor expert in the mid-1980s about the emerging "barbell economy." "You know," Rob explained, "where people are either on the poor end or the rich end, and no one's in the middle. At the time I didn't think things would turn out like this guy said. But he was right: there are fewer and fewer people in the middle."

The upper-class parents I interviewed frequently mentioned the growing inequality in income and wealth in our society, often explicitly linking the topic to their concerns about how it would impact their children. As Marissa Donald said,

> From what I can glean from new reports, it's harder [economically]. There's been a polarization of the economic wealth in the country. I've been polarized on one end, and I think there are a lot of people that have been polarized on the other end. My fear is that my children will be the working poor.

And Simon Chow told me,

> I think the rich are getting richer and I think the poor are getting poorer, and the middle is getting squeezed. The differences between the haves and the have-nots are even greater than ever before. And so I think it's very hard. You feel for your kids. You just sort of say, "What's it going to be like when they're grown up?"

These parents also expressed concern about the impact of globalization. Rob Newman recounted a cocktail party conversation:

> I had drinks with Bill Gates and some other technology people, and we were talking about globalization about five years ago, and Bill Gates said, "Well, I have two thoughts about it. One, on an intellectual level, I think it's great that people in disadvantaged countries are getting the opportunity to equal the playing field and compete for the advancements available in life. But two, as a father, it scares the hell out of me."

In particular, these parents worry about the declining position of the United States relative to the developing countries. Winston Durham, a money manager, explains:

> In this area, people are working for venture capital firms and technology companies that are doing things in India and China. And so I think maybe around here there's more of an awareness of what's going on in the global economy . . . There are going to be Chinese companies and Chinese people that will, if they can, take work that would in the past have been done here, and they can do it and they're going to want it. And this whole outsourcing thing, there's going to be foreign competition for things that in the past the U.S. would be dominant in. It may not be that we're completely dominant. I think we'll be very strong. But [the Chinese and Indian] educational systems are gearing up to produce more and more people who are really well educated, who are really motivated, and in some cases they'll work for less money than what people here get paid to do the same work . . . I've talked to other parents about how our kids had better be pretty well prepared to go into the workplace.

Rob Newman added:

> When I grew up, the U.S. was well ahead of the rest of the world in its standard of living, in its innovation, in the strength of its companies on a global basis. And all of that is now much more diminished. By the time our kids get to the workforce, it will be totally gone. And the opportunities available to our kids will not be unfairly weighted in their advantage. When I graduated from college, success was unfairly weighted in your direction if you were American. You got a better education . . . the strong companies were in the U.S., and the vast majority of people outside the U.S. weren't as well trained. So that's all changed. You have to be competitive on a global basis as an individual and as a company, and that is certainly a factor that all of our kids will have to deal with.

For their children to contend with increased global competition, these parents demand top-flight education and lots of it. Marissa Donald says, "I think you've gotta have a good education ... An education is more important [now] than it was when I was growing up." And Winston Durham says, "The key is to make sure you get a good education and that there's something that you can do to differentiate yourself ... that just makes you more easily employable. Getting a good education is a little bit of an insurance policy as far as being able to have some kind of a meaningful career." And part-time business development consultant Ditra Chopra says,

> There was a time when you went to school, you went to college, you got a job, and you would plod along. That's not true [anymore]. [Globalization] is changing the way the world works ... [I tell my kids,] You must be in direct contact with the customer or have a skill that's unique, or a knowledge set that's unique, because if your knowledge set is generic and your interaction is not direct to the customer, your job is going to end up in some other country ... So I feel it is my responsibility as a parent to get my kids through a master's degree. I don't think a bachelor's qualifies as an education because in any profession today one needs to go beyond a bachelor's level in order to have a meaningful career.

Among this group of parents, a "meaningful" career means one that can withstand the pressures of the global marketplace. What they want for their children is a profession that will enable them to remain "haves" in a country and a world they see as increasingly polarized between the "haves" and the "have-nots."

Yet despite their familiarity with the changing rules of the game and their readiness to intercede on their children's behalf, this group of parents remains anxious and unsure about tomorrow. Like the early Calvinists, who devoted themselves to worldly success to ease their doubts about future salvation, today's upper-income parents dedicate themselves to their children's schooling in order to mollify their doubts about the economic future.[6] And just as the Calvinists sought increasing financial returns to maintain the belief that they were among the elect, today's upper-income parents seek ever more impressive credentials and achievements for their children to sustain the belief that their children will make it. College isn't enough; graduate school is also essential, and both degrees must be earned at elite institutions. Nor are educational qualifications sufficient; these must be supplemented by personal characteristics like "motivation," "stick-to-itiveness," and "aggressiveness." Indeed, the list of what upper-class children need (and what they lack) is seemingly endless.

Once again, this set of upper-class concerns is in marked contrast to the attitudes of middle-class and working-class families, who seemed less aware of broader economic trends. Caleb Bristow, a mechanic, told me, "Well, I consider myself middle class and I think I'm doing good. I think [concerns about the middle class], that's just people pointing the finger at other people." And Jenny French, an administrative assistant, said, "I've heard a lot of gripes [about the rich getting richer], and honestly I just don't even get caught up in it . . . I just don't like to be bothered with it. It's something that's gone on for generations and . . . I just don't like to hear people gripe and I don't like when I do . . . It's like if you don't like your circumstances, do something about it." When I asked Owen Meehan, a technician, whether talk of a middle-class squeeze worried him, he said, "No, it doesn't, really. Those numbers are fluid. Ten years from now the whole thing could change. I mean, it all depends on how you define it and who defines it. As far as I'm concerned, it's kind of a marketing thing. It's like these guys say that this is what's going on. And the reality is that these things are happening, but what does it really mean as a whole? I don't know. And I don't think that it matters a whole lot."

Most parents in my study, no matter their class, want their children to go to college, noting that nowadays a college degree opens up many more opportunities. But genuine worry about macroeconomic forces and their impact on their children is restricted to upper-class, highly educated parents. Others in my sample have more faith that their children will find their way. As Owen Meehan puts it, "[My kids'] options are really wide open. They can do pretty much whatever they want."

WHEN THE WORLD IS FLAT

Unlike Owen Meehan, Brooke Mah spends a lot of time wondering how her children will turn out. Again and again she questioned whether her children would have what it takes to make something of themselves, saying things such as, "They have strong names but not strong personalities." And like other upper-class parents, her anxiety—in particular her worry about her kids' science, math, and critical-thinking skills—is bound up with a sense that the rules of the economic game are changing.

Interestingly, Brooke realizes that she worries a lot: "I read a lot of the paper, so I probably worry about more things than people even know to worry about." From reading widely about various education-related issues, Brooke identified some key areas of concern that fueled her push to keep Alec interested and challenged in science and math. Driving to pick up the children after school, she said to me, "The U.S. is falling behind in math, science, and technology, and that's where the economy is going. We've got to emphasize that. That's why my focus is on curriculum." She added,

> Math has gotten a lot of press lately—math and science, with the whole, you know, "the world is flat" phenomenon. It seems from my research that the relative weakness in the United States in math was starting in elementary school. It wasn't that we're not doing a good job in high school. It's the foundation [that's a problem]. A lot of the foundations aren't being met in elementary school. So [my push at Alec's school for science] kinda fit into this perception of how we're not really a world economic power anymore. It's because the world is flat. And, you know, a lot of things are being outsourced, and if you want to keep a vibrant economic community in Silicon Valley, or really anywhere, [you need science and math].

I heard other parents refer to journalist Thomas Friedman's book *The World Is Flat,* which argues that technology has helped to create a level playing field among nations and individuals around the world.[7] Summarizing a newspaper article she read that detailed America's relative weakness in math, Brooke exclaimed, "It concluded by saying that to be prepared for the future, children need to be proficient at math." From Brooke's vantage point, there is a direct link between Alec's fifth-grade math skills and his future ability to compete in a flat world. This connection frames her assessment of the situation and serves to generate her anxiety.

Brooke also worries that the United States is in decline because its citizens lack critical-thinking skills and an independent voice. One night during dinner, talk centered on how Brooke and Paul felt that Americans were fooled by the Bush administration into supporting the Iraq War. Brooke said, "Sometimes I think Americans are just too stupid to remain powerful. Other powers will pass us by." To prevent her children from sinking with the rest of America, Brooke tries to ensure that they possess critical-thinking skills and are unafraid to express their opinions:

> We go vote all the time. And I bring my kids with me when we vote so that they see you need to be in the habit of being informed and having a voice. Kids need . . . to be able to independently assess what information they get and whether it makes sense and be an informed electorate. And that's one of my pet concerns is that I really want to do as much as possible to make sure that we don't become an ignorant country and we just start following people who have the glossiest brochures. I mean, people [need] the ability to look at things beyond a superficial way.

Brooke's belief in the need to stand up and speak one's mind seems to frame her concern about Jacob's shyness. If Jacob is a follower rather than a leader, if he lets others speak for him, he may get duped or left behind.

Though Paul worries about the children a bit less than Brooke does, he too wonders whether Jacob and Alec are aggressive enough to make it in the globalized economy:

> For me to be where I am today, do I think I've needed to be aggressive? A little bit, but not a lot. Do I think I've needed to work hard? Yes. And I think by virtue of hard work and applied intelligence, I've been successful. When I started working, the way the business world worked was that there was a whole bunch of opportunity. Every year for the graduating college kids, there were jobs. I'm concerned that, as the global economy changes, that the kinds of jobs that are available and the number of jobs that are available here in the U.S. are going to shrink. I think for my kids, coming into the workforce in ten or so years, that the kinds of jobs will be different and the number[s] are going to shrink because more and more of the work is being done in China and India and other developing countries.
>
> Within all of this changing stuff—look, I mean, if my kids have to compete with other kids in their AP calculus class in high school, I'm not worried about that. But if they've gotta compete with a kid in China who's just as smart, who's willing to do everything that an employer is asking for one-tenth the price, I don't know that they know what they're in for . . . I worry about their level of aggressiveness, whether they're aggressive enough. They've always been a little more on the passive side, and I worry about that in terms of will they be able to compete as things move forward?

And I do worry. It's been part of the American mythology for several generations now that each succeeding generation should be more successful than the previous one. I don't know that that is actually true for my kids. I think there is a significant probability that they will not be as successful as I am, and I worry about that. I worry about what that does to their psyches. I worry about what it does or will do to the way they raise their kids. And whether America as a nation, over the next couple of decades, goes from being the world's leading super [power] to being a dinosaur, to being the economy on its last legs and we get usurped by China and India and other developing countries. I think that that's a big issue.

Paul has decided that both he and his children need a better understanding of the role India and China now play in the world economy. For Paul, this means working in those countries: "One of the reasons I am working at my current company is that some of our development is being done in India, and I wanted to figure out how that worked, and what kind of implications that would have. I was over in India earlier in the year, and I've been to China maybe a dozen times over the last decade, both for work and for pleasure." He and Brooke have arranged for Jacob to spend several weeks this coming summer in China, where he will stay with relatives and study Mandarin. Paul explains, "Part of why he's doing that is parental brainwashing of the fact that something's going to change the world and you need to be conscious of it . . . I think that China's going to change the world in the next decade. It's changing the world right now. And for him to be successful in the world economy over his productive lifetime, I think speaking Chinese, dealing with China, leveraging his heritage would be a huge asset for him." Sam Bishop, another upper-income father in my study, also feels it is important for kids to experience the global economy firsthand. Sam had his teenage son, Nick, accompany him on one of his business trips through Asia. Sam said,

> And part of the reason for taking Nick to Asia was because I think that the cultural and economic forces behind globalization and immigration are phenomenal. And they are more likely than anything else to change what happens . . . I wanted him to see the global economy. I wanted him to see how the rest of the world works. I wanted him to see how people fit in. I wanted him to see how things were different and similar. Part of me wanted him to see how hard people work in Asia. One of the things Nick said at the end of the trip was, "Everybody spoke two languages and some people spoke

three or four. I gotta go back and learn a language. I can't speak just one." And I thought, "Yeah!" That was one of the things I wanted him to learn.

The Mahs and the Bishops are not alone. A *Wall Street Journal* article details how many American CEOs are now having their children learn Mandarin and travel to Asia to gain on-the-ground experience and a long-term competitive edge.[8]

Like other upper-class parents, Brooke and Paul see education as the tool that will help their children stay afloat in an increasingly globalized and competitive world. Brooke says, "Things have changed a lot. College is more like high school now, and you probably do need extra training to get into the kind of career you want. In fact, from what I read, graduate school is really important. It's not really what college you get into, it's the graduate school program. It's where you go to get trained in graduate school that makes the most impact on where your career is going to take you." Paul backs up Brooke's sense that graduate school is important, saying, "I think to be successful—again, that's a subjective statement—but to be successful in whatever career [my kids] choose to pursue, I think that the odds are that both of them will [need to] go."

The Mahs also want their children to attend the best educational institutions possible. Brooke's view is based on her own experience. She said, "For me, a top school opened a lot of doors just by virtue of the resume quality of the name. And you want your children to have as many opportunities as possible. So I still buy into going to a good college is a good move." Paul agrees:

> I do think that different schools open different doors. And this is a very elitist thing to say, but I think there is some truth to it. I think it stems from the alumni network. I think it stems from the competitive nature of the college-admissions process, where if you're going to school with a bunch of other overachievers and that becomes your social peer group, then, as you progress on out into the workplace, you've set a certain standard for yourself and for the kinds of folks that you'll hang out with. And I think that all of that has an impact on how people's careers and attitudes and so forth evolve.

Paul's personal experience of the value of his own network has reinforced this belief: "Have I been fortunate and blessed with having a great network? Yes. But, again going back to the whole discussion about the [rankings of] schools, that's why I think going to a Stanford or a Berkeley has value . . . because part of what you're establishing is that network."

Even though their children were only twelve and ten, Brooke and Paul were already concerned about their getting into good schools. One evening Brooke told me that lately she had been having a difficult time with Jacob. Brooke said,

> The last week has been stressful. Jacob has ignored our requests about doing his homework, and he's been just defiant. I finally got time to talk with him in the car today, and I asked him, "Jacob, do you want to go to a good college for me or do you want to go to a good college for you? Because if you want to go to a good college, what do you think you are going to have to do to get in? Be smart, work hard? But there are a lot of kids like that out there." I told him, "Here are the steps," and I broke it down for him. Here's what you're going to have to do to get there, and doing your homework is part of it.

The Mahs came to an agreement with Jacob that for a week they were not going to fight with him or make him do his homework. He could decide if he wanted to do it, and they were leaving it up to him to manage his time. Brooke said, "He can decide to do it if he wants to, if he thinks it's important." But this agreement did not last very long, as one afternoon Brooke caught Jacob playing solitaire on his iPod for an hour even though he still had homework and chores to do. Paul chimed in, saying, "But if he's too immature to discipline himself, then we need to do it for him. We need to micromanage him."

The Mahs' concern about the world's globalized and competitive future provides the broader context that helps to explain their unease about their children. If we focus narrowly on incidents like the Mahs' effort to perfect Alec's violin performance for his recital, their anxiety seems excessive. But when we widen our angle of vision, we see how the tension that filled their house that evening is connected, like links in a chain, to the macroeconomic changes that the Mahs feel threaten their children's security. In their minds, Alec's violin performance might determine which junior high he gets into. The junior high may determine how prepared he will be for high school, the high school may determine the college he attends, and the college will affect where he goes to graduate school. So the violin performance was much more than a violin performance. It was the linchpin connecting the building blocks that will position their son, providing him with the best opportunities in a shifting and uncertain future. With the stakes so high, it's no wonder that the Mahs view "perfection" as a necessity. This process of perfecting children is a central part of affluent families' response to the economic changes occurring in the world around them.

THE DIVISION OF WORRY IN UPSCALED SECURITY PROJECTS

As scholars like Sharon Hays and Stephen Ball have noted, the work done to reproduce advantage and privilege in children draws "heavily upon the unpaid work and emotional labor of mothers."[9] My study confirms that among upper-class families, women are primarily responsible for securing their children's futures. Most of the sixteen upper-income mothers I interviewed had dramatically curtailed their work schedules in order to focus on their children; only two worked full-time and earned about what their husbands earned, while six worked part-time and eight stayed at home full-time. This left men with the primary responsibility for securing the family's financial well-being.

This traditionally gendered division of labor seemed to catch these couples by surprise, since prior to having children, most of the wives had had professional careers. Leonard Weiss, the CEO of a biotech start-up who met his wife at business school, said, "Surprisingly, we've fallen into much more traditional roles than I ever would have imagined." Moreover, despite the "home" focus among these mothers, they and their husbands tended to view what these mothers did in less traditional terms. For example, when Paul Mah was completing the section of my questionnaire that asked for background information, he asked, "Can I really write that Brooke is a homemaker? That seems wrong." Opting instead to write "full-time mother," he said, "That sounds better I guess."

Among these families, the work that mothers do to help their children and enhance their schooling is viewed in quasi-professional terms. As Sam Bishop noted, these mothers "administrate the heck out of their communities . . . and what they're doing contributes extraordinarily to the fabric of society and to the community." These mothers aren't at home to bake cookies or make sure the house is clean; they are professional mothers who specialize in securing their children's futures. In the Mahs' case, for example, Paul often does the cooking, since Brooke's evenings are filled with meetings for her children's schools. This slightly different twist on the stereotypical gendered division of labor leads me to describe these marriages as *neo-traditional*.[10]

In thirteen of the sixteen neo-traditional marriages I studied, worry about children and concern about finances are divided between husbands and wives. Nonetheless, when it comes to child-related issues, these fathers are quick to respond to both practical issues and emotional concerns raised by their wives. For example, they will work with the children to improve their math skills or meet with experts to address a child's learning disability. By contrast, when it comes to dealing with financial matters, the husbands are largely on their own.

Paul Mah's explanation for why he was the point person for the family's financial issues was "'cause I'm making the money. [He laughs.] I'm the person responsible for fixing it if there's a problem." Brooke adds, "Because my focus is the kids." Leonard Weiss explains that he was in charge of his family's finances because his wife lost interest in them:

> We've talked about this. My wife worked on Wall Street for a little while, but once we met, like, a threshold of having enough money where we didn't really have to worry about it, she was totally uninterested in it—which is kind of weird for somebody with an MBA. So to get her interested at all in, like, how to invest money . . . I mean, she could not be less interested. So I'm responsible for that . . . and so I consult her on those decisions about, "Well, should we invest in that?" But it's really hard to get her directly tied in.

Another mother explains why her husband was in charge financially by saying, "It's probably our personalities," while another father says, "It's just a natural alignment with our interests and abilities." Ultimately, the dynamic that appeared to be at work in these families was that because the fathers had always exhibited such keen interest in the financial aspects of their security projects, and because the mothers had become so absorbed with their children, this division of work and worry was viewed as practical and equitable. As the next chapter will show, this neo-traditional division of worry is quite different from what I found in middle-class and working-class families.

THE UPSCALING OF FINANCIAL FUTURES

If the security benchmarks for upper-class children are extremely high, so are the financial security benchmarks that upper-class fathers strive to achieve. For example, several fathers with more than a million dollars in assets told me that they did not feel rich. Bret Colson says, "I don't consider ourselves wealthy. But on a national basis, we're probably at the top 1 percent." Paul Mah echoed Bret's feelings: "We are probably in the top 1 percent of all American households, which probably puts us in the top quarter percent of all worldwide households, right? . . . So I can't complain . . . [but] I still don't feel rich." When asked what it would take for him to feel he had complete financial security, Paul says,

> For me, the financial metric, given the world today and everything, I think I would need to have—it's a very arbitrary number—but I'd say if I had ten million dollars in the bank in investments right now, then I'd feel at that point [secure]. Again, would I feel I was rich? No. But would I feel that that was enough money that I could basically say, "To hell with it. I'm not working anymore. I'm just going to figure out what I want to do and do that?" Yes. That still wouldn't mean enough for me to go buy a private jet or fly a helicopter and do that kind of stuff, but at that point I would feel financially secure. Totally financially secure. And I'm not there right now. Do I think it's likely that I'll get to ten million dollars? Not likely. Can I get half of the way, two-thirds of the way there? Yeah, I think that's possible. And if that's true, then again, I think at that point our lifestyle in retirement will be fine.

Exploring what Paul means by "everything I think I would need to have" illuminates the factors that drive upper-class fathers' upscaled financial projects.

For most of the families in my study, the goals of their financial security project were to make ends meet, perhaps save for retirement, and maybe set aside something for their child's college. But for fathers like Paul, paying the monthly bills was not the issue. They are focused on more far-reaching security concerns. As Paul explains,

I have a certain responsibility to ensure that [my kids] are educated and prepared for the world. And I view education as an important part of that equation. Some people don't. I have always assumed that part of my parental obligation was to put my kids through college, absolutely. My parents put me through college and grad school. They put my brother through college and grad school. I think I have the same obligation with my kids. At the same time, I want to make enough money to make sure that I can retire at a reasonable age and Brooke and I can do whatever we want to do. So those are goals . . . And from that perspective, we still have not saved enough to be sure that we'll be able to live in the lifestyle I'd like to live until we pass away and continue to help the kids if they need help and so forth.

An additional concern in the back of Paul's mind is buying property as an investment that can be used to help his children get a start in their adult lives by providing them with a down payment on their first homes. This sort of upscaled security package is a common goal among fathers like Paul. As Sam Bishop explained,

So probably the thing that most concerns me and most consumes me is making sure that I have enough financial resources to take care of the kids, to take care of [my wife], and retire. And I don't. Yet, I mean, I don't need to, right? But it absolutely concerns me. And part of me feels very guilty about that . . . I do think about that. And I'm pretty quantitative. And actually on one level we do have enough. We could certainly sell the house, move to the mountains, and there would be enough to retire and send the kids to college. But we wouldn't have the lifestyle that my wife would like to have. We certainly can't retire and live in an upper-middle-class community on the Peninsula.

Despite their lack of day-to-day financial problems, the upper-class fathers in my study experienced a palpable level of anxiety about achieving their lofty economic goals. For example, Michael Handley, an engineer, often worries about how he will pay for his child's education and his own retirement if a hoped-for influx of cash from stock options does not materialize. He said, "I'm consciously aware of where the nest egg is and, okay, if I got to ride this the whole way, how do I manage it? What does that mean? What's the trajectory? What are my options? What's my plan B here? You must have a plan B. It's not enough to say, 'Oh, this will work out.' You can't have that kind of confidence [if] you're not always kind of working your angle."

Prior to striking it rich from stock options, Rob Newman also worried about his family's financial security, despite his high salary. "If I was on a plane going someplace and I was working and I wanted to just take a mental break, I'd take out my calculator and I'd recalculate my net worth and I'd look at all my financial obligations and kind of figure out how much I was really worth and how long it would last if I lost my job. So I was probably hypersensitive to accumulating financial security." Safeguarding their family's financial future is a worry that many fathers experience every day. Leonard Weiss says, "I think of where we're going to be fifteen years from now almost every day. Like where will we be and are we on track to be taken care of, kind of like our parents are on track. But they have different things . . . pensions, and they live in areas with a lower standard of living." Lori Thorson explains that her husband checks on their financial project often, saying, "He definitely looks at our stocks day to day . . . he looks at it daily. He has a goal." Charged with the task of keeping the finances on track, the men in these upper-class families play the part of their family's designated planner, the person charged with managing risks and investing for the future so that the right foundation is laid for the next generation's social and economic trajectory.

As opposed to the families in my study whose precarious economic circumstances make it difficult or impossible to plan, the upper-class families live in a steadier world, where creating long-range goals and executing them is possible. Reflecting this privileged position, many fathers have been planning and diligently supervising their financial projects for a long time. As Paul Mah explains,

> About twelve years ago I created a big Excel spreadsheet that went out from then to fifty years from now and said, "Hey, we've got so much saved, and I'm going to need to replace a car every ten years. I'm going to need to put a new roof on the house every ten years. I gotta plan for my kids' weddings. I've got to worry about grad school." Part of it was trying to eliminate some of the uncertainty. Part of it was trying to quantify some of the uncertainty, or quantify some of the goals . . . I did that once a year kind of thing for a while until I got to the point where I figured out, "You know what, Paul, you're okay. You may not be perfect, but you're close enough."

To manage his anxiety, Sam Bishop created a software program that over the years has analyzed his finances and alerted him to the exact stock price his company's stock must reach in order for him to hit his magic retirement number. Bret Colson's upscaled security project has also been years in the making: "I personally have thought about these things for ten, twenty years."

Paul Mah explains his financial management strategy as follows: "We have a variety of different investment vehicles, one of which was more internationally focused, the rest of which were more domestically focused, and then large cap and small cap funds, and so forth. And we've just tried to stay reasonably balanced across all of those, such that if one does well and another doesn't do so well, that on average your investment's going to continue to grow, and if there is a fall off in any given market, you're somewhat protected." In addition to possessing their own high levels of financial acumen, many upper-class fathers also work with financial advisors who help them keep their financial projects on track.

This obsession with planning and attempting to control their financial futures is a strategy used by upper-class fathers as a way of addressing their anxieties about insecurity. The emotions that result can seem paradoxical or even irrational. A *New York Times* article entitled "In Silicon Valley, Millionaires Who Don't Feel Rich" explores the upside-down world of affluent people who worry about the rising costs of health care and college and continue to put in long hours at work in the hopes of earning even more money, despite enjoying levels of wealth nearly all Americans would envy.[11] The article notes the high cost of living in the Valley as well as the unusual standard of comparison there, where keeping up with the Joneses can mean not only owning a house with a pool, but also owning a mansion, a private jet, and a vacation home. In such an environment, as one informant observes, "You're nobody here at $10 million."

In similar fashion, a report by the financial services firm Barclays Wealth that surveyed high-worth individuals came to the conclusion that a million dollars is not what it used to be.[12] According to the report, today's gold standard for wealth is closer to ten million dollars. The increase is partly due to inflation, partly due to a rise in costs associated with a life of luxury, but it is also a result of the proliferation of billionaires and multimillionaires, which has altered the understanding of what it means to be rich. A wealth expert cited in the report notes that in his work it is a common occurrence to "see affluent individuals, with what we would think of as sizeable assets, who still don't feel that they are truly wealthy because they are comparing themselves with people who are wealthier than they are."[13]

Other studies confirm these findings. A survey conducted by Worth-Roper Starch found that the majority of Americans in the top 1 percent of earners do not think of themselves as rich.[14] Another survey by PNC Advisors, a wealth management firm, found that for their clients to feel financially secure, virtually all of them would need to double their level of net worth or income. Those with $500,000 to $1 million felt they needed $2.4 million to feel secure, those with $5 million or more felt they needed $10.4 million, and those with $10 million or more needed a median of $18.1 million.[15]

We could write off these attitudes as simply another example of the hedonic treadmill, which posits that as people's incomes rise, so do their expectations, thus leading them never to be satisfied with what they have. Yet rising expectations are shaped by the social world and the particular form of stratification in which they are embedded. If the rungs of the class ladder were closer together, rising expectations would rise only so high. It is in the context of extreme inequity, then, when vast fortunes begin to dot the horizon, that expectations become limitless and the upscaling of security becomes a widespread phenomenon. The financial anxiety of upper-class fathers—like their wives' worries about the schooling of their children—is thus tied to broader macroeconomic circumstances, including the rise in inequality and the shift of risk onto individuals and their families.

Consider, for example, the transformation in risk that has occurred in tandem with the emergence of the new gilded age of the superrich. According to Milton Pedraza, the chief executive of the Luxury Institute, the reason $10 million has become the current standard of wealth for people like Paul Mah is because that is the "level of wealth where people feel protected from the hazards of the world."[16] Interviewee Winston Durham identified a similar threshold: "Yeah, for me it had to be more than ten million, which is kind of ridiculous. I admit that now. But it sort of took it getting to that point [to feel secure]." And this, it seems, is what the goal has become at the top—the ability to be impervious to risk, to be immune to the ups and downs of life while remaining completely self-reliant. This ethic is most clearly revealed by the sentiments of Rob

Newman, who was able to feel secure only once he had become independent of everything and everyone else:

> I kind of felt secure with 25 million dollars cash in the bank and no mortgages, but even then I didn't feel totally independent. I don't know why, I mean, it's hard to spend 25 million dollars . . . [At that point] I was spending less than the money was making every year, so I guess intellectually I thought, "I'm independently wealthy." And for anybody, particularly somebody with a mathematical mind, you'd think, "Well, of course, look at the numbers. You're independently [wealthy]—you don't have to be concerned." But when you throw in the emotional insecurity about really wanting to be financially secure . . . I'm not sure I felt that until I had 30 or 35 million dollars. Sometime after that I started feeling [we were] financially secure and probably our kids would be financially secure, because at that amount of money you are definitely not spending what you're making every year, nor will your kids be able to.

Through this ratcheting up of what it takes to feel secure at the top, we can see the internalization of the ownership society's commandment that people build their own safety net. The desire to be invulnerable reflects the emotional response among the affluent to the privatization of security in the era of neoliberalism. Upscaling, then, reveals the squaring of emotions to fit affluent individuals' location within the shift in risk. In this world, being independent is within the realm of possibility, so it is the goal for which they continually strive. But the huge price tag affixed to this goal inevitably leads many fathers to feel as if they are coming up a little bit short.

THE COSTS OF UPSCALING

As Alec's response to the violin incident makes clear, there are psychological and social costs to the upscaling of security. The pressure placed on upper-class children is enormous. One upper-class mother says, "My daughter pushes herself a lot. My challenge with her is, 'You will *not* do all the extra credit that's assigned to you. Take it easy.'" Some upper-class children I interviewed were taking antidepressants to manage their stress. The intense pressure on children caused a friend of Simon Chow's to leave the area:

I have a friend, actually, who has been very successful . . . but he decided to move to New Hampshire, where he grew up. Because, you know what he says? In New Hampshire you can have average kids and they can feel like they're successful. Here, if you have an average kid it makes them feel like a failure. So being average is not going to cut it here. And my friend said, "I don't want my kids to grow up thinking that because they aren't exceptional at something that they're failures."

Another familial cost of the upscaling project is the absence of fathers who work long hours to build the family nest egg and often have to travel on business. One teenage boy told me, "My dad is at work a lot. I don't talk to him a whole lot. And I like to hang out with him on the weekends and stuff, but I'm not really close with my dad so much as my mom." Rob Newman talks about being a high-level technology executive: "The negative obviously is that family dinners during the week are totally nonexistent. Zero."

Additionally, many fathers don't enjoy their daily work, seeing their high-paid jobs as merely a means to an end. Bret Colson switched jobs for financial reasons: "I took an additional layer of responsibility at my job several years ago. It's probably a little beyond my comfort zone. And part of the reason was that I could increase the benefit out of this pension plan [they offer], and some of the financial rewards are better. I frankly don't like the job I'm doing now as much as what I was doing before." Lori Thorson comments on her husband's job: "I have a husband who is working in an area where it just doesn't fit him, but he makes good money . . . enough for me to stay home and for us to do things that we'd like to do. But he'd much rather go back to school and be a writer and do things that just don't pay well [she laughs]."

Brooke Mah talked at length about how unhappy she thought Paul was, saying, "I always think he's not a happy person because I don't think he enjoys work. He just knows that he has to do it. And a lot of the time he tells the kids, 'It's not always fun, but you have to do it.' So I kind of feel bad for him. He sees himself in that role. I do think one day, when he turns fifty or something, he'll have a midlife crisis like, 'Look what I've been doing my whole life.' Really. I think he'll have that." Paul admits that he doesn't really like the work he does: "Do I like it? Not particularly. I do it because it pays the bills. But the nature of what I do day to day, am I competent at it? Yes. Do I love doing it? No." He adds, "Looking at the next five to ten years and then what's after that . . . you know, from a psychic income perspective . . . I would much rather be working in a company that was oriented to solving global warming than doing what I'm currently doing. But if I were to go do that, I would not be leveraging my network, leveraging what I've done, and what I know, and I'd take a 50 percent pay cut, and right now that's an inappropriate thing to do."

Of course, many people, perhaps even most, work in jobs they do not love. Yet these well-educated fathers ostensibly have more options than other workers. The fact that they have chosen to prioritize making money over doing something they enjoy underscores the importance they place on supplying their families with a particular package of security.[17]

Despite the long hours they work in jobs they often don't like and the fact that they must shoulder the family's financial concerns largely on their own, the high-income fathers I studied did not seem to resent their spouses or the burdens they carry. (In this they differ from the "designated worriers" we will meet in the next chapter.) Undergirding this lack of resentment seemed to be the neo-traditional nature of their marriages. Being in charge financially was congruent with these fathers' notions of masculinity and femininity, with what seemed normal for fathers and mothers to do. As a result, they did not view shouldering the financial responsibilities on their own as an unequal division of labor, and consequently they were not frustrated or annoyed by it, as were the designated worriers. Another reason these men are content with their neo-traditional marriages may be that they receive extraordinary benefits from controlling the purse strings in their families. They net "patriarchal dividends" in the form of power, influence, and stature from this division of labor.[18]

As the sociologist Douglas Massey points out, studies of inequality have tended to concentrate on the lives of the poor while neglecting the affluent.[19] But, as Massey rightly argues, in order to understand fully the "newly emerged system of stratification" that results from rising inequality, we need to study the lives of the affluent as well.[20]

Through an examination of how affluent families do security, I have sought to shed light on this relatively neglected social sphere. And while I expected to find those at the top feeling at ease with their privileged position, instead I discovered a palpable unease and a desire for more and more in order to feel secure. In a world of great insecurity and volatility, even those at the top worry about permanence. Ironically, upper-class families' intimate knowledge of the way the world is changing and what they need to do to protect themselves in the face of such changes does not reassure them. Rather, their understanding of the new rules of the game generates heightened levels of angst, leading affluent families to focus on negatives more than positives and to try to manage their anxiety by attempting to perfect the world around them. These responses involved scaled-up notions of security, a persistent and at times unrealistic ratcheting up of needs that often leaves the members of this group feeling as if they are behind.

5 Holding On at the Middle

GINA AND SAM CALAFATO

You know Gina, she probably thinks I don't worry enough.
I don't really make a big deal of many things. And that's
why I say it's a good thing she is the way she is. But yeah,
I'm not the kind that really, you know, worries. I guess
maybe in tough times I should.

Sam Calafato

It's 8:00 on a warm Tuesday evening in September, and Sam Calafato is helping his fourteen-year-old daughter, Mindy, with her geometry homework. Over the last hour, Sam, who is wearing denim shorts and a blue-and-white-striped T-shirt, has intermittently cleaned up the kitchen, putting dishes in the dishwasher, scrubbing pots and pans, and drying clean dishes with a red-and-white-checkered towel while fielding Mindy's questions.

Mindy, a usually cheerful girl with long, wavy blond hair and large green eyes, is feeling very stressed. Only a month into her first year of high school, she is overwhelmed by the amount of homework and studying on her plate. Sam is trying to help her complete a set of math problems, but he's having troubling remembering the basics of geometry. Running his hand through his hair, Sam says to me, "You know, I haven't done this in probably thirty-six years. I can't remember what I did yesterday." As Mindy reads problems to Sam, he responds with questions like "What's an integer?" and (with a laugh) "Complementary angles are what? Angles that say nice things to each other?" and thumbs the pages of a math dictionary searching for answers. When they get stuck on a particularly hard problem, Sam turns to me and jokes, "Gee, Marianne, it would be really helpful right now if you were a math major."

As the evening progresses, it becomes clear that Sam is helping Mindy not just with his dimly remembered math expertise but also with his joking. At one point Mindy drops her head into her hands and says, in complete frustration, "I hate math with a passion!" then adds, "I hate biology with a passion, too!" Sam replies in mock astonishment, "Wow, you have a lot of passions!," and he playfully bats her ponytail to get her to smile.

Minutes later, Mindy says in a very irritated tone, "This is so stupid. How is geometry going to help me in real life?" "It won't," Sam says flatly, then cackles loudly as if to say, "It sucks to be you." In response, the corners of Mindy's mouth curl up as she tries not to laugh. Sam's teasing, I see, has become a tool that Mindy can lean on to help her manage her frustration and anxiety about her sense that she is falling behind in school.

At this point Gina Calafato, Sam's wife, arrives home. Still dressed in her work clothes (fitted black pants and a long-sleeved red blouse), she has been attending a meeting at the junior high school her son, Trevor, attends. There she helped organize a fund-raising event for the coming weekend. Walking into the kitchen, Gina glances at Mindy and asks, "Do you need a hug?" They hug and Mindy grumpily returns to her chair at the kitchen table, complaining, "I have no free time this week because I'm falling behind and I have a test tomorrow."

"Don't worry about it," Sam responds. "Worry is a wasted emotion."

Taking a different tack, Gina says, "Well, Mindy, some weeks will be like that. You just have to put your head down and get through it. You just need to look forward to when it's all going to be over. But you also need to talk to your teacher [about how you are falling behind] . . . We can meet with her if you want us to."

These two responses to Mindy's stress illustrate Sam and Gina's different ways of coping with problems. Sam takes a let-it-go, things-will-work-out approach, while Gina is action-oriented, focused on the work Mindy needs to do and the possibility of meeting with her teacher. As we will see, these differences reflect two contrasting ways of doing security—though both are versions of a broader set of strategies that I've come to describe as *holding on*.

HOLDING ON

Forty-nine-year-old Sam Calafato is a perpetually smiling man. Large in stature, he also has a large presence in any room with his constant banter, teasing, and staccato bursts of laughter. By contrast, his wife, Gina, is soft-spoken, restrained, serious, and deliberate, the natural foil for Sam's never-ending comedy act.

For example, when I stopped by to have the Calafatos sign their consent forms to be in my study, one minute after starting to read his form, Sam yelled triumphantly, "I'm done first, I get the two hundred dollars!" The two children laughed in response, but Gina, her reading glasses poised on the tip of her nose, merely glanced up, said, "Shhhh, I can't read while you're talking," and returned to reading the form.

"You can't?" Sam responded, then turned to me and said, "I think you should write that down."

After two decades of marriage, Gina is accustomed to her role as the "straight woman" in the family. But with the serious economic issues the Calafatos have faced in recent years, that role has begun to take a toll on her, as this entry from my field notes suggests:

> To make conversation, I mention to Gina that MTV is turning twenty-six years old this week. Gina rolls her eyes and says, "Seriously? God, I was in college when MTV started, has it really been that long?" In response, Sam says, "You know, even though we've been together for nineteen years, I don't feel any different, any older, it just feels the same to me." Gina says, "Oh, I feel it. I've noticed I'm starting to get more gray hairs, and I'm tired. My heart might not be getting old, but my body is."

It may seem curious that Sam, despite being three years older than Gina and having undergone surgery and chemotherapy two years ago for prostate cancer, feels younger than his wife. The explanation lies in how the Calafatos have shaped their security project. When macroeconomic forces and Sam's own actions threatened to derail the Calafatos' family security, it was left to Gina, the "designated worrier," to hold on to the life they had built for themselves and to keep the family afloat.

The Calafatos' story documents how changing economic trends interact with gender to produce a very differently configured division of security work in middle-class and working-class families than in upper-class families. It is the women in these families who are their family's security guard, charged with the responsibility of maintaining, or, if need be, resuscitating their family's security. It's no wonder that women like Gina Calafato, who bear such burdens, sometimes feel they're growing old before their time.

Twenty-six of the two-parent families in my study were middle-class or working-class. In fourteen of these families, women were the designated worriers, while men were the designated worriers in five of the families. In seven families the parents seemed to share the responsibility. Actually, the pattern is stronger than this breakdown suggests. Of the five families in which the man was the designated worrier, three were immigrant families in which traditional gendered divisions of labor tend to be more durable.[1] When looking at just the twenty American-born middle- and working-class families in my study, there were only two families in which the father was the designated worrier. This pattern is quite a contrast from the high-earning, highly educated families in my study, in which men were in charge of the financial aspects of their family's security projects the vast majority of the time. The eight other families in my study are single-mother families, and consequently, it is the women here, too, who are the designated worriers for their families.

Because the women are in charge of the more "serious" matters in the family, they carry around high levels of stress and anxiety. Even though some designated worriers downscale their security at times in order to cope, they are nonetheless the point person in managing the day-to-day stresses of trying to make ends meet. They carry around and live with worry. The designated worrier is the one who must foresee upcoming expenses like property taxes and school field trips and perform the mental calculations to ensure that the needed money is available. It's the designated worrier who checks the bank account regularly, who feels a twinge of dread in her stomach when things get too tight, and who loses sleep at night when the bills go unpaid.

By contrast, the husbands of these women seem less stressed, more carefree, and at times almost childlike in their ability to continue to have fun even during very difficult times. This unequal division of emotion reflects the unequal division of psychic burdens in these families. That women generally do the work involved in protecting the security of the middle- and working-class families when a destabilizing event like a job loss occurs, is important in understanding how gender, class, and the shift in risk are shaping Americans' experience of security.

THE CALAFATO FAMILY'S SECURITY PROJECT

Gina and Sam Calafato live with their fourteen-year-old daughter, Mindy, and their eleven-year-old son, Trevor, in a two-story home on what they describe as a "nice, quiet" suburban street in a midsize city in Silicon Valley. With its red shutters, inviting porch, and basketball hoop in the driveway, the house gives off a quintessential middle-American feel—at least until you notice the missing slats in the shutters, the peeling paint, and the large crack in the living room window. Symptoms of deferred maintenance are visible inside the house as well: threadbare patches in the brown shag carpet, grout missing between the tiles in the first-floor bathroom, and the dilapidated backyard hot tub that Mindy says goes unused because "it costs too much."

About eight years ago, when money and time were not as tight, the Calafatos updated their kitchen, installing black quartz countertops and new linoleum flooring. But as the economy worsened, the Calafatos began postponing what they called "the extras," like fixing the deck or applying a new coat of paint. Today, conversations between Gina and Sam include frequent references to the "extras" they are deferring. Thus, when Sam finishes watering the back lawn using a handheld hose, he remarks to Gina, "We need to get a new sprinkler system," to which Gina responds sarcastically, "Yeah, add it to the list."

Unlike the very low-income families in my study, the Calafatos, who together earn about $110,000 annually, can supply their family with food, shelter, and clothing without much difficulty. Yet their definition of security extends beyond survival to include what they—and Gina in particular—consider "opportunities" for their children. Consequently, their family security project now centers on things like Trevor's dream of becoming a professional soccer player; addressing issues at Trevor's public school, especially those related to his learning disability; helping Mindy transition from junior high to high school; and saving for their retirement. If there is anything left over, they try to squirrel that away for their children's college educations.

With its emphasis on education, the Calafatos' security project echoes the upper-class security project detailed in the previous chapter. However, they are trying to finance the project on less than half as much income, which means they can't buy their way out of concerns they have with their lower-performing public schools (for example, through a flight to private schools). Furthermore, the high cost of supplying opportunities to their children means that the Calafatos must spend an inordinate amount of time and energy scrimping, saving, and fund-raising. Finally, whereas upper-class families generally divide the economic and child-rearing components of the security project between husband and wife, in middle- and working-class families like the Calafatos, these responsibilities reside squarely in the hands of just one person—the wife. By exploring "who did what" in relation to the Calafatos' security project, and who and what kept their security project on track when forces threatened to derail it, we are able to see how some of the families in my study held on in the face of real insecurity.

SURVIVING THE CRASH

For the past twenty-five years Sam has worked for just two companies, doing a very similar job and earning about the same amount of money. Sam earns $45,000 per year fixing and maintaining cash registers and ATMs. After high school Sam took a few college-level courses, intending to earn a degree, but he decided against it because he preferred work to school. Sam disliked having to study and do homework, preferring work because, as he says, "When I get home it's my time. I can do whatever the hell I want."

Sam likes his job, not necessarily because of what he does but because of the life it allows him. Sam likes the fact that his work hours, from about 8 A.M. to 4 P.M., enable him to do what he enjoys most, which is spend time with his children. "You know the MasterCard commercial—This costs this much, this costs that much, this is priceless? To me, if I had a job where I made three times as much but I was working sixty to eighty hours a week and I was missing out on all these experiences I have with my kids, to me it wouldn't be worth it."

Unlike most workers without a college degree, Sam enjoys great benefits—a comprehensive health-care plan, a pension, a 401(k) plan, an employee stock purchase plan, disability insurance, and, at this stage of his tenure, a month of paid vacation a year. (Gina's company also offers benefits, but they are much less extensive than those Sam gets from the larger company that employs him.) Unfortunately, paying for those benefits takes quite a chunk out of Sam's salary. According to him, "I don't get paid that much. Once you take out money for [all the benefits], with what's left, it's not even enough to make the house payment. That's where Gina comes in. [He laughs.] People crack me up when they ask, 'Oh, does your wife work?' If she didn't work, we'd be living in a cardboard box!" Indeed, Gina's salary from her job as a software account manager provides the family's cash flow, the money the family really lives on. This is why the downturn in the early 2000s that created hard times at Gina's software company and resulted in a 15 percent cut in her base salary was quite a shock to the family's system.

At forty-six years old, Gina is proud of the fact that she is the first person in her family to graduate from college. After attending a large state school in Southern California, where she majored in marketing, Gina began a career in software sales and account management and steadily moved her way up in various companies. Her long hours at work translated into a good living, with her take-home pay, including commissions, reaching as high as six figures.

With the future looking bright, Sam and Gina decided to take advantage of low interest rates and refinance their mortgage. They changed from a thirty-year to a fifteen-year loan, willing to increase their monthly payments in order to pay off their house years earlier. However, soon after they refinanced, the economy took a dive and Gina's company faltered. The cutbacks began with one mandatory unpaid day off per week, then shifted to layoffs and a 15 percent reduction in salary for the employees who remained. Gina survived, but with her base pay lowered and her commissions decimated by a depressed economy, she now takes home just $65,000 per year, which she describes as a "mediocre income." Surviving what Gina calls "the crash" after their mortgage payment went up and their income went down proved to be "one of the worst times" in her life—a time that was undoubtedly made worse because of the solitary nature of her endeavor.

MANAGING INSECURITY: THE UNEQUAL BURDEN

The first thing Sam tells me about Gina is that it is she who is the more financially responsible of the two: "When the kids ask me if they can get something, I'll say, 'It's fine with me, but go ask your mom.'" Sam explains how Gina recently decided that, due to high gas prices, they needed to sell their older SUV and replace it with a newer, more fuel-efficient car. Sam says he would have preferred to buy a new SUV: "With all the soccer traveling we do, and coaching that I do, and all the stuff that goes along with that—bags, equipment—it's just easier to load an SUV." But Gina insisted on a more economical choice, a new Toyota sedan. After driving it for a while, Sam did a few calculations. With eyebrows arched in surprise, Sam enthusiastically exclaimed, "In three weeks, we've driven a thousand miles and have saved $80 in gas already!"

This story nicely frames the marital dynamic between Gina and Sam. Gina is the enforcer of planning and responsibility, while Sam is the somewhat reluctant supporter. "If it were up to me, we would buy an SUV, we would have a big plasma TV," Sam said. Yet he appreciates his wife's prudence, recognizing that it helps to keep him in line and the family's security project on track.

"Gina and I are opposite in a lot of ways," Sam observes, "and it's actually a good thing. I mean, you have to be compatible; otherwise, forget it, it's not gonna work out. And you obviously have to have things in common and all that. We're not completely opposite. But, you know, she's the one that does the bills and she's the more responsible one . . . She's the one that pays the bills; she knows how much we have in savings and all that kind of stuff."

I observed a similar dynamic among many of the middle-class and working-class families in my study. One of the husbands in the group, Michael Clifford, says, "I tend to be more spontaneous, if you will, than Debbie is, and that's why it's good, because she can take a look at more things and analyze stuff where I just go, 'I'm going to get that. Let's go get it.'" Michael's wife, Debbie, agrees, although she describes the difference more pointedly: "Michael has no financial responsibility. I've always made more money. I've always paid the bills. I've always made sure the bills were getting paid."

Another middle-class wife, Heather Webb, echoes these sentiments: "I'm just more practical when it comes to [finances]. As we say, 'I'm the saver, he's the spender.' That's been my role. It's not Nick's strength; it's more mine. I think the ultimate veto power is mine. If I said, 'No, we can't afford a car,' he wouldn't go out and buy a car."

What's the explanation for this gender distinction? Sam Calafato says it's simply the result of how he and Gina happen to divide the household tasks:

> I think we used to both pay the bills, and at first I did it, but then she just started doing it. And I had no problem with her doing it. [He laughs.] It's not like it's something fun, you know. [He chuckles.] So yeah, she does it. I don't know, I have a certain role and she's got certain roles, and there's certain things I do and certain things she does. Like I said, I always clean the bathrooms and mop the floors. I'm usually going to practice with the kids and all that. So, you know, I got my things to do and that's one of the things she does.

By contrast, Gina seems more inclined to attribute the task division to personality differences. She says, "Sam's personality is, well, he hardly has a pessimistic bone in his body. He's always very upbeat, always trying to lighten things through his humor or funny stories or whatever. And to me, a lot of times he will just ignore stuff. It's just ignore, ignore, ignore, whereas I hit things head-on and I want to get them tackled and done right away."

However, when I finally asked Gina directly why she had always been in charge of paying the bills, she sat silently with a quizzical expression on her face for a long time. Finally, she responded, "Yeah, I don't know why. It's funny that you ask that. I don't know why. I always just did it. When we first got married, we kept our separate checking accounts for a while, and then we merged those, and I think from then . . . I just kind of always paid the bills . . . Yeah. It was just the task I took on." Because Gina had always been in charge of keeping the Calafato security project on track, it fell to her to guide them through the two-year-long bout of insecurity her family experienced when her pay declined and their mortgage payment increased. Gina was caught off guard by the severity of her family's economic fall: "I never expected for the economy to just [drop], for my industry to just plummet." Beset with worry and feeling beleaguered by the layoffs at her company, Gina nonetheless set to work to right the family ship. She cut expenses by canceling the biweekly housecleaning service. She told the kids to switch their shopping from Macy's to Target or the local thrift store. The family stopped going to movies and out to eat. They even curtailed their social life. "We used to have a lot more gatherings, with people coming over for parties," Gina says. "Those were expensive. We don't do that anymore."

Gina spent many evenings going over the family's budget in her head and anxiously entering their expenses into a spreadsheet, adding up their bills and trying to square their costs with their lagging income. She was finally forced to cut back on the monthly deposits she had recently started making to save for the kids' college educations. She was also forced to sell some of the stock they owned in Sam's company. "It was a struggle," Gina says, "to keep ends meeting by not using your credit card or not getting into debt because of the situation."

Managing this insecurity took a toll on Gina's relationships with family and friends. "It was really stressful," Gina laments. "Sam and I would get in fights about money, and Mindy and Trevor would be upset if we couldn't do this or that. It's very stressful on a marriage and on your relationship with your kids, and it kind of rubs over onto what you are doing with your friends, because you can't always do things with them."

Though both Gina and Sam described this period of insecurity as difficult, it was harder for Gina since she was the person in charge of holding on. Gina said that it was a very tense time in their marriage because she and Sam would fight about their finances. Many fights were triggered by Sam's love for the 49ers, the local NFL team for which Sam had long held season tickets. To Gina's profound displeasure, Sam continued to purchase these tickets when, in her mind, they could no longer afford them. As Gina angrily explained, "Struggling, you don't go to 49ers games . . . To me, it was like, you know, 49er tickets are like 80 bucks apiece, and then you've got parking, and then you've got the food. And it's like every Sunday you leave at 6 A.M. and then don't go home until 6 P.M., and that money could be used somewhere else, and he's not only got one ticket, he's got four." Sam's brother-in-law chipped in to help cover the cost of the tickets for a couple of seasons, and Sam was often able to sell the extra tickets he didn't use, but the football games remained a battleground. When they would fight about the tickets, Gina says that Sam would always tell her that she should go out and do something fun, too, but Gina had forsaken such things: "I used to have season tickets to the symphony, and I used to do that as kinda my thing. I gave that up a looooong time ago."

While Sam attended football games, Gina grew weary of being the designated worrier. She grew tired of worrying about the uncertainty, grew tired of monitoring their bank accounts, grew tired of making ends meet without running up debt on their credit cards. She started to ask Sam to share in her burden. Gina said,

> And sometimes I would just ask him, "Can you just be the bill payer for a while? Just so I can get away from having it always be in my face." Because he wouldn't, he wouldn't, and he would see money in the checking account and think that it's there to spend. I'm like, "Come on! You have got to understand that just because you see money in there, it doesn't mean that it's not already spent." So, things like that. He did it for like a month. [She laughs.] I was trying to make him understand and see exactly how frustrating it was for me, because when you know what money is coming in and where it's going, and if it's short, it's more stressful when the other person isn't paying attention to it at all. He is aware of it, but he's not . . .

Sam, too, remembers this as a stressful time and remembers that Gina asked him to take over paying the bills. When he took on this burden, however, Sam's approach did not respect Gina's line in the sand that the family remain free of credit card debt, so Gina took the job back from Sam in order to prevent him from taking what she considered to be a reckless step. Sam explains,

> It was stressful. Because I remember one time she was so stressed out, she goes, "You do it." So to me, if say our Visa bill was—this is an example, I don't know what it was—but let's say it was two thousand dollars. Well, we're used to paying our Visa bill every month, 'cause you know you don't want to pay those interest charges. But because money was so tight, to me when I was gonna do it, [I thought], "Okay, the Visa bill's two thousand dollars, we can only afford to pay four hundred dollars of it. Well, hell, that's all I'm gonna pay of it then." You know what I mean? [He chuckles.] But, I forget, she

didn't agree with that, so I don't even know what she did. But then before you know it, she took it over.

Gina is a stickler for avoiding credit card debt, having watched friends suffer under the weight of such debt. For Gina, credit card debt represents a threat to her family's security that she is determined to avoid. She says, "It has always been very firm with me . . . that always was one of the things, as hard as we were struggling, I was not going to have credit card debt. But no, we never [had debt] because I do all the bill paying and all, you know." Gina also didn't want to cut back on the family investments (though ultimately she was forced to). When Sam suggested lowering their contributions to his 401(k) plan and employee stock purchase plan, Gina initially insisted on the importance of maintaining the maximum contribution: "Sam always suggested that, too, 'Let's not do the max stock buying, just for a while.' I was always like, 'No, I think that's really important, that stock is growing, that stock is making money. It's money we are putting away.' To me, it was not what we were going to touch."

Given Sam's greater tolerance for going into debt and reducing their investments, Gina was faced with a choice: either continue to manage the family's financial security project on her own, or to share the burden with Sam and risk it getting off track. Gina chose to go it alone and remained her family's designated worrier.

One option the Calafatos did have was to lower their mortgage payments by refinancing the loan for a thirty-year term. However, Gina was reluctant to refinance because her job was so unstable. She worried that they might not get the loan if she lost her job while in the middle of the paperwork. Eventually, though, things were just too tight, and Gina and Sam decided to refinance, giving themselves room to breathe once again.

This step significantly reduced the Calafatos' financial troubles, but they were still under pressure to make their dollars stretch every month. As Gina notes, "When I am making more money, we can do a lot more things. We don't have to think about going to a play or sports event or taking a vacation." But in the wake of Gina's pay cut, the Calafatos had to think about every penny, especially when it came to holding on to opportunities for their children, like having them continue to participate in extracurricular activities.

THE FUND-RAISING CHALLENGE

At the time I was doing in-depth research with them, the Calafatos' lives were dominated by their son's participation in a traveling soccer team. Describing why it was both so expensive and so important for Trevor to be on the team, Gina said,

> The traveling soccer league costs a lot of money to travel to different places, going to hotels; we went to Nevada last year. So that was lots of money . . . [But] for me those opportunities are going to help my son. His goal is to be a professional soccer player. So what not better a thing to do than be on a traveling team and then be scouted. If he's not in those tournaments or he's not in those places, he wouldn't have that opportunity for his future, for his choice of career.

Gina and Sam were both hopeful that if Trevor continued to excel at soccer, he might be able to go to college on a soccer scholarship. Many other middle- and working-class families eye scholarships as a doorway to college for their children. As property manager Angela Barbieri says, "Well, we're hoping for scholarships. I mean, that's basically, you know, that's what we're banking on." So the Calafatos considered it essential to preserve Trevor's ability to play on his traveling soccer team and thus perhaps earn a scholarship for college. But funding it was difficult. Consequently, it became critical for them to raise money from outside sources in order for Trevor to be able to stay on the team.

Though each member of the team was expected to raise a total of $1,000 to help offset the costs of an end-of-the-season trip to soccer tournaments in Oregon and Northern California, many of the other families on the team had more discretionary income than the Calafatos. So if the more affluent families didn't earn all the money, it wasn't a big deal; they could make up the difference out of their own pockets. For the Calafatos, however, raising that money was vital. And—unsurprisingly—the task of managing the fund-raising fell to Gina.

One of the main ways the team members raised money was by selling candy. The previous year Gina and Sam had sold most of the candy, but this year Trevor's coach wanted the kids to be more involved—a challenging task for a somewhat shy kid like Trevor—so Gina picked up the slack.

She and Sam brought candy to work to sell to their colleagues. And when the family attended a neighborhood picnic in the park one evening, it was Gina who reminded Trevor to bring the candy and Gina who pointed out people they knew well who would be likely customers. Still, Trevor dragged his feet. Finally, at a glance from Gina, Sam reluctantly grabbed a box of candy and walked off with Trevor to make a few sales, though not before muttering in a low voice, "I hate doing this."

Gina also encouraged Trevor to earn money by setting up a lemonade stand and running a neighborhood car wash. In addition, she wrote to friends and family soliciting donations. So did Sam, though only after much prompting from Gina. Sam explained to me why he disliked writing these letters: "I don't know people or have friends with extra money like that."

Overhearing our conversation, Gina interjected, "You never know. Last year I sent out an email and managed to raise $380."

Sam replied, "Yeah, last year didn't it [the stipend] pay for the seven nights of hotel?"

"No," Gina replied. "It barely covered half the nights, but still . . . that's why it's great to get the money."

Gina followed up her letter with phone calls to the people she'd written to, and she urged Sam to do the same. Even Trevor's soccer coach got into the act. Hanging up the phone one evening, Sam explained to me, "Trevor's coach said that I should bring the letter up with the dad of one of Trevor's friends the next time I see him, and I'm like, 'Oh, okay.'" But shaking his head, Sam said, "I'm *not* going to bring it up."

Gina dismissed Sam's reluctance to raise funds as an aspect of his nice personality, telling me, "That's the way Sam is. He's the type of person who is always doing favors for other people but hates to ask anyone for a favor." It's certainly true that asking people for money seems to make Sam uncomfortable, but his reluctance also seems to be related to his passive role in managing the family finances. Sam was never the point person for coming up with the funds for Trevor to participate in the soccer tournaments in the first place. It was Gina who knew that last year's stipend covered only half of the hotel bill; it was Gina who researched airfare and hotel options online and determined that driving to Oregon would be $800 cheaper than flying. Because Sam did not do this kind of security work, he could both practically and psychically distance himself from the burden of raising the money. Gina could not. Accordingly, Sam played a more minor role in the ongoing fund-raising efforts while Gina took center stage. She even spent her scanty free time in the evenings making jewelry, which she later sold to raise additional money.

GETTING HELP WITH THEIR BURDEN

Other designated worriers in my study were more forceful than Gina in attempting to get their husbands to share their burdens. After Michael Clifford was laid off from his sales job and stayed home for several months, his wife, Debbie, laid down the law. She'd grown irritated over being responsible for everything, including child support payments to Michael's ex-wife:

> It just bothered me for a very long time. He wasn't making any money and I thought, "I'm not doing this. I'm not making enough money to support every-body under the sun. Your ex-wife, your kids, and you, because somebody thinks that they don't need to get up and go to work every day or they don't need to make more than enough to put two nickels in their pocket." So at one point I finally said, "Fuck you, I'm not giving you any more money . . . If you're not putting any in, you're not getting any out. Sorry. It's not the way it's working when I'm struggling so much. And I say 'I.' I mean, we are starv-ing, but because you decide not to recognize that, apparently you don't feel like you're struggling. I feel like I'm struggling."

Some of Debbie's anger subsided when Michael started a car-washing business. But as opposed to Gina, who continued to manage the burden all on her own, Debbie decided to deal with her burden by taking a page out of her husband's playbook: she began to care less about the family security project. She says, "His tolerance for a lack of money is a lot higher than mine. And his tolerance for having a messy financial situation is a lot higher than mine. So I've kind of learned from him. I've given up and said, 'Okay, if it doesn't matter to you, it doesn't matter to me either.' Which is not a great plan to have, but it's kind of like, 'Okay, I can't handle all this, I can't do all this, I can't.'"

Heather Webb dealt with her husband's unemployment differently than Debbie Clifford. Heather's husband, Nick, who works in sales, has been laid off numerous times. During these times Heather embraces the power of positive thinking and tries to focus on the good things and not fixate on the negative things: "When we did have hard times . . . I've always tried to think, 'Okay, what's the positive side of it?" and just go from there. 'Cause there's been quite a few. I mean, he's probably had fifteen jobs." After her husband's latest layoff, Heather decided to focus on the ways it helped her to have her husband home, especially since her work hours had recently increased: "We try to look at things as the glass half full. Like, okay, Nick's not necessarily working right now, but with my daughter in summer camps and with me working a huge amount of hours, Nick being unemployed . . . it's good, he can pick our daughter up after school and I can work late hours. I can go in early 'cause Nick can take our daughter to school . . . or pick her up from summer camp." For Heather, focusing on the positive is "just easier. It's so draining not to be positive about it."

Despite her optimistic take on things, Nick senses Heather's resentment toward him, especially when he is unemployed. To ward off her annoyance, when he is not working he keeps a daily list of things he's gotten done as a way to show that he is doing his part. Nick said, "There are days when Heather comes home at eight o'clock at night and wonders what I did today. But I always have a list . . . I'm prepared for that . . . I am always prepared to tell her what I did that day, 'cause I don't want her to feel that she's the only one that's supporting the family or contributing to what needs to be done." Although there are different ways that designated worriers attempt to get their husbands to help them shoulder the burden, such as laying down the law or checking over their husband's to-do list, these very acts illustrate who is ultimately in charge. Despite wanting their husbands to help them out, or wishing that they were capable of doing so, either way designated worriers are shouldering the majority of the security burden on their own.

SECURING OPPORTUNITIES: ANOTHER UNEQUAL BURDEN

Sam and Gina place a high value on being present for their children. Both avoid taking on management responsibilities at work so they can spend time with their children, with Gina helping out at school and Sam coaching their sporting events. However, just as Sam does not share equally in the burden of managing the financial aspects of the Calafatos' security project, he also does not share equally in the work of securing educational opportunities for their children. It is Gina who is always in charge and always on guard while Sam stands on the sidelines and offers comic relief.

A few years back, in the midst of the Calafatos' period of greatest insecurity, they learned that their son, Trevor, has a moderate form of dyslexia. Though a third grader, he could do math and reading at only a first-grade level. To get Trevor "caught up," the Calafatos took him for one-on-one tutoring twice a week for almost a year at the cost of $400 to $500 a month.

The tutoring helped enormously, but Trevor continues to have some difficulty keeping up with his classes. To address this disability, the Calafatos, after what Gina describes as a "long and frustrating" struggle, established a formal plan with Trevor's school, outlining a special instructional approach and services, including extended time for test taking. The complicated task of managing Trevor's dyslexia is another burden that is borne primarily by Gina: "I'm always making sure that all the teachers know about his plan, that they are following it, and that the school is updating it, and that there are special conditions where he should have the opportunity to take [a test] in another classroom, with a longer period of time, with breaks, because sometimes he can't finish [tests on time]. And a lot of times his teachers just forget." Though Gina is always on alert about Trevor's special needs, events that occurred the fall before my research with the family required her to be even more vigilant.

The first sign of trouble was the class schedule Trevor brought home from his school orientation, in which a placeholder name, "Jane Teacher," appeared next to his three main classes. Gina was puzzled until she learned, after Trevor's first day of school, that he had been placed in a seventh-grade class that had not been assigned a permanent teacher. In the interim, a substitute teacher would teach Trevor's class.

Gina told me the story while driving Trevor and me to meet up with Sam and Mindy at Mindy's softball game. Stopped at a red light, Gina looked over at me, drumming her fingers on the steering wheel with annoyance. I grimaced to acknowledge her frustration with the situation.

"Thank you!" Gina declared. "So it's not just me!?" and outstretched her arms as if to say, "Finally, someone gets it."

I asked Gina what she planned to do. She replied, "Well, I've already e-mailed the principal and set up a meeting with him tomorrow, and I e-mailed someone we know on the district school board. Unfortunately, he's out of town, but, I mean, when I get on a roll, I don't waste time." After we arrived at the softball field and Trevor scampered out of earshot, Gina explained in a low voice exactly why she was so angry: "Trevor has a special program. He doesn't like to talk about it because he's embarrassed, but the school is very well aware that he has it and they go and put him in the substitute's class anyway. He's a slower learner, and now the things they are studying are more advanced, [so] it just gets harder. Every year I have to talk to his teachers and make them aware of it, and now it's like there's no teacher to talk to yet, and who knows when there will be."

Walking across the field toward the bleachers, Gina said, "You know, I just feel really dissed by the school . . . really dissed, especially after all we do for that school." Gina refolded the thick plaid blanket she had brought along for us to sit on and explained that she wanted Trevor switched into the class taught by Mrs. Anderson, who had been Mindy's teacher the two previous years. As if succumbing to the weight of her frustration, Gina sank down into her seat. She paused for a moment and then said in a mocking tone, "And Sam's just like, 'Whaaat . . . whaat's the problem?'" As she said this, she made a "duh" sort of expression on her face with her eyes widening and the corners of her mouth turned down. She shook her head from side to side as if to say, "I can't believe he doesn't get it." After silently watching the first pitch thrown, Gina turned to me and said, "It gives me a heart attack."

A week later, after meeting with the principal, Gina managed to get Trevor transferred into Mrs. Anderson's class. Meanwhile, however, her anxiety about the confusion further fueled her insomnia. For the past four years, as "probably a side effect of all the stress," Gina has been waking up in the wee hours of the morning. With thoughts about her family and her job racing through her head, she is unable to fall back to sleep. "Finally, I'll just get up," she says, "and it's really when I do my chores—laundry or get on the computer, clean out the e-mail, clean the kitchen, do my crafts, or read." On the morning when I first interviewed Gina, she had been awake since 3:15 A.M.

By contrast, Gina says, "Sam can fall asleep anywhere." This pattern isn't confined to the Calafatos. A study in the United Kingdom found that men with lower levels of education sleep better and suffer less insomnia than better-educated men, while low-income, less-educated women have higher rates of insomnia than women with more schooling.[2] Moreover, a survey of couples going through bankruptcy found that wives reported experiencing more stress-related sleep problems than did husbands.[3] These findings mirror the gendered and classed patterns of worry I found in my study. A few designated worriers I interviewed experienced insomnia when they were stressed out about their family's situations. As one mother said, "I've lost sleep over it." Debbie Clifford's worry manifests itself in other ways. "I drink too much," she says. "I drink more than I want to be drinking. But it's like, 'Okay, I'm having a glass of wine tonight. I just need a glass.'" Debbie has also suffered from heart palpitations for the last five years, which she thinks are related to her anxiety.

HOW THEY MAKE IT WORK

Because of her concern about the family's finances, Gina would happily move from the Bay Area: "If it were up to me, I would absolutely move away from this area, [because] it's so expensive." Sam understands Gina's thinking. If they sold their house in the Bay Area and moved somewhere like Arizona, he observes, they could buy a house for cash and "wouldn't have that financial burden as much as we would here." But Sam is unwilling to move. He says, "I don't want to move. [He chuckles.] I love it here. I love the Bay Area. I love the 49ers. I love the Giants. All our friends are here. Most of our families are out here. Like I said, it's another one of those things where, you know, like the MasterCard commercial, the priceless things."

For Gina, having family nearby is not enough: "My family is here, too, but that wouldn't keep me from moving to another area." With Gina wanting to leave and Sam wanting to stay, the reason they remain in the Bay Area is, as Gina says, that such a decision must be made jointly; it is not "up to" her alone. Sam echoes this perspective: "If you're gonna make a decision like that, both people would have to agree, and she knows I don't want to move."

That Sam's desire to stay put should trump Gina's desire to move when it is Gina who shoulders most of the responsibility speaks to the fact that although Sam may not share equally in the security work, he is an integral and very loving member of the team. He cooks and cleans, picks up after everyone, goes to the grocery store, drives the children around, coaches their teams, and helps them with their homework. Moreover, though he makes less money than Gina, his earnings and particularly his benefits are crucial to maintaining the Calafatos' security. Thus, while Gina is the captain of the ship, Sam is the competent and witty first mate who, out of respect and love for his wife, yields to her in all matters of navigation.

What's more, as the eldest of four siblings, Gina seems to gravitate toward the leadership role. At times she exhibits a predilection for micromanaging and an unwillingness to share responsibilities with Sam, most likely caused by a combination of factors: Gina's self-described "perfectionism," her dissatisfaction with Sam's past performance, and his seeming cluelessness about issues that Gina considers vitally important (like the problem with Trevor's class assignment).

Given the uneven division of emotion and worry work in the Calafato household, one might expect Gina to harbor a tremendous amount of resentment toward Sam, yet her resentment generally seems fleeting. This is partly explained by Sam's active presence at home, and partly by the fact that their straight woman / funny man dynamic forms the basis of their marital relationship. This dynamic is so entrenched that Sam even acknowledged it in an anniversary card he gave to Gina. The card, taped to the wall above Gina's desk at home, reads

> Well darling, since there are many times when I should be serious, but instead I joke around.
>
> To somewhat make up for it, instead of joking around . . . I'm going to be serious.
>
> Happy Anniversary darling, I will love you forever.

The same dynamic is reflected in the family's holiday card. A picture of Sam and the children making funny faces appears on the top of the card. On the inside of the card is a solitary picture of Gina looking a bit perplexed with a bubble above her head that says, "All I want for Christmas is a vacation from my crazy family." Gina is portrayed as the serious one in the family, while Sam and the children are the comedians.

Not all designated worriers can work through their resentment as easily. Debbie Clifford is quite bitter that her husband doesn't share in her concerns. She says, "I don't like that responsibility. It's like, I don't want this. I don't want to have to be a superwoman. I don't like the fact that I have to give birth to the babies and earn all the money and pay all the bills. I'm having a problem with all that responsibility." Debbie's resentment has taken a toll on her feelings for her husband, forcing her to reevaluate the relationship:

> It forced me to recalibrate what I thought of my husband and how much I respected him. And why I respected him or why I didn't, and what I respected about him. I had to decide, how does this matter to me? And how much does it matter to me? I had to decide if I respected my husband as much. And I decided I do for different reasons. I mean, he's a good guy. And I didn't fall in love with him because he was rich. I fell in love with him 'cause he was a nice guy and he was really good with kids. And having children with him has been a great thing.

Heather Web, too, is resentful toward her husband due to his repeated unemployment. Though she knows that he has often been a victim of economic forces beyond his control, she also feels that his work ethic is lacking: "I have a very, very strong work ethic. I don't miss days. I've had maybe four sick days in seven years. With Nick, honestly, his work ethic isn't quite as good as mine. And when he says he's working really hard, I think he could work harder." After noting that difficult financial situations such as the unemployment of a spouse can "destroy a marriage," Heather complains, "I'm tired of being the stable one." And later, "There's been times where [I thought] marrying him was the absolute worst thing I could have done. And did I settle?"

If marriages like these are going to last, the resentment and annoyance that designated worrier wives hold toward their husbands must be reconciled. For Debbie and Heather, who appeared to have much more anger toward their husbands than did Gina, addressing the conflict required a historical revision of the very definition of a good husband. For Debbie, a good husband has become someone who is good with children, not necessarily a man who is a good provider. For Heather, a good husband has become someone who is available to pick up the extra slack at home, not necessarily a man with a strong work ethic and a steady job. By redefining—or, in Debbie's words, "recalibrating"—what it was that they valued about their husbands, designated worriers muted their negative feelings toward their spouses and instead cultivated an appreciation for the things their husbands could provide them, such as a rich family life and the opportunity to work more.

Although the designated worrier dynamic can have a very negative effect on marital relationships, Gina's annoyance with Sam is much more limited. Perhaps this is because Gina is a mostly willing participant in the implicit security bargain she and Sam have made. As the family's holiday card reveals, she doesn't mind being the more serious grown-up in the family. Moreover, compared to the bargains Debbie and Heather have struck with their husbands, the bargain Gina has with Sam is an easier one to accept. In contrast to Michael Clifford and Nick Webb, Sam has been steadily employed throughout their marriage; he gets good performance reviews at his job; and, with the exception of the 49er tickets, Sam dutifully defers to Gina when it comes to the finances. Nonetheless, Sam's jovial persona can annoy Gina at times, especially when she feels he is ignoring important issues. And just as Debbie and Heather try to focus on the good characteristics they see in their husbands despite the bad or annoying ones, so does Gina.

On a few occasions I noticed Gina pointing out the upside to Sam's lightheartedness. For example, Gina often expressed real appreciation for Sam's ability to brighten her children's spirits with his sense of humor. On the night that their daughter, Mindy, was so overwhelmed with her schoolwork, Gina praised Sam's silly antics and said, "I think that's sooooo good. Mindy is so stressed out, she needs to laugh." Even though Sam's optimistic outlook frustrates Gina during hard times, in other contexts his funny persona and his glass-half-full take on the world are things that she truly cherishes about him.

As long as Sam maintains his end of their security bargain, Gina keeps her cool. But she reacts with anger if Sam strays outside its bounds and behaves in ways that Gina believes put the family's security project in jeopardy.

Two years ago Sam began having pain in his lower back and his upper thigh as well as problems with urination. True to his philosophy that "worry is a wasted emotion," Sam assumed everything would be fine and that eventually he would feel better. But when his symptoms persisted for two months, Sam finally told Gina, and Gina sent him to the doctor, who diagnosed Sam with prostate cancer.

Sam's doctor underscored the role women often play in worrying about their husbands, telling him that married men live longer than single men. This resonated with Sam: "Because me, I'm a typical guy. If I have something, I'll wait till it goes away." Fortunately for Sam, the cancer had not spread, though the treatment was still aggressive, involving surgery and a course of chemotherapy. In total, Sam missed two months of work.

For families like the Delgados, catastrophic medical costs can spell financial disaster. However, Sam's comprehensive benefits protected the Calafatos, covering his medical care and paying almost all his normal wages while he was out on disability. Still, during the time it took to get Sam's biopsy results back to see how extensive the cancer was, the Calafatos' security project that Gina had so dutifully maintained appeared to be at serious risk. She says, "I had a lot of anger about that. It took me a long time to work through that because, to me, [by waiting to see the doctor] he put our family in so much danger. He could have died! So there wouldn't have been half of our income and all of our benefits." Gina's company does offer benefits, but they are much less extensive and much more expensive than those Sam gets. Thus, Gina felt that Sam's behavior had crossed the line separating carelessness from sabotage.

THE INSECURITY SHIFT

If we analyze the Calafato family in terms of who does what in the second shift (housework, child care), we would find a mostly egalitarian couple almost evenly dividing up domestic work between them. But when we analyze the Calafato family in terms of their security project, we find a decidedly unequal division of emotion and labor. By invoking the lens of security, I am purposefully trying to bring to light a distinctive type of work done in families that is a permutation on the second shift; it is the insecurity shift. This type of work is becoming increasingly common due to the rise in instability among many families as a result of the volatile nature of the new economy and the shift in risk.

And this work is performed overwhelmingly by women. Other research points to the feminization of security work, noting that when insecurity strikes families, it is the women who deal with foreclosure notices, seek credit counseling, negotiate with bill collectors, and decide when it's time to file for bankruptcy, and they suffer from the stress and depression associated with such difficulties.[4] My study echoes these conclusions. Among the middle-income families and working-class families in my study, it is the women who take the responsibility for holding on to security. But why?

GENDERED AND CLASSED DIMENSIONS OF SECURITY

When I probed more deeply in the interviews about why someone's spouse worried more or less than he or she did, my interviewees often attributed this difference to personality, gender, or some combination of the two. For example, Michael Clifford said, "'Cause she's yin and I'm yang," while Nick Webb said, "It's not my personality . . . Heather does enough worrying about it for the both of us." And when I asked Salvador Garcia about why his wife worries more than he does, he said, "It's just, she's the woman. [He laughs.] To put it bluntly, you know, that's just her personality. She's always been the one to worry about things." Salvador's wife, Glenda, agreed, saying, "Women just worry more."

If women simply worry more than men, then we should expect this pattern to occur in all families, regardless of income. But as chapter 4 illustrated, the gendered division of "worry work" looks different in upper-class families, where the primary responsibility for the economic and child-related aspects of security projects are divided between the husband and the wife. These findings that the gendered division of security work differs by social class and by educational attainment points to a more complex explanation, reflecting these families' different positions in relation to recent macroeconomic changes and developments.

In my study, the most striking examples of the feminized designated worrier role are in families where the women have more education and/or higher earnings than their husbands. Mothers had higher levels of educational attainment in eleven out of the fourteen designated worrier families, with the most common pattern being that the wives had a college degree and the husbands did not (six families). In the remaining three families, the parents had the same level of education. In nine families, the mothers outearned the fathers. In eight of the families, the mothers had both more education and higher earnings. Though some designated worriers had college degrees and others only high school diplomas, what united them is that they are all married to men who did not graduate from college. These less-educated men have been left behind as the economy transitions from one based on manufacturing to one based on services.

Nowadays, good jobs are primarily reserved for those with at least a college degree. According to the Bureau of Labor Statistics, the earnings of men with only a high school education declined by 15 percent between 1979 and 2005.[5] In contrast, the change in real earnings during the same time period has been more favorable for women at all levels of education, such that the wages for women with only a high school degree increased by 7 percent.[6] Women fared better partly because they were playing catch-up with men, as their earnings have historically been lower than men's; partly because of an increase in the proportion of college-educated women in the workforce; partly because of a rise in the number of women in professional and managerial positions; and partly because of a movement toward more full-time, year-round employment for women.[7]

Women are also faring better than men in regard to education. Women now outpace men in graduating from high school and college. By the early 1980s, the college enrollment rates of male and female high school graduates had reached parity.[8] Since that time, women's enrollment rates have exceeded those of men by an average of 6 percent a year.[9] For more than a decade now, women have earned about 57 percent of all the bachelor's degrees awarded.[10] This gender gap favoring women is expected to continue over the next decade.[11] Reflecting these gender and education trends, the number of marriages in which the wife has reached a higher level of educational attainment than her husband has grown from 7 percent in 1960 to 23 percent in 2011.[12]

These educational trends likely correspond to a rise in the number of households where women earn more than their husbands. In 1981, women earned more than men in only 15 percent of households.[13] By 2011, the percentage of couples in which the wife outearned her husband had grown to 28 percent.[14] Furthermore, women now make up half of all workers in the United States, and mothers are the primary breadwinners or co-breadwinners in nearly two-thirds of American families.[15] This worsening situation of less-educated men and the improving situation for many women frames the tendency among middle-class and working-class men in my study to prefer to have their wives take the lead in matters of security. But this gendered and classed dynamic is not an altogether new finding.

Other scholars have found that women tend to be in charge of the management and expenditure of family money, especially when families face economic difficulties.[16] In her 1976 study of working-class families, sociologist Lillian Rubin found that more than 75 percent reported that women were responsible for managing and paying the bills. Rubin argues that the reason for this gendered pattern among working-class families is that men have the power to turn over tedious tasks and, more important, that it allows men to avoid facing the painful reality that they are not earning enough money to provide everything their family needs. Thus, when money is short, the husband can blame his wife for her deficiency in money management rather than his lack of income. By turning this task over to their wives, husbands are able to protect their identity as breadwinners. In contrast, Rubin found that among the professional, upper-middle-class households in her study, men were responsible for the money in three-quarters of her sample. Moreover, she found that among working-class families with some discretionary spending, the men took over decision making. Together, these findings lead to the conclusion that when there is extra money in the household to be managed or invested, it is the men who control it, whereas when money is tight, women are in charge of the everyday management.[17]

Coming thirty years later, my study largely confirms the gender and social class patterns Rubin found. However, there are two important differences. First, in my study this designated worrier dynamic exists not just in working-class households but among solidly middle-class families as well. And it existed even in working- and middle-class households that had some discretionary spending, such as setting aside some money for savings. Consequently, this type of gendered division of security work may be moving up the class ladder as economic insecurity spreads into the middle class—into homes where the person best equipped to deal with it is, increasingly, a woman. Second, the reasons behind the gendered division of security work seem different than the ones Rubin pointed to. From my discussions with these men in middle- and working-class families, their lack of involvement in managing the family finances seems less related to salvaging a masculinity based on being a breadwinner. Living in an age where two paychecks is the norm, these men never really believed they could support their families on their income alone. Instead, having their wives be the designated worrier allows them to embrace a different kind of masculinity, one that celebrates the freedom of not being the one who has to carry such burdens. This was certainly true for Sam.

Sam never clung tightly to the idea that he should be the breadwinner. As he explains, there are "probably guys who grew up thinking, [with] the way they were raised, that you should always make more than the wife. There's probably guys that think the wife should stay home. I mean, when we got married, I used to think that ideally that's what I wanted. But obviously when [we had children], it was obvious that wasn't gonna happen because I didn't make enough money." When Mindy was born, Sam even tried to move into sales since, if he excelled at it, he could earn more money. But his attempt seemed halfhearted. "I couldn't do it," Sam said. "I hated it." He felt as if he was duping people into buying things they didn't need. Sam said that he never had a desire to get to the top. "Some people want to advance in their company and one day be in management," Sam said. "I was just never driven by that."

Years later, when Gina's salary decreased and she started earning about the same or even less than Sam (see the epilogue), he didn't welcome this new parity in their earnings. Instead, he pined for when she used to earn much more than he did. "I was happier when she made double of me, are you kidding? [He laughs.] . . . I don't have that kind of ego, 'Oh my God, my wife's making twice as much as me. I feel useless.' [He laughs.] No. Are you kidding? I always look at it like it's the same pot that it goes into." Alluding to men who might think they are the dominant one in their relationship because they earn more than their wives, Sam said, laughing, "Thank God I don't suffer from that."

Although early in his life Sam may have thought about being the breadwinner, he quickly accepted the reality of their situation—that Gina would also need to provide. Having Gina manage their finances, then, didn't protect Sam from a reality he found painful. Instead, having his wife take charge is, in Sam's view, a smart move since she is better at it anyway. Noting that Gina was always on top of things, Sam said, "Thankfully, Gina's not like me." Sam accepted things as they were. In fact, he even embraced them. Sam began to see that he was getting a pretty good deal.

When Sam talked about security work—paying the bills, figuring out the finances—he typically described it in negative terms. "It's not like it's something fun," he said when explaining why he was fine with Gina doing it. Other times he referred to it as "all that crap" and would quickly add, "I'm lucky; Gina does it." From Sam's vantage point, being the breadwinner and doing all the tasks that it entailed were not all they were cracked up to be. The day-to-day reality of it was a complete drag. In comparison to other men who suffered from their "egos," Sam was grateful that he didn't bear any of these self-imposed masculine burdens. Who, Sam thought, would want to carry that burden anyway?

By stepping away from traditional markers of masculinity, Sam inverted their meaning. Instead of feeling as if he didn't measure up, Sam seemed to feel like he had dodged a bullet.[18] He was "lucky" that he had married Gina, who was perfectly equipped to take the lead in these matters, which meant that he didn't have to. Indeed, their "arrangement" enables Sam to have a more carefree existence. Although Sam does a lot of work around the house and is actively involved with their children, he is not the one on call to right the family ship. Thus, when you compare Gina's life with Sam's, in many ways she got the short end of the stick.

Yet by being cast in the more carefree role, Sam is able to be the optimistic one in the family. He can be the one whose job it is to lighten the mood. Just as the Calafatos need Gina's diligence to help them stay on track, so, too, do they need Sam's comic relief to keep their spirits up. In this way, Sam's upbeat personality serves a similar function as did Laura Delgado's rosy repackaging. When families are on the edge, someone needs to reassure everyone that everything is going to turn out okay.

If Sam has dispensed with the traditional breadwinner role, he clings tightly to a masculine identity rooted in sports, athleticism, hard rock (his favorite kind of music), joking around, fun times with friends at pregame tailgate parties, and being an involved father. Reflecting aspects of this identity, Sam dutifully maintains a large collection of sporting memorabilia. A few years ago his collection of bobble heads, photographs, and jerseys became so large that he took over a corner of the garage, put a small TV out there, and built shelving so he could display his collection. On warm summer evenings Sam will sit in the garage surrounded by his collection, sip a beer, and watch a Giants' baseball game with Trevor.

Sociologist Deborah Thorne, who interviewed couples filing for bankruptcy, discovered a division of security work that was similar to the one I discovered among the middle- and working-class families in my study. She found that it was the wives who were in charge of the debt management chores, ranging from dealing with debt collectors to doing the research to file for bankruptcy. Professor Thorne discovered two reasons for this pattern. First, the women wanted to be in charge because their husbands were too irresponsible to be counted on to competently address their complicated financial issues. Second, the men apparently had the power to veto requests from their wives for help. The husbands were "allowed" to decide not to be bothered by the financial distress.[19]

Echoing these findings, my research indicated that many of the wives I interviewed felt that their husbands couldn't be trusted to manage the finances responsibly. I also got the sense that the fathers I interviewed considered dealing with financial pressures a real pain, and so they were eager—as well as relieved—to have their often more competent wives take over. But being able to turn this job over to their wives or ignore requests from their wives to be involved didn't always seem like an expression of power. In many ways these men were almost infantilized in their relationships. Like children, they often had to get approval from their wives about what they could spend money on. In the end, most of the women in this group of families had the final say on almost all matters. In these households the wives were the ultimate authority.

As the responsibility for managing economic risk shifts from the government and employers onto individuals and families and as economic volatility rises, these forces take on gendered and classed dimensions, affecting families in different ways. For, as my study shows, the vigilance or "worry work" required to keep economic risk at bay is largely a male endeavor at the top and a female endeavor at the middle and below.

This finding speaks to men's differential position in relation to macro-economic changes. Men at the top, whose skill set is in demand, have sufficient education, money, and power to grapple effectively with risk, while men toward the bottom do not. Incomes mark this pattern. Earnings for men with graduate degrees have increased by almost 40 percent, while earnings have stagnated for men with only some college and have decreased for those who have only a high school diploma.[20] Armed with graduate degrees and in-demand skills, upper-class families have done well during the rise of the new economy, with most of the upper-class men in my study earning more than $200,000 a year. It is thus possible for upper-class men to absorb the responsibility for their family's economic security, even if at times they would like their wives to be more involved. By contrast, the new economy has not been so kind to men without a college diploma. With their wages stagnating at best and often declining while costs continue to rise, these men are unable to fund security projects on their own and must instead rely on the financial contributions of their wives. These men's structural position means that they are hampered in their ability to grapple with insecurity. From an emotional point of view, then, worry becomes, as Sam Calafato says, "a wasted emotion."

Salvador Garcia, a working-class father, agrees: "I try not to worry about much. [He laughs.] 'Cause, I mean, financially, if we're behind on something, it's kind of out of my control. It's not like I can just fly out and figure out how to make the money that we need." These men thus leave the burden of holding on to their often better-educated and higher-earning wives.

On a follow-up visit with the Calafatos about six months after I completed my in-depth research with them, I learned that Gina's job had recently become more stressful than ever. Feeling that she was being "worked to death," she was diagnosed with clinical depression and put on antidepressants as her insomnia grew worse. Unable to withstand the pressure, Gina decided she needed a less stressful job. She found a new job within two months after she started looking, but the sales account she was hired to help manage soon dried up, and so, after only four months on the job, she was let go.

When I spoke with Gina, she was actively looking for work. The toll of the last few months showed clearly on her face: she looked exhausted and her eyes seemed almost expressionless. Worse still, when she mentioned that Trevor once again had a substitute teacher for his main social studies class, she expressed none of the dissatisfaction that she had the previous year. The fight, it seemed, was drained out of her.

During my visit Sam was his same jovial self, sticking his head into the room where Gina and I sat talking and saying teasingly, "If she says anything bad about me, it's not true!" If Gina seemed broken, Sam seemed remarkably unchanged.

Recalling the question raised at the beginning of this chapter, we now know why Gina feels old while Sam feels young. Gina feels old because of the unequal division of the work required to hold on in the face of economic insecurity. As the designated worrier, Gina does most of the work and carries most of the burden; it is Gina who loses sleep at night.

The Calafatos' story serves to highlight the way gender and class come together and shape how families do security. Carrying the heavy psychological and emotional load of the insecurity shift, as Gina does, may become increasingly common for middle- and working-class women in a world where economic risk and insecurity are both continuing to grow, while women's rates of college attendance continue to outpace those of men and the number of marriages in which wives earn more than their husbands continues to rise.

6 When Religion Fills the Gap

LAETA AND KAPO FALEAU

If you need help, you just got to ask. Without church . . .
very difficult. We give up.

Laeta Faleau

It is 8:30 on a sunny Sunday morning and six members of the Faleau family are sitting quietly in their minivan as they make the twenty-minute trip
along a freeway and over a bridge to get to their Mormon church for services. There are Mormon churches that are closer to their home, but they
prefer this one because they like its equal mix of white, Latino, and Pacific
Islander families.

When the Faleaus arrive, they hurry inside the church. With only a few
minutes to spare before the services begin, the Faleaus hastily settle into a
pew in the back. Kapo, the forty-seven-year-old patriarch, sits at one end of
the pew; he's wearing a navy suit and a red-and-black-striped tie. Laeta, his
forty-four-year-old wife, dressed in a green pantsuit and with her hair
pulled back into a bun, sits at the other end. Between them sit four of their
five children, one boy and three girls, who range in age from six to twenty
years old. Their eldest son, Peter, is away at college.

As the Faleau family waits for services to begin, other families stream
into the church, many carrying copies of the Bible and the Book of
Mormon in brown leather cases. Most of the adults in the pews have several children with them, and many, like Laeta, are focused on keeping the
youngest ones quiet. As the bishop begins speaking he is barely audible

over the din from the congregation, to which Nonni, the Faleau's six-year-old daughter, is contributing.

After the bishop welcomes everyone to the church, the congregation sings a hymn. Laeta sings passionately in high tones that contrast sharply with her low speaking voice. The Faleau children also sing with conviction, while Kapo just mouths the words silently.

After the bishop announces some upcoming events, he invites a Latina woman in her early thirties to the podium. Each week a different member of the ward (the Mormon term for congregation) gives a talk, and this woman has been asked to describe her experience living in Silicon Valley for three years while her husband pursued graduate studies in social work.

The woman's voice shakes and her hands tremble, but the emotions she wants to convey come through clearly. She talks about the difficult transition from living with her parents in Utah to getting married, moving to California, and starting a family. Her anxieties, however, were soon eased by the warm welcome she received from members of the ward. They helped her and her husband in a variety of ways, from babysitting their children and teaching them about parenting to having them over for dinner and mentoring her husband in his professional studies. As a ward, she says, "We have covenanted to share in one another's burdens. To do this, we must first learn of each other's burdens by listening with patience and respect. In the ward family, friends know each other's needs. Such a calling [to help each other] creates bonds of love. The positive effect of the calling is to give service to others. By doing this, you develop feelings of caring, and our service becomes more spontaneous." Her voice breaking, she concludes, "My deepest gratitude to the ward for welcoming us and sharing with us. I am grateful to the Heavenly Lord for this ward family. The ward is part of the plan, part of God's plan. It is an ingenious structure designed by God so that we can be more like him."

As the woman returns to her seat, Laeta nods her head and then leans toward me and whispers, "Every time I struggle, I call someone from the ward to help me out. The church is like a family to us."

Like the woman who has just spoken, the Faleau family relies on the church to help them deal with their burdens. Yet as a large immigrant family from Samoa, their burdens are not only emotional but also economic.

Consequently, the Faleaus depend on the church not only for spiritual uplift, but also, at times, for their very survival. This is the fourth type of security project I found in my research: families relying on their churches and their faith to help them manage and address their security needs. I call this approach to doing security turning to God.

Although many participants in my study were religious, the interviews in which religion came up most frequently were those with participants who had experienced the most extreme and consistent economic hardship. This finding suggests that religion may play an especially important role in the way those at the lower end of the class spectrum do security. Recent research supports this finding. A study found that women in poverty have higher measures of personal religiosity than their nonpoor counterparts, despite the fact that, ironically, the poor attend church less often.[1]

Understanding how the families in my study used their religious involvement and spirituality to cope with life stressors is an important topic to explore as the government increasingly turns to faith-based organizations to provide social services to the needy. This examination bears in mind the possible negative implications—including the potential for coercion—that arise when religious organizations fill the social service needs that government and employers are increasingly neglecting.

"THE NEWER DEAL"

Over the last decade there has been a major shift toward relying on religious organizations for the delivery of social welfare. This "newer deal" was institutionalized at the national level with the passage of the Personal Responsibility and Work Opportunity Reconciliation Act (POWRA) in 1996 during the Clinton administration.[2] The act includes provisions frequently described as mandating "charitable choice," which make religious organizations eligible to receive state contracts for the provision of social services if the state uses funds made available by POWRA. Moreover, religious organizations can receive funding without changing their internal governance, removing religious artifacts like icons or scripture, or altering their religious practices and religious expressions.[3] They may also restrict their hiring to those who share their religious views, though they may not discriminate against recipients of their services on the basis of religious belief.[4] These provisions eliminated conditions for receiving government contracts that faith-based organizations (FBOs) had previously been required to meet.[5]

The move to expand religious groups' involvement in social work took a substantial leap forward when, in the second week of his presidency, George W. Bush signed an executive order establishing the White House Office of Faith-Based and Community Initiatives. The order created eleven faith- and community-based offices in federal agencies ranging from the Department of Housing and Urban Development and the Department of Labor to the Agency for International Development.[6] This initiative ensured that governmental agencies that contract out services would be receptive, both administratively and ideologically, to working with faith-based organizations.

Some have argued that the inclusion of religious organizations in the welfare system marks a final stage in the retreat of the federal government from its formerly central role, after the New Deal, in securing the welfare of its citizens.[7] As professor of social work Robert J. Wineburg and his colleagues point out, since the 1980s a kind of New Federalism has been implemented in which responsibility for welfare provision has been steadily shifted to lower tiers of government and society, including private-sector organizations. The approach began with President Ronald Reagan, who asserted that states and counties could understand the concerns of the needy better than the federal government could. The approach continued under President Bill Clinton and reached its zenith during the administration of George W. Bush, at which point welfare provision became decidedly religious in nature. Since Bush's executive order, eighteen states have set up "faith-based liaisons" or created programs to help religious groups establish relationships with government antipoverty programs and to apply for government funding.[8] Under President Obama faith-based initiatives continue to be supported. Although hard numbers are difficult to come by, it is estimated that during President Obama's tenure the number of FBOs receiving grants has increased.[9]

The same neoliberal ideological stance that promoted the shift in the management of risk from a collective endeavor to an individual responsibility is also at work in the devolution of welfare. Particularly in conservative circles, social problems are no longer seen as societal problems requiring collective national solutions. Rather, they are viewed as personal failings to be solved through individual transformation. For example, Clinton's POWRA emphasized teaching work values and family values to welfare recipients.[10] If social ills are believed to be a result of personal problems, it follows that churches and religious organizations that cater to individuals' spiritual and moral needs are particularly suited to dealing with the needy.

Advocates of charitable choice argue that FBOs are well positioned to deliver social services because they are better than nonreligious organizations at providing intensive one-on-one, holistic services that focus on personal transformation, behavior change, and the development of long-term self-sufficiency.[11] By changing the conversation surrounding welfare from the New Deal language of "entitlement" to "Newer Deal" terms like "personal responsibility" and "rehabilitation of sinners," the political movement behind charitable choice has, in the words of sociologist Robert P. Weiss, transformed "a political right and governmental obligation into an appeal to altruism, dispensed at the discretion of sectarian interests."[12]

Studies testing the belief that FBOs are well equipped to deal with the needy have had inconsistent findings.[13] It is thus impossible to draw any firm conclusions about the scope and efficacy of religious organizations' work in social services.[14] Nonetheless, religious groups do play an important role in delivering services to the poor. Researchers estimate that, among the nation's 350,000 houses of worship, the typical congregation has about five human service programs and allocates close to 20 percent of its income to their activities.[15] However, these congregation-level services represent just a small fraction of the social services delivered by religious organizations. Although advocates of charitable choice often focus on congregational activities, large religious service agencies such as Catholic Charities play a much larger role. In fact, only about 3 percent of congregations receive money from the federal government for social service programs. However, a survey of more than a thousand FBOs found that 36 percent of congregations were interested in applying for government money to fund their social service programs.[16]

Currently, there are few studies about the manner in which congregations provide social services.[17] But with so many churches expressing interest in receiving government funding for these programs, it seems important to learn more about how such congregation-level services might be provided. As religion scholars Mark Chaves and William Tsitsos note, their "inclusion in large numbers in our publicly supported social welfare system would constitute a qualitative change in church-state relations regarding social services."[18] And as economic and social changes like the privatization of risk continue to erode more traditional sources of support, we can easily imagine more people turning to congregations to find the security they need. In light of the dramatic transformation in the American social welfare system and the increasing prominence of FBOs in this transformation, much insight can be gained about the "Newer Deal" by learning more about religion's role in providing families with security.

THE FALEAUS' SECURITY PROJECT

Hanging above the black leather couch in the Faleaus' living room is a framed poster of a curving stretch of sandy white beach dotted with palm trees and surrounded by crystal-clear water. Noticing me gazing at the poster, Laeta remarks, "We like it because it reminds us of the island. That's exactly how it looks. It might be Tahiti. We don't know." She laughs easily at the notion that the picture, which is supposed to represent the Faleaus' homeland of Samoa, might very well depict some other Polynesian paradise.

Whatever its provenance, the picture captures many aspects of the story of the Faleau family, who left Samoa in search of more opportunities but now miss home and, in some ways, the ease of the life they left behind. The picture's relaxed vibe contrasts starkly with the hardship the family has endured since they left Samoa seventeen years ago.

Kapo and Laeta Faleau grew up on "the Island," as they call it, where they met while attending the same high school. Both wanted to attend college, but family circumstances intervened. Kapo's father died when he was a teenager, and as a result the money that had sent the two oldest of his ten siblings to college dried up. Kapo went to work in construction. Laeta's mother died when she was a young child, her father when she was twelve. After high school Laeta decided she needed to work in order to help support her youngest siblings and make sure they finished high school. After working for a few years, she and Kapo married and had a son, Peter.

Like other immigrants in my study, Kapo and Laeta were dissatisfied with the job opportunities in their homeland. Kapo decided to join his brother's family in Nevada for a year or so, hoping to earn enough money to build the house and life he and Laeta wanted back in Samoa. After arriving in the United States, however, Kapo quickly realized that without citizenship, the jobs available to him would pay poorly and that it would take him much longer than a year to save the money they needed. Kapo and Laeta decided that she and Peter should come to Nevada. At least they would all be together. They would apply for work visas, and if they couldn't make a go of it in the United States, they could always return to Samoa.

The Faleaus' first few years in the United States were extremely difficult. In the beginning they shared an apartment with Kapo's brother and his family, but sharing close quarters with so many relations was stressful. After Laeta got pregnant with their second child, she decided they should move to the Bay Area to live with one of her sisters, since she thought she would feel more comfortable living with her own family. The move eased day-to-day tensions, but life was still hard. "I would cry all the time," Laeta recalls, "I was just complaining that it's really hard . . . We wasn't going really anywhere. I saw that it's much harder than in the islands. It's much better back there than here. 'Cause over there I can get free food and stuff, you know . . . You don't need a lot of money. People have land, have crops, grow food, or go to ocean and fish, get something to eat. The hospital is free. Here, if you don't have money, you don't eat." For several years the Faleau family, now five in number, shared a two-bedroom, one-bathroom apartment with Laeta's sister and brother-in-law. They scraped by with Kapo doing odd construction jobs. Beth, the Faleaus' second-oldest child, remembers, "I mean, it's been hard. I know sometimes we would have no money to pay the rent."

Worse still, they could afford to live only in a low-income community plagued by violence. Peter explains, "Well, when we first moved, it was, like, really dangerous. We always would hear gunshots in the night. It was always crazy like that." Laeta adds, "When we moved here, there were drive-bys and hanging out on the corner. I try to make sure no bullets get in here." As if to illustrate, she shrinks to the ground and shields her face with her hands. Kapo and Laeta kept the children inside as much as possible to protect them from their violent surroundings: "I would run to the car, run back," she recalls.

As with other immigrants in my study, lacking citizenship or permanent legal permission to work has been a huge obstacle for the Faleaus. Over the years they have been able to get work visas, but it is a constant problem. Driving to a party one night, Laeta stares aimlessly out the window as she describes the difficulties: "It's so hard because my visa is always running out. I call about a job and they want to see my work visa, and I say, 'I'm renewing it, I don't have one right now,' and they say, 'I'm sorry, we need one for taxes.' And I say, 'I understand.'" She sighs and shrugs. Kapo has run through a string of jobs, intermittently having to leave when his visa expires.

Things eventually got better for the Faleaus. Staying in the apartment all the time proved to have an upside, since it allowed Kapo to get to know the owner of the apartment building. The owner liked Kapo and offered him low rent ($400 a month) in exchange for work around the building. Then Laeta's sister and brother-in-law moved out, leaving the Faleaus with the two-bedroom place all to themselves. Laeta finally found work as a nanny. The family understood her visa situation and helped her file paperwork periodically to get it renewed. The job lasted for almost ten years. And best of all, through a family friend Kapo got a job in operations for a freight-hauling company right after he got a two-year extension of his work visa. It was the best-paying job he had ever had, paying $20 an hour.

Kapo and Laeta both liked their work, and for about four years they were earning enough money to meet the needs of their five children. What's more, the dot-com boom meant a modest gentrification of the Faleaus' neighborhood, an increased police presence, and decreased violence. "It was good money," Kapo says. "We could afford to buy a minivan, and we could afford to buy a car. And the needs of my children [were being met]."

The good times came to an end after the terrorist attacks of September 11, 2001. The ensuing economic downturn led to layoffs at the company where Kapo worked. Kapo lost his job, and, with his work visa about to expire, other potential employers were not willing to hire him.

Grappling with the financial setback was difficult. Kapo says, "I get used to have a check every two weeks. And suddenly they cut it. The needs of my family have to be cut . . . I don't know how to describe how painful [it was] . . . It was very painful, you know. And we struggled."

But equally hard for Kapo to deal with was his shock at falling backward when he had thought his family was finally getting ahead. For Kapo, his job at the freight company had symbolized the opening of a "door for our family [to] go through," passage to a better life. Then suddenly "the door slammed"—a possibility that Kapo had never even imagined: "I'm never thinking about that. I'm thinking I go in. That's it! . . . But after September 11, then boom. Door closed . . . I don't know where to go." For several months Kapo was depressed. Finally, his brother flew out from Nevada to console him and tell him that he had to move on.

In the aftermath of the September 11 attacks, the entire immigration and work visa system came to a standstill. With Kapo unable to quickly renew his visa, the family decided that it was best for him to stay home and focus on caring for the children, driving them to and from school and taking them to their various activities. Although his days were primarily filled with caring for their children, to make extra money Kapo would do handyman jobs that lasted a few a days at a time.

Laeta still worked full-time as a nanny. However, after a few years the children in the family she worked for no longer needed to be watched all the time. So Laeta began to work more sporadically for the family as a housekeeper. The reduced hours suited Laeta's needs in some ways, since she had a new baby, her youngest child, Nonni, at home, but the cut in income was difficult to absorb. As eighteen-year-old Beth says, "I would say we were pretty stable during that span [when Laeta was a nanny]. But lately, I think within the past two to three years, it's kind of up and down."

During my research with the Faleaus, Laeta got a full-time position as a caretaker for an elderly man and began earning a steady income once again. Yet Beth points out that, with such a large family, if her dad doesn't supplement Laeta's income with odd jobs, "it's not enough to sustain all of us."

The Faleaus have a lot of mouths to feed. As Laeta explains, "The hard thing is the food. That's the most money we spend is on food." Kapo and Laeta often talk about the fact that they are "doing okay" because their children have enough to eat, and, indeed, food appears plentiful in the Faleau home. At one end of the kitchen is a large oval table perpetually stocked with at least five boxes of cereal, a bowl of apples or oranges, and a box of

Top Ramen noodles. But the Faleaus don't always have the right kinds of food for the children, particularly food they can take with them to school.

Some of the Faleau children talk about not having anything to eat during the day. Eleven-year-old Rebecca tells me, "I don't have lunch. I eat when I get home. I get hungry. But when there's hot food days and people don't want their food, I'll eat it . . . I don't get a lunch." When I ask her why she doesn't eat lunch, Rebecca says, "There isn't anything for me to take for lunch. I can't take noodles, because there isn't a microwave. I could take a banana. There's nothing else."

Rebecca says that she usually doesn't eat breakfast either, adding excitedly, "I didn't eat breakfast for a whole week once and I went blind." She then tells me the story of how she passed out at school—"It turned black when I blinked"—and was taken by ambulance to the hospital, where she was met by her mom. According to Rebecca, the doctor at the hospital asked, "'Did she eat breakfast?' And my mom said, 'No.' 'Did she eat lunch?' And my mom said, 'No.' The doctor told me that I needed to remember to eat all the time. But I know I'm going to eat something when I get home, so I don't really care."

Rebecca says that Monday is the best day for food because that is the day her parents go shopping, "There is food on Monday. I know there is going to be food, and I'm usually the first one home," she said with delight. Given their low income and the fact that four of their children were born in the United States, the Faleaus are eligible to receive welfare assistance, including food stamps. But the lawyer assisting them with their citizenship application told them not to apply for this help, since it could affect their application status if the government is concerned that the family cannot support itself.

The Faleaus know that getting U.S. citizenship would drastically transform their lives, but they are waiting in a type of immigration purgatory for the government to review their case. Laeta's sister became a citizen by marrying an American, and in 1999 she filed for amnesty for Kapo, Laeta, and Peter. "It's been many years now, waiting," Kapo explains, adding, "The lawyer said it could take ten years, maybe twenty-five, except if the law changes." Kapo often expresses frustration about the seemingly endless wait: "In America, it's a lot of opportunity to go. But I saw the other way. The only way to go [is] to have a U.S. citizen." Kapo adds, "I think my life is not good. [He pauses and thinks.] Good, but I think it's up and down."

Yet the Faleaus are committed to staying in the United States to give their children a better life. Kapo says, "I promise I'm going to struggle here for them to go to a good university no matter what. That's why we come, for the opportunity. We can't give up."

"CHARITY NEVER FAILETH": THE MORMON WAY OF WELFARE

> It has always been a cardinal teaching with the Latter-day
> Saints, that a religion which has not the power to save the
> people temporally and make them prosperous and happy
> here cannot be depended upon to save them spiritually, and
> exalt them in the life to come.
>
> Joseph F. Smith, in Leonard Arrington's *Great Basin Kingdom*

Though extended family members have helped the Faleaus with job leads and places to stay, in some ways their church has been more instrumental in helping them navigate the difficulties of the immigrant experience. By supplying them with help, hope, and opportunity, their church has given the Faleau family—and particularly the Faleau children—a path to the "American dream" that might not be available to them otherwise.

Since its founding, the Church of Jesus Christ of Latter-day Saints (LDS)—commonly known as the Mormon church—has focused on providing for the welfare of its members, as evidenced by the church motto, "Charity never faileth." By the late 1800s the Mormon church had already established a kind of welfare system that assisted poor members by employing them in building temples or church buildings and by giving those in need basic provisions. The church's current system for aiding the poor was established during the Great Depression.[19] Crops that Mormon farmers were unable to sell in a depressed market were harvested and stored in church-sponsored warehouses for distribution to the hungry. Based on these beginnings, church-run "welfare farms" were soon created, bishop-administrated "storehouses" were opened for food storage and distribution, and a church-run transportation system moved food from place to place, depending on need. In 1938 Deseret Industries, a workshop program similar to Goodwill Industries, was created to provide jobs and job-training to the unemployed.

Today the Mormon church provides a vast array of welfare services. The church runs several hundred agricultural production projects, which by the late 1980s were dispersing about $30 million yearly in food aid.[20] Worldwide, it has two hundred employment centers offering job listings, job training, and career counseling.[21] In the western United States, the church has fifty Deseret Industries operations that provide work and training to thousands of people.[22] The church also has sixty-five social services offices that counsel those in need.[23]

Moreover, the LDS church has substantial financial resources. Although it is difficult to obtain precise financial information, one investigation in the late 1990s estimated that the church has between $25 billion and $35 billion in assets. Annual revenues approach $6 billion, $5.3 billion of which comes from member contributions, who, according to church doctrine, are expected to give 10 percent of their annual income (a "tithe") to the church.[24]

Bridging the link between the worldwide LDS welfare system and individual members are the local wards, each headed by a bishop, and the Relief Society, a women's organization that provides compassionate services. Bishops are directed to be alert to the circumstances of the families in their wards and to provide assistance when necessary, drawing on the wards' financial resources and the help and services ward members can offer one another depending on their occupations and skills. Typically the ward derives its financial resources from the "fast offering," a monthly two-meal fast that is supposed to be the source of a cash donation to the ward, as well as from additional donations that individual members may choose to make.

The Mormon faith cultivates an ethic of service both to the church and to other members. There is no paid ministry at the local level. Instead, members are expected to volunteer their time to fulfill church needs, from teaching Sunday school to giving a talk during church services to filling higher leadership positions. Such volunteer efforts can be enormously time-consuming; one study finds that bishops spend about twenty-seven hours a week on their duties, while a Relief Society president spends thirteen.[25]

Furthermore, as the opening vignette of the chapter illustrates, members have covenanted to "bear one another's burdens" (Mosiah 18:8). This commandment seems to engender an orientation toward helping out other ward members, especially those in need, in ways from babysitting and mentoring to providing financial assistance.

The main objective of the LDS approach to welfare services is to foster self-reliance.[26] Accordingly, the church focuses on instilling and upgrading skills through education and training so that members can support themselves economically without relying on the church or the government for support. In this spirit, the former president of the Mormon church, Gordon Hinckley, counseled members to "get all the education you can. . . . Cultivate the skills of mind and hands. Education is the key to opportunity."[27] To further encourage self-reliance, church directives urge members to create financial goals, avoid debt, pay their bills, save their money, and have adequate health and life insurance.[28] Yet this emphasis on self-reliance is linked to a belief in the interdependence of family members, neighbors, and ward members. For Mormons, interdependence means being in a position to assist others.[29] Thus, although the LDS principle of self-reliance echoes neoliberal discourse, the church acknowledges that individuals experience hard times. The church stands ready to assist in times of need rather than leaving people to fend for themselves.

THE WARD'S HELPING HAND

Over the years the Faleaus have depended on their church both to help them address immediate needs and to assist them—and especially their children—in achieving a better life. This reliance on the church predates their arrival in the United States. When Laeta was orphaned at the age of twelve, the church stepped in to help take care of her. Before his death, Laeta's father worked as a custodian at a local school, where he became close with a Mormon missionary woman who helped out at the school. When Laeta's father died, the missionary cared for twelve-year-old Laeta and her siblings and made arrangements so that they could continue their education. As Laeta explains, "The church school helped me pay for my tuition when they found out that [my father died]. The church [has] scholarships for kids like that. So they paid for my school the whole time and my sisters the whole time. So it's easy. They help pay for the apartment so that we can stay there. We have no place to go."

Since their arrival in the United States, the church and individual ward members have helped the Faleaus in a variety of ways. Early on the church provided them with food and other basic necessities that they could not afford. Their son Peter explains, "My mom and dad didn't work when they first came from Samoa, so they didn't have much money and we didn't have any food. They would call the church and say, 'Is there a way maybe my dad could work or something in the church and we could get food?' And they said, 'Don't worry about it. We'll get you some food.' And here they come in the morning with boxes of cereal for us to eat." When in need of food or diapers, Laeta would contact the Relief Society at her church. She explains, "We're in the Mormon church. If I needed the help, it's there. Because they have the bishop's storehouse, it's got food and everything. Diapers if I want for babies . . . Once a month, I called the Relief Society lady [to say] I needed diapers. I can't afford to keep buying that . . ." Their church also sometimes assisted the Faleaus with paying their rent and other bills.

The Faleaus have also received dental and medical care from fellow church members. Pointing to a middle-aged white woman sitting two pews in front of us at church one Sunday morning, Laeta said, "Vanessa is a dental hygienist and does our teeth stuff for free whenever I have a problem. Vanessa [is] always there for our teeth." And when Laeta cut her hand cooking, ward members connected her with doctors who stitched up her hand for free. The Faleaus' daughter Beth explains,

> Health care has always been a big issue, especially with my older brother, who isn't a citizen. So it was kind of hard to figure out things. But there are doctors in the church. There's always, like, someone in the church. It's kind of like there's always somewhere, some way, someone can help you. Like, for instance, with my mission, I need to get another hepatitis booster. I don't have an actual doctor. So I let the church know and they said, 'Oh, that's not a big deal. We've got plenty of things.' So I'm going for that shot in a couple weeks. They figured it out. Same thing with dental . . . We've got church connections there.

The church has also supplied the Faleau children with educational help and opportunities. Church members told Kapo and Laeta about free preschool programs for their children and helped them fill out the paperwork. Others helped Laeta deal with Beth's learning problems. Laeta wanted Beth, who was struggling in school, to repeat a grade, but "the school don't listen to me. But they listen to white people." Laeta told some women in her ward about Beth's problems, and they went with Laeta to the school to talk to the principal. "They know what questions to ask," Laeta said. "They asked for her to be tested, and we found out that Beth learns different. She can't learn from reading, more by hearing. It was so helpful to know what was wrong. The school listen."

Time and again, when the Faleaus have expressed worries about their children's educational opportunities, the church has provided support. When Kapo told a friend from church that David, their middle child, was struggling and getting into trouble at his public high school, the friend said, "Well, why don't we see if we can move him to a different school." Kapo and Laeta didn't think much would come from their friend's remark, but weeks later, after filling out an application, David found out that he got a spot at a local public college-prep charter school. The church also helped with extra funding so David could go on school trips to places like Washington, D.C.

The church has even provided financial assistance for the Faleau's older children, Peter and Beth, so they could go to college. When Peter was approaching high school graduation, Laeta wondered how they would pay for him to go to college. She was disheartened when a counselor at Peter's high school told her that, since he was not a citizen, he was not eligible for most scholarships or much financial aid. Then Laeta learned that the Mormon church has an educational foundation that provides college assistance. An elder at her church helped arrange a scholarship for Peter to attend a state university in Arizona. As Laeta explains, "Our church, they pay for everything. They give Peter money every month to support him in school because we just can't afford it. Otherwise, they're not going to go to college." Peter's younger sister Beth also benefited from church aid and, after attending a local community college for two years, now attends a state school in Utah.

Explaining the ward's commitment to helping members achieve their educational goals, one of the ward leaders told me, "We think education is so important . . . [that for] those who have a sincere interest in going to school, who can't afford it . . . we'll fund it."

Curiously, the elder in the ward the Faleaus attend downplays the enormous amount of help the church has given the Faleau family over the years: "They're pretty self-reliant. [We've helped them], but it's not a lot. They're not here every week knocking on the door and saying we need help. We help them some. We've helped them with rent. We've helped them with food occasionally."

Kapo and Laeta, however, are keenly aware of how crucial the church is to their security. As Kapo explains, "So that's why we feel secure. If we don't have food we've got the bishop . . . If you don't afford the rent, we can ask . . . It really helps." Laeta feels the same way, saying, "That's why we're still survive around, the church. But I don't really want to depend from the church always. But they are there. You don't have limits. You can ask anything, they'll do it." Kapo echoes Laeta's sentiments: "When we really need help, we call for them and they never turn us down. They never do."

In addition to helping the family procure food, shelter, and clothing, the church has also helped the Faleaus keep their children on the right track. With drugs and gang violence widespread in their neighborhood, the Faleaus knew that trouble lurked just around the corner. Laeta and Kapo worried that without the church and the teachings of the gospel, their children "would go in a different way" and take drugs or abuse alcohol. Laeta said that if her family didn't have their faith, they would probably be like other Samoan families in which, she said, drinking and violence were rampant. "Without church," Laeta said, we "be like other Samoan family. Only one [person] good, and four [people] bad." Underscoring how central the church is to their well-being, Kapo told me recently, "The church is our life. The life of our family is because of the church."

Perhaps the ward elder views the help that the church has given the Faleaus in a more limited fashion because he sees it as part of the path to greater self-reliance that the LDS supports. Furthermore, the Faleaus participate in the culture of interdependence by giving back, for example, by babysitting for other families in the ward and by volunteering for construction projects.

Churches provided several other families in my study with different types of assistance (though none received as much as the Faleaus). When Jenny French was going through a divorce, her mother, Cecilia, told her evangelical Baptist church about Jenny's struggles, and a fellow church member offered Jenny a part-time position as an administrative assistant. A few years later, when health problems prevented Jenny from working, church members delivered food to her and helped pay her rent.

In other cases churches helped families by providing learning opportunities and career assistance. Diego Rivera was a recovering drug addict and former gang member just out of prison when he decided to change his life by attending an evangelical Christian church. Through introductions by church members, two businessmen took him under their wing and taught him the construction business. The transition was tough, Diego says: "I still had a lot of old background, you know, I was not really being a man of my word. I was not really fulfilling my commitment. I was just surviving. I still had that mind-set of surviving, and it kind of didn't do good with the relationship with the clients." But over time his fellow church members taught him how to interact with clients and how to land jobs, and he has remained steadily employed and worked his way up in the company.

Diego and his wife, Danielle, also received help with what Diego calls learning to be a "functioning family." After suffering difficult childhoods marked by serious neglect, Diego and Danielle had four children of their own by the time they were in their early twenties. Church friendships helped the Riveras learn how to bring order to their chaotic lives and improve their parenting skills. Diego says, "The good thing about the church that we go to is it has some functioning families that are actually helping other families function in the right way, normally. [Like] getting the kids to get up to go to school and having them lined up, structured, with their clothes. That's still hard, especially if you don't have that training."

Danielle says the church also taught them life skills, such as "learning how to save, learning how to pay debt, learning how to value money . . . My pastor sat us down last week and he was speaking about order—getting your lives in order and making sure you have a plan. Making sure you have your will, that you have life insurance . . . and know the plan."

As these stories suggest, churches offer opportunities to acquire what sociologists call "bridging social capital," which connects individuals of diverse backgrounds, life experiences, and communities, supplying them with resources and opportunities to which they might otherwise not have access.[30] Such social capital can then be converted into the kind of knowledge and skills that allow families of less means to improve their lives. For example, because of the Faleaus' limited education and their lack of computer skills, they were often unable to help their older children with their studies and homework assignments. "It's very painful when the children came home from school and say, 'Dad, can you help me?' And I said, 'I can't. But don't worry. I'll look for somebody to help.'" The Faleaus could not afford to hire tutors for their children, so instead they reached out to students at a local state university who attended their church. These students tutored the Faleau children for free, enabling them to keep up their grades.

For the Faleau family, the church has been crucial in helping them eke out an existence and advance the lives of their children. Thanks to the assistance of the church, many of the Faleau children will likely achieve their own version of the American dream.

RELIGIOUS COPING

Not only do churches provide social supports, but the religious beliefs they espouse also provide spiritual support. As religion scholar Kenneth Pargament argues, much of the power of religion lies in its ability to provide resources for coping with the demands and difficulties that people experience throughout their lives.[31]

This power can be seen at work in some of the humblest settings imaginable. The Reverend Shannon Rust, a member of the Assemblies of God, runs a chapel at a truck stop in Breezewood, Pennsylvania, out of an eighteen-wheel tractor-trailer. Rust has noticed an uptick in the number of travelers who attend his Sunday morning service since the recession began. Rust says that truckers "used to always ask me to pray for their families to be safe while they're gone. Now they just want me to pray for their marriages, their homes, and their jobs."[32]

Research has established the importance of spirituality in dealing with difficult life events, from illness and aging to bereavement and domestic violence.[33] Yet as sociologist Susan Sullivan notes, there is little research examining the way religious and spiritual beliefs operate in the lives of those who face economic hardship.[34]

So how do religious beliefs help people cope with economic difficulties and create security in their lives? In my study I discovered two interrelated types of religious coping: the belief that God has a plan and will provide, and the belief that God rewards the faithful with material blessings. These beliefs seem to genuinely comfort interviewees as they deal with trying economic and emotional circumstances.

Laeta Faleau engaged in this kind of religious coping, with prayer being a tremendous source of comfort to her whenever she was worried. For example, after being rejected for many jobs because her work visa had expired, she interviewed for a nanny position that she desperately needed. "I just kept praying every day that I'm going to get it," she recalls. When she got the job and her employers agreed to do what they could to help her renew her visa, she took it as a sign that God was looking out for her.

Another time, explaining to me what she does when she's really stressed about money, she shut her eyes tightly and said, "I just keep praying. I just keep praying and wishing that some kind of a miracle happen." Opening her eyes, she continued, "I just stay focused reading the scriptures . . . The scripture says, 'It's okay, see like this person here in the Bible, when they went through this tough life, [it got better]' . . . It just kind of give me comfort. And I believe in it, because all of a sudden somebody will call me, they offer me something, you know. It just comes . . . This is the answer to my prayer."

Despite the difficult economic times the Faleau family has faced over the years, Laeta even sees herself as lucky, saying, "I feel like we've been so blessed with people. They love us and they want to help us. It's just there if you need it. You feel so lucky that, even though we don't have things, if I wish for something . . . it just happens. I never feel like things that I wish for or I want, I never get it. It's always some way, somehow, I'll get it."

Laeta offers examples of her luck, such as someone offering her children free tickets to an amusement park, a relative unexpectedly dropping off extra food during an especially tight week, or a friend winning a bingo tournament and splitting the winnings with her because they had gone together. "It just happens," she says. "You feel like somebody's reading our mind." Reflecting on the good things in her life Laeta tells me, "We don't have much money, but man, how lucky are we . . . We struggle, but I'm still happy . . . I feel that I'm rich and blessed already."

In Laeta's view God is responsible for her luck, operating behind the scenes and sending blessings her way. "I think he's taking care of me," she said. "In my mind, he's watching over my family." She often alludes to God's intervention when talking about how a difficult problem was resolved. For example, when she found out that the church would help pay for Peter to go to college, she thought, "The Lord provide a way to help our family."

Kapo, too, takes comfort in prayer when his family faces really hard times. And like Laeta, he interprets their ability to get by and occasional bouts of good fortune as blessings from God. With his head bowed, Kapo let me listen to his prayers. He said, "Lord, we are here as a family. We don't have enough to feed our children. Show me something I can do to help to feed the children. I don't know what to do."

Many years ago, when Laeta's hours working as a nanny were reduced and her pay was cut to only $200 a week, Kapo and Laeta said a prayer like this before going to bed. After falling asleep, Kapo had a dream. In the dream, his deceased grandmother directed him to a local shopping center and told him he would be able to find work there. The dream was so vivid that when he woke up he told Laeta about it. Unsure and a little embarrassed by the dream, Kapo nonetheless decided to try to find this shopping center. He dropped off Laeta at work and the kids at school and then drove in the direction that his grandmother had told him to go. After about fifteen minutes, to his disbelief, he came upon the shopping center that his grandmother had showed him in the dream. He parked his car and went into a home improvement store. There he encountered a couple who were trying to shop while being pulled in different directions by three young children. He asked them if they needed help. "Do you work here?" they asked him. "I don't," he said, "I'm just coming to see if somebody needs help." "We need help!" they said. So he walked around the store with the husband, helping him load lumber and plants into their cart while the wife entertained the kids. After they checked out they realized their purchases did not fit in their car, so Kapo offered to load their purchases in his car and drop them off at their house. "How much do we pay you?" the husband asked. Kapo replied, "I need a job. I don't know how much it pays, but I need something to do because my wife and my children, we need money." The couple agreed to hire Kapo to bring everything to their house and help plant the flowers and fix their deck. After working all day and agreeing to come back the next day to finish the work, Kapo went home. As he was leaving, the wife handed him an envelope. When he got home, he looked inside the envelope and found $500 inside. He walked into his apartment in disbelief. "I was crying to my wife, saying, 'We are blessed!'" After completing the work the next day, the couple gave Kapo another $500. That night Kapo thanked the Lord before he went to bed. He said, "Thank the Lord. I was able to feed my children." After telling me this story, Kapo said, "You see, the miracle happened because we believe [fully] in prayer . . . The Lord show us what to do."

Other interviewees share Laeta and Kapo's sense that God personally intervenes in their lives. Grocery clerk Lydia McDaniels says, "I feel a very strong presence in my life, you know, something that has guided me and has provided for me." They also pray for God's help in tough times and interpret good news as caused by God's actions. Lupe Galvez, an illegal immigrant who works as a house cleaner to support her three children, explains that when she gets really desperate for work she gets on her knees and prays. "I know God think of me," she says, "and will send work." Just when Lupe thinks she will run out of money, she says, a client will call to ask for extra help, bringing Lupe enough money to get by. "God is with me," Lupe concludes.

Jenny French, too, talks about how she prayed for help when a serious medical problem left her unable to work: "I have gone to church pretty much my whole life off and on. And I mean, like, back in the days when I thought I was dying [she laughs], we were basically just paying our rent and we did have food. I mean, it was just like bare necessities. And there was times that I would just pray about it, and people would call me up— 'How you doing?'—and just leave food at my door. I mean, it was really pretty awesome." After recounting other ways she has felt God's presence, Jenny adds, "I absolutely, beyond a shadow of a doubt, truly believe that Christ is risen. That he is there for us and that he will provide for us."

Charlene and Santo Medina are having problems with their flower business that have left them $60,000 in debt. However, their belief that God provides for them and has a plan for them relieves their worry. As Charlene says, "I do think God provides for us . . . He does do what you ask for . . . It's like there's no need to stress. We're not here to stress. We're not here in this world to figure out every problem there is. We just have to let it be in God's hands and he'll deal with it, and whatever happens we'll get through it." Santo explains that he doesn't worry about their security or their ability to pay their bills: "No, I don't think about that. I don't. Like I said, I'm spiritual. I leave it to God's hands." Later he adds, "This is where God wanted me, so this is where I am."

Running throughout these stories is the notion that God rewards the faithful with material aid and other concrete blessings.[35] Beth Faleau explicitly makes this connection when she speaks about her upcoming mission. (During a mission, young Mormons spend two years away from their families spreading the gospel and engaging in community work, often in a foreign country.)

> As far as the mission goes, I mean, we believe that if we just go on the mission and serve and preach and let everyone else know of its truth, blessings will come to you and your family. And I know this now, too, especially. My mom basically told me that if it wasn't for me, she wouldn't have gotten that [new] job. She said, "If it weren't for you leaving on your mission, I would not have gotten that job." 'Cause she hadn't been working for like a good year or so. She said, "Beth, it was basically when you decided to go on your mission and you got your calling that things kind of clicked back into place with the family." She said that all of a sudden jobs are just springing up and down for her.

Danielle Rivera, who joined a church with her husband once he got out of jail, echoes the link between faith and material blessings: "My husband and I have no high school diploma. We have no education . . . And when you take people like that in an impossible situation and what God will do with that, it's mind-boggling. It's like my husband makes almost a hundred thousand a year and this is someone that never graduated. The way we see it is it's a favor of God. It's the blessing of God. It's living righteously. It's living right."

Laeta also emphasized the importance of being a true believer. She compared herself to friends who decide to live righteously for a few days, who pray to the Lord for something and "want an answer right away," but then a week later go back to their old ways. Laeta said, "Some [of my friends] say they pray, but they're not lucky like me." Explaining why she thinks more of her prayers are answered, she said, "I think you have to have faith on it. You don't just give up. I stick to what I believe no matter what. Sometimes it doesn't come the way I want. When I keep praying and things just not coming the way I want, I still believe. No matter what, I don't give up." Eventually, Laeta said, "The Lord answer my prayers."

These beliefs—that God will provide, that God has a plan, and that faith will be rewarded with material blessings—provide these interviewees with emotional and psychological resources as well as coping mechanisms to weather difficult times and nurture a sense of security in highly insecure situations. To date, many views of religious coping have seen it, rather simplistically, as a form of denial and as a passive defensive strategy.[36] But religious scholars Kenneth Pargament and Crystal Park suggest that we should instead view religion as a way of coping, either effectively or ineffectively, with life's most troubling issues.[37]

My study, however, raises different questions: Why is religious coping primarily seen among those at the bottom of the class ladder? And why do upper-income people generally not say things such as, "My faith in God led to a 20 percent return on my 401(k) last year"?

In his discussion of the future of the working class amid growing inequality, economist William K. Tabb offers some insight into this question: "Facing relative deprivations or simply living surrounded by social breakdown and disturbing signs of a disordered culture, a personal savior and acceptance of an inerrant authority of Biblical literalisms can have greater appeal."[38] We see, then, a connection between different types of coping mechanisms and different social class positions. Although many people from every class may turn to religion to cope with cancer or the death of a loved one, the use of religion to create security and to deal with financial hardship proved to be a highly stratified practice in my study. People in more difficult circumstances—those experiencing greater emotional and psychological burdens as a result of their deprivation—may "need" to seek psychic relief from religion and spirituality in ways that those with more resources do not.

In a parallel fashion, other studies have found that those in disadvantaged positions are more likely than those in higher socioeconomic groups to feel connected with God and believe that God controls the things that happen to them.[39] Reflecting this sense of divine control, Jeff Kenney, an out-of-work construction worker, told me, "I wish I had control. I have no control . . . I'm definitely a believer that God is in control. I mean, my higher power is in control."

Rather than viewing religious coping among those with fewer resources as merely a form of denial, then, we can conceptualize it as a reasonable—even rational—means of dealing with and responding to the difficulties they face in a life over which they have little control.

OTHER SOURCES OF COMFORT

Interestingly, in addition to religious coping, Kapo has other techniques for relieving his concern. "Sometimes when we need money, I say, 'Maybe we should go gamble,'" Kapo said, adding, "We don't do it all the time, but . . ." Kapo's sense that gambling can solve his problems is derived from the fact that on several occasions the Faleaus have won large amounts of money during outings to nearby casinos. One time Laeta won $6,000, and another time Kapo won $2,000. On one occasion, after lamenting that he did not have enough money to repair the minivan, Kapo said to me, "But I buy lotto ticket today. Maybe tomorrow you see my picture on TV and you go, 'Hey, I know that guy!'" Kapo's dream of striking it rich from the lottery is shared by others who are facing similar kinds of economic hardship. A study of state-sponsored lotteries found that ticket sales go up, particularly among low-income people, as the economy worsens.[40]

If Kapo sought relief through visions of winning the lottery, Laeta took comfort in their dense network of friends and family. In the Samoan culture, extended families and good friends always assist one another, especially to help fund wedding celebrations, pay for funerals, or help others through particularly hard economic times. Describing this cultural value, Laeta said, "We always help each other. If something happen, we help, we give money . . . No Samoan ever get rich. The more you have, the more the family expect you to give. [She laughs.]"

Laeta's reliance on this resource caused her to worry about what would happen if her children ended up marrying white Americans. "White people just help their own family," Laeta said, her hands forming a tight ball to illustrate a nuclear family. "That not the Samoan way." With her hands expanding to form a large circle, she said, "We always help out the *whole* family."

At the time I was doing in-depth research with the Faleaus, their eldest son, Peter, was dating a white woman. When Peter came home for a visit, Laeta took him aside and told him he shouldn't marry her, saying, "It's not good idea. Whites don't understand. When you marry a Samoan, you marry the whole family." Recalling her conversation with Peter, she said, "I don't think your girlfriend want that job, for life! [She laughs.]" According to Kapo and Laeta, a lot of marriages between whites and Samoans don't work out because of these kinds of cultural differences. And even if the relationships last, marrying a white person can put a wedge between you and your family. In this regard, Kapo's cousin was considered a cautionary tale. After marrying a white woman he became cut off from the family. "His wife make a budget," Laeta explained, "and all the money budgeted so he can't give if something happen. So no one thinks to call him. I think he's lonely."

In addition to relying on her friends and family for support, Laeta also copes by trying to ignore her financial burdens. Focusing on her money woes just makes her sad. She said, "I don't really worry much about bills that I'm behind on. It happens. And when I think too much about it, it will make me feel depressed." Kapo interferes with her desire to ignore things. He often checks in to see which bills have been paid. This annoys Laeta. "We always argue because I'm always behind with the different bills that need to be paid," Laeta said. Laughing, she added, "I just try to ignore hearing him . . . Who cares? [We can pay] bills later. I'm always telling him, 'Let me handle the bills. That's gonna be [paid] later. It's not a big deal.' I don't really worry about bills."

Not thinking about the bills is part of a larger strategy Laeta uses in her life. Like Laura Delgado, Laeta tries to focus on the positive and tune out the negative. "If I hear about negative things, I will be unhappy . . . I like to just focus on what will make me happy." If a depressing thought started to creep into her mind, Laeta said, "I just ignore it." The way Laeta saw it, people can choose to be happy or sad, so why not choose to be happy.

Laeta's insistence on being happy likely contributes to Kapo's sense that he worries more about their economic situation than Laeta does: "My wife thinks everything is okay. [He laughs.] Sometimes when I was stressed out, she said, 'What is wrong? What are you stressed out for?' But I know our income is not so much, and I think of how do I get more. But somehow my wife think it's okay."

Their daughter Beth, on the other hand, thinks her parents worry equally. "Whenever it's me and my mom," Beth recalled, "she just kind of sometimes throws in her worries," and she said, "I would always talk with my mom, and she would, like, vent her emotions about family struggles." As an outsider, I shared Beth's perception that both Laeta and Kapo worry, although Kapo's worries are more explicit and open, while Laeta's are more internal and hidden. Whereas Kapo will voice his concern about their looming bills, Laeta buries her worry away, first through prayer and second by actively ignoring things. At one point she even told me that she doesn't really worry about money. Instead, she just puts her trust in God: "I'm not really worried, financially or whatever. It feels good for me to just keep praying." Despite her assertion that she doesn't worry, many times she talked about being very concerned. For example, she recalled being beset by worry years ago when she couldn't find a job; she worried about how to pay for Peter's college education; she openly worried that her income might be reduced when the family of the elderly man she cared for considered reducing her hours; she anxiously called relatives and friends to try to find a buyer for a table Kapo had made so they could get the money needed to go to a family get-together in Northern California; and she often prayed to God to help her find a way to get the things she desperately needed for her family.

In my view it is not accurate to say that Laeta did not worry or that Laeta worried less than Kapo did. It is more accurate to say that Laeta put more energy than Kapo did into trying not to worry. Like Sam Calafato, Laeta seemed to be the person who reassured everyone else in her family that things would work out. Being that person meant that she could not voice her concerns as loudly as Kapo did. Instead, she quietly reserved her worries for God and for her daughter, perhaps so that the rest of the family could sleep more soundly.

Though Laeta and Kapo have different ways of expressing their worry, they work together to manage their security project. In their current arrangement, Laeta earns more of the money and Kapo has more caretaking responsibilities. "I feel like that we both work together," Laeta said.

"Even though I'm the one [who earns the money], I think he's working, too, because he's the one who's taking me to work, he's taking the kids to school. He's home. It's both of us, this is what we get." Laeta and Kapo feel it's important that one of them is home with the kids to keep them from getting into trouble. Kapo said that if he didn't pick them up from school and they had to wait for the bus, "maybe they [get into a] fight or maybe [other kids] give them stupid things [like drugs] . . . and go to jail. Then I'd rather pick them up when they come out at school."

Although they may have differing opinions about which bills to pay first, in general they work as a team to decide how to spend their money. Laeta said, "We both decided what we going to do with that money. It's not my decision, or what he thinks; we both have to agree to that." Perhaps because they are both so involved in managing the family budget, when I interviewed them separately, each told me that he or she is the one in charge of dealing with the bills. Both feel that they are shouldering more of that burden.

SOCIAL SERVICES AND THE DANGER
OF RELIGIOUS COERCION

The Faleau case study reveals the many upsides that can result when the needy turn to churches for support, but there are downsides as well. Scholars analyzing the increasingly central role that faith-based organizations are playing in the provision of social services have pointed to these downsides, like the concern that when religious groups are in charge of dispensing help, such help may come with strings attached. As some observers have pointed out, to those on the political right, the personal transformation sought by religious groups in order to assist and solve the behavioral and moral problems of the needy may mean "accepting Jesus Christ as a prerequisite to making that personal change."[41] Sociologist Robert P. Weiss warns that "assistance by charitable organizations will be predicated on a profession of faith and behavioral conformity. Clergy and local leaders will emerge as social control agents."[42] The Faleaus' story sheds light on these concerns.

Peter Faleau had expressed interest in going on a mission when he was in his late teens. However, Eric, the LDS elder in charge of coordinating scholarships and missions in the Faleaus' ward, discouraged that notion. Since Peter was not a citizen, he would be unable to serve on an overseas mission because he could not leave the country and count on being permitted to return. Instead of serving on a mission, Peter took full advantage of a scholarship to attend a state university in Arizona.

A few years later Congress passed a bill making it legal for noncitizens to serve in church programs, including missions, as long as they remained in the United States and didn't drive. Eric invited Peter to meet with him to discuss the good news. Eric recalls, "I had Peter come in, and I said, 'Peter, it's a miracle. Now you can serve a mission.' And he said, 'I'm not sure I want to go.'" As he tells me this, Eric arches his eyebrows in surprise and drops his jaw to illustrate his shock.

The result of Peter's decision was that Eric terminated his scholarship. It wasn't easy for me to discover this fact. When I first asked Eric about why Peter's funding was terminated, he told me that the ward's usual practice is to assist members with their educational expenses for a limited time: "We helped Peter two years and now he's back on his own . . . It's just a matter of getting them started and then having them be self-reliant." As the interview continued, however, it became clear that the main reason Peter lost his funding was because he would not go on a mission. Eric said,

> It's church money that did the scholarship for him, and I wanted to make sure that Peter understood that it was contributions from the church that allowed him the education and that at this point he ought to . . . "pay back" is not the right word, but he ought to honor that help. And early on he wanted to serve a mission. So I made a decision. I'm not sure it was the right decision, but I made a decision, and I said, "Peter, with what the church has helped you with, if you choose not to go on a mission and go back to school, the scholarship is not available."

Relaying his decision to Kapo and Laeta, Eric told them that, because Peter didn't want to serve on a mission, "I'm really not comfortable sending him off to school with a full scholarship. I think he needs to mature. I think he needs to understand that he has a responsibility."

Apparently certain aspects of Peter's behavior also entered into Eric's decision, although Eric was vague about this: "There are certain areas that they have to adhere to to get the scholarship and also adhere to to go on a mission . . . They have to be chaste. They can't live with someone. They can't rob stores. They have to be honest. There's a range of issues." Returning to Peter specifically, Eric said, "There are certain things they have to do and things that we don't like them to do. And I'm not sure that did not enter into my decision. Later on, as I looked at some things, Peter would have had to change his life a little. And hopefully he has."

As for Peter, he didn't want to go on a mission because he felt that he was too old and he wanted to finish his undergraduate education without interruption. Kapo and Laeta respected Peter's decision as well as the elder's decision not to provide funding for Peter anymore. Laeta said, "Peter wants to finish schooling. If they go [on a mission] or not, it's up to them. Some do, some don't." Regarding Eric's decision to end Peter's funding, she said, "I think they're being fair because that's their rule of their scholarship thing. But it's just time for Peter to take action for himself."

Despite thinking the situation was fair, Kapo and Laeta were nonetheless extremely worried about how to fund Peter's remaining years of college. Beth told me that Laeta openly expressed worry about the situation, saying, "I don't know if he's going to go [on a mission]. I don't know how we're going to be able to pay for his school." Fortunately, Laeta's former employer (for whom she had worked for ten years) offered Peter a loan to cover his tuition for the next semester. But Kapo and Laeta are on the hook for Peter's living expenses, which greatly worsens their financial struggles.

To my knowledge, the Faleaus faced no other repercussions as a result of Peter's refusal to go on a mission—perhaps in part because their second child, Beth, did go on one. Her reasons include her sincere faith in the church and her sense of obligation to it: "The church has been there for me. There've been so many times where I've needed something, and the church has gotten it for me." Beth was told that when she returns from her mission, she will likely continue to receive funding for school.

Like Kapo and Laeta, many may think it is fair that the church stopped providing Peter a scholarship after he decided not to go on a mission. Yet the quid pro quo underlying Peter's scholarship highlights the coercive implications of turning to religious systems for social support. When people do not act in accordance with religious beliefs, expectations, or teachings, individuals can be reprimanded, as Peter was when he lost his school funding.

It is important to note that the Mormon scholarship program that supported Peter and Beth does not receive government funding. If it did, it is unlikely that such a blatant form of punishment would be imposed. Nonetheless, this story sheds light on the issues that may emerge as armies of faith replace the federal government in providing social services. Favoritism toward applicants who share an organization's religious beliefs, backlash against those who do not, and forced conversions among those who may fear that they will not be helped unless they are seen as "true believers" are just some of the disturbing problems that could arise in the years to come. These worries are heightened by the fact that those who receive help from FBOs are often the most disadvantaged.[43] This reliance by the most vulnerable members of our society on religious groups that seek to encourage church attendance creates a situation that is rife with the potential for misuse.[44]

It is also interesting to ponder which religions best address the problems arising from growing economic instability. Although this subject falls beyond the scope of my study, my findings point to a connection between the rise in insecurity and the fact that Mormonism, which has significant financial assets and offers a network of social services, is growing rapidly. By the early 2000s, the LDS church had 5.5 million American members, outstripping denominations such as the Presbyterians, Episcopalians, and Lutherans.[45] A recent study tracking religious affiliation found that between 2000 and 2010, Mormonism was the fastest-growing religion in the United States, gaining 2 million members in that period.[46]

Interestingly, recent converts to Mormonism tend to be those who are on the bottom of the economic spectrum, meaning they are often in desperate need of more security. According to a study by the Pew Research Center, new converts to Mormonism are less educated than lifelong Mormons.[47] Sixteen percent of converts lack a high school diploma, compared with just 6 percent of lifelong members. Converts earn less money than lifelong members: 40 percent of converts make less than $30,000 a year, compared with 21 percent of nonconverts. And converts are also more likely to come from minority racial and ethnic groups and are three times as likely as nonconverts to be immigrants to the United States.

When welfare security changes from being a political right or entitlement to being dependent upon an appeal to charity, certain religions are better positioned to respond to that shift than others. There is evidence suggesting that the LDS church may lead the pack in this regard.

Highlighting the buffering role that churches often play, economist William K. Tabb notes, "The church offers a heart in a heartless world of economic dislocation and deprivation."[48] As welfare provision is curtailed and increasingly shifted away from government and toward faith-based organizations, churches are becoming some of the only havens left, and God the only one to whom the poor can turn.

7 Debt and Hope

EDDIE AND CHELSEA JENNER

We're middle class, but I'd say we're on the higher end of it.
We still do the month-to-month thing, but . . . I have been
at the other end. When I was growing up, I've gone to the
grocery store with my friends to buy candy bars and I'm the
one that stole the $5 food stamp out of my mom's purse and
went to the grocery store and they said, "No, you can't buy
candy with this." I've kind of been at that end, so . . . I may
not be upper class now, but I kind of feel like it from where
I've been before.

Eddie Jenner

On a cool, crystal-clear spring morning, I turn into a cul-de-sac in a
middle-class neighborhood in Silicon Valley and park my car in front of
the Jenner family's house. Like many other neighborhoods I've visited
over the last two years, this one is filled with single-level California-style
ranch homes circa 1950 or 1960. Like its neighbors on either side, the
Jenners' dark gray house with white trim has a low roofline, window shutters, and an attached two-car garage. The front lawn, dead in patches from
the winter, bears the artifacts of the Jenners' child-focused life: bike hel-
mets, two red scooters, a deflated soccer ball, and a Superman backpack.

Ten minutes early for my interview with Eddie Jenner, I pass the time
watching twelve-year-old Corey ride his skateboard. Oblivious to the cold,
Corey wears a faded blue T-shirt and a pair of black nylon shorts as he skates
back and forth across the street, repeatedly jumping the curb. Though there
are six other homes that share the cul-de-sac, Corey is the only one outside.

At 11 A.M. I ring the Jenners' doorbell. Eddie Jenner responds. Forty-five years old, Eddie is six feet six with a stocky frame; I remember thinking he looks like a rugby player. His dark-brown hair is closely cropped and he wears an old pair of Levi's with a hole in the left knee, a red-flannel shirt, a gray fleece jacket, and a pair of Nike running shoes.

Eddie ushers me inside with a quick smile and calls Corey to come inside so he can watch his five-year-old brother, Keenan, while we talk. Not excited about this proposition, Corey asks when his mother will be back. "She'll be home soon," Eddie says with a smile. "Don't worry. Just turn on the TV and you guys can watch a video until Mom and Katrina get home." (Katrina is their ten-year-old daughter. Nelson, Eddie's twenty-year-old son from his first marriage, is staying with his mother this weekend.)

Keenan wanders in. Dressed only in his Curious George pajama bottoms, he is dragging a teddy bear behind him. "Hey, Keenan," says Eddie, "this is Marianne, and I'm going to talk to her for a little bit. You and Corey are going to watch a video. Mom and Katrina will be back soon." "Okay," replies Keenan, eyeing me a bit suspiciously. He and Corey disappear into the family room, and in a few moments we hear the high-pitched voices and happy music of a children's video.

This is my second visit to the Jenners' house. Since interviewing Chelsea, Eddie's forty-three-year-old wife, the week before, I've been pre-occupied by her story. When I interviewed Chelsea, I was almost two years into my fieldwork, and I had reached the point in my research when most of my interviews had become variations on similar themes. I might hear someone say, "I try not to worry about things," and immediately think I was hearing another story of downscaling, or I might hear a working-class woman say, "Oh, I worry way more than my husband," and promptly conclude I was seeing another case of a designated worrier holding on.

But on the rainy April day that I interviewed Chelsea, I was hearing something new and I wasn't quite sure what to make of it. At times the story Chelsea told me suggested she was downscaling, but at other times it sounded as if she might be upscaling. At one point she told me that she worries more than her husband does, but then she was quick to add that, really though, they do a lot of the worrying together. Chelsea's account of the Jenner family's security project didn't fit neatly into the patterns I had discovered. I had a hunch that the difference might be linked to Eddie's job, so I came back to interview Eddie to try to sort out the conflicting signals I had received about the Jenners and their security project.

A LUCKY BREAK

"My husband is all about the Sharks, the Giants, the A's, and Budweiser," Chelsea had told me. He's a "very mellow guy," she added. As I watch Eddie sit in an oversized recliner surrounded by sports memorabilia, I think that Chelsea's description of Eddie seems apt.

For my interview with Eddie, we sit in what could have been the Jenners' living room. Instead, they have converted it into what Chelsea cheerfully describes as "a space for my husband." "When we got the place," Eddie explains, "the room was really formal, with orange flowered wallpaper and brown carpeting. We never came in here. So we decided to turn it into a game room and get some use out of it." Chelsea had described the room conversion the same way: "It was so ugly! We didn't use the room. I decided that my husband should have the room to put all his sports stuff out." Chelsea and her sister-in-law painstakingly scraped off the old wallpaper, smoothed the walls, and painted them bluish gray. Then they installed a pool table, a mini pinball machine, two comfy chairs, and several neon red Budweiser signs. Grinning broadly, Chelsea recalled, "Eddie was so excited to get his stuff out of the boxes and put it out."

This room, along with the rest of the Jenners' four-bedroom, two-bath, 2,000-square-foot house, make Eddie feel that all is right in his world. When I ask Eddie what security means to him, he waves his hand around the room and says, "Having a house that the kids can grow up in, since I always grew up in apartments all my life. That's kind of a goal of mine . . . Having functional cars. [He laughs.] [Growing up] we always had a beater. I wasn't going to park in the first row of the high school parking lot with a car that was [falling apart]. [He laughs.] . . . So stuff that I didn't have growing up kind of makes me secure that I have them now." As we'll see, Eddie's sense of upward mobility grows largely from the security his employer has provided.

"My dad left my mom when I was six and my brother was four," Eddie tells me. Eddie's mother then remarried and moved the family from

Southern California to San Jose to be with her new husband. Her second husband's alcoholism led to their divorce seven years later.

Raising two kids by herself was a struggle for Eddie's mother, Bonnie. Money was very tight, and she relied on food stamps to get by. To improve her prospects, she went to night school to become a nurse. But between Bonnie's day job and her nighttime classes, Eddie and his younger brother, Charlie, were on their own a lot, and it became Eddie's responsibility to take care of Charlie.

Once they reached high school age, when Charlie didn't need so much supervision, Eddie began staying away from home as much as possible: "I don't even remember being at home from, like, my sophomore to senior year. I was either playing organized sports . . . or cruising around. I think I spent weekends a lot with friends who had houseboats or at sleepovers and stuff . . . We just had a little two-bedroom apartment, so it wasn't the most popular place to hang out. Other people's houses were always better. So I didn't spend too much time at home." Living several hundred miles away and going through a series of marriages and divorces of his own, Eddie's dad was not a big source of support either. "There was never anyone pushing me along," Eddie said. "[I] was all on my own, I would say."

Chelsea didn't have an easy childhood either. She grew up in San Jose in a family with four children. Her parents divorced when she was young, and her mother was overwhelmed with the task of raising so many children largely on her own. Chelsea's family was better off financially than Eddie's, since her father was a mailman who earned a steady income and made steady child-care payments. But, like Eddie, Chelsea was left to her own devices much of the time.

This lack of parental involvement in their own childhoods has shaped the Jenners' approach to child rearing. Corey, Keenan, and Katrina are rarely left on their own. Each child plays sports, attends various church activities, and participates in Boy or Girl Scouts. And Chelsea and Eddie are very involved in their children's lives. Commenting on how their own childhoods have shaped their parenting, Chelsea said, "I want them exposed to as much as possible. I think my husband and I were maybe limited [as to] what we were exposed to. And so I think both of us are of the mind-set that we just want to make sure that they have exposure to everything and those things that they enjoy they'll continue to do." When

I asked Eddie how involved he is in his children's lives, he said, "Yeah, probably too [involved]. Maybe that's an overkill for what I didn't have growing up."

Looking back on his early years, Eddie feels lucky that things have turned out as well for him as they have. "I could have easily gone down the wrong path," he says. "I met a lot of kids in the same situation. There were drugs and stuff when I was growing up . . . but I had sports on my mind . . . So I'm glad it worked out okay."

Indeed, as Eddie approached high school graduation, his prospects were limited. He wasn't a great student. "I maintained like a 3.2, but that included PE and woodshop and everything. It wasn't Cal State type of grades." But in his last semester of high school, Eddie got a lucky break. A counselor from a local business college came to his drafting class to recruit students for the college's new design program. As an inducement, the college was offering grants to pay for half the cost of the program. To this day, Eddie doesn't know why he raised his hand, but he did. Upon graduation, he took out a loan to pay for the other half of the cost and he set to work earning his design certificate.

At the end of the program, the business college's job placement office told Eddie about an open design position at Burcell, the medical device division of a large pharmaceutical company. The job was just a six-month contract position, but Eddie jumped at the opportunity, hoping it might become permanent. "That was in 1983, and I'm still there," says Eddie. "I've had several jobs [during my time there], but since my twenties I've been here with the same company."

After high school, Chelsea spent a few years working in retail and taking courses at a local community college, but she was never able to focus on her studies. Lamenting the fact that she never graduated from college, she says, "I wish I would have gotten more guidance [from my parents] and been maybe prompted a little more into that direction . . . My parents, they got married young and had four kids. So they separated after my sister was born . . . and so it was kind of more of just managing all these kids in the house and not really thinking about college or anything."

After working in lower-level accounting positions for several Silicon Valley tech companies, Chelsea decided to become a cosmetologist. She now works two days a week giving facials, and she cares for her children the other days of the week. Chelsea enjoys her work but earns very little money, "maybe $15,000," she said, after subtracting day-care costs from her take-home pay.

THE LAST OF A DYING BREED

But the rewards provided by Eddie's job almost make up for Chelsea's modest income. The security package provided by Eddie's employer is substantial, reaching levels almost unheard-of nowadays. He enjoys robust health benefits, two retirement programs, including a generous pension and a 401(k), four weeks of vacation, and, most important, higher-education tuition assistance. This educational benefit has been a key factor enabling the Jenner family to build their security.

Eddie worked as a designer for several years, slowly climbing up the ladder. But then his company decided to streamline operations, laying some people off and moving others to another part of the country to save money. Only the most sophisticated, software-intensive design work would remain in Silicon Valley. Eddie's manager urged him to upgrade his design skills and gain more technical capabilities. "My boss said, 'Get back to school or you're going to get laid off' . . . So I went back, and it worked out good."

For three years Eddie attended an accelerated program in advanced design systems at a local college, working during the day, taking courses at night, and studying on the weekends. His schedule was grueling, particularly with two young children at home. "It was not very often that we saw him," Chelsea says. "It was very, very challenging."

Eddie says, "It was hectic but it went by fast," adding, with a laugh, "I finished in '93 and I haven't wanted to pick up a book since." What made the situation more manageable was that Eddie felt as if he were getting paid to go to school. Burcell covered 75 percent of his tuition bill up front and then reimbursed him for the rest once he graduated. Unlike today's typical college student, Eddie graduated debt free.

Armed with a college degree and improved technical skills, Eddie was a shoo-in when he applied for a leadership position in Burcell's design project management group. At the time I interviewed him, Eddie was in charge of six people and was earning about $95,000 a year.

Eddie's company also facilitated his entry into the Bay Area housing market. Back in 1988, when Eddie had been working at his company for five years, his friend's father suggested that Eddie buy a house. At the time, Eddie was renting a studio apartment and was not planning on buying. But his friend's father said, "Just trust me. Just do it. Find a house. It doesn't matter if it's a good one or bad one, just do it . . . All you need is 10 percent [down]." Eddie heeded this advice. He borrowed about half of the $25,000 he had saved in his 401(k) and bought a small house in Santa Clara, near San Jose, for $125,000.

Eddie lived in the house for more than fifteen years and paid back into his 401(k) the nearly $12,000 he had loaned himself to buy it. Then, in 2004, he sold half the house to a friend and used that money as the down payment for the bigger house where the Jenner family currently lives. He and his friend now rent out Eddie's former home, which is now worth approximately $450,000. The Jenners bought their new home for $550,000; by the time I interviewed them, it was worth about $800,000.

The Jenners' real estate holdings supply them with a sense of security. As Eddie explains, "I always think that my security, if it ever comes down to unemployment and food stamps and all that, we've got half of [my first] house and a couple hundred thousand equity in this house. We could move to Oregon or something and pay cash, and we'd be set. It's not like we are ever going to be homeless . . . So I think the real estate is maybe a false security, but we work with it. [He chuckles.] If needed, we could move." Chelsea adds, "We always know that if we needed to, we could sell this house and we could walk away with probably about three or four hundred thousand. We could go live over [at our first house]. Pay that mortgage off. We would be in a cramped little three-bedroom house, but we would have a house." Monitoring the fluctuations in their real estate investments is an ever-present concern for Chelsea and Eddie. "We always go on Zillow.com [a real estate website] and look," Chelsea told me, explaining how they keep track of what homes in their neighborhood are selling for.

Another source of security for the Jenners is the savings Eddie has built up in his 401(k)—some $260,000 at the time I interviewed him. He contributes 8 percent of his monthly paycheck to the account and receives company-matching funds worth another 5 percent. Eddie set up his 401(k) with the help of financial planners at the brokerage firm that manages retirement accounts for Burcell employees, investing his money in a few different funds. "I just kind of pick and choose on their advice," Eddie says. "I have eight different things and they all have $30,000 in them. I kind of play a little game—when it goes up to $34,000, I'll take that extra four [thousand] and I'll put it down into something more secure, like a bond or something, just in case . . . It's kind of like a video game." Eddie adds, "Chelsea doesn't even see [the 401(k)]. It's just at work, and I just know it's there and tell her, 'Hey, look what we're up to now' type of thing."

Like the "upscaling" Mah family, the Jenners assign investing to the male partner. However, in comparison to Paul Mah, Eddie monitored his retirement account a lot less. Though Eddie and Chelsea do not meet with advisors from the brokerage firm on a regular basis, they did meet with a financial planner that their church connected them with. "Those guys did look at my portfolio and said that it looks like I'm on the right track for what we want to do, so that's kind of an insurance. [He laughs.] Okay, I won't change anything then . . . So I guessed right."

Eddie's company also provides a pension plan: "If I retire at sixty, I get like 70 percent of my salary or something. If I wait till sixty-five, then I get 80 percent. If I work to sixty-eight, you get a hundred percent of it." The Jenners are hoping to retire early. Eddie says, "I'd like to get out in ten years and then do something else . . . I just don't want to sit behind the desk till I'm sixty-eight. There are too many people that have done the forty-year thing at my company and a week later you read their obituary— you know, 'Worked forty years for one company. Hooray!' [He laughs.] What a life!"

The fact that the Jenners can talk about early retirement underscores the fact that Eddie Jenner is one of the few American workers still blessed with a rich array of company-sponsored benefits. In many ways, Eddie is one of the last of a dying breed.

THE JENNERS' INSECURITY

Despite having assets to draw on, the Jenners still struggle on a month-to-month basis. Chelsea says, "When I look at the 401(k), I think, 'This is a nice tidy little [nest] egg we have here.' So I feel like we're probably doing better than most [people], even though I feel like we're always broke. And Eddie's like, 'That's 'cause we're always paying our bills.' [She laughs.]"

Eddie provides more detail about their monthly struggle: "We live check to check, it seems like. We just hope Bank of America doesn't say you bounced a check on the last day. 'Cause I get paid monthly, so it's kind of a long time in between paychecks. You pay all your bills at the beginning of the month, and then you do your one big giant Costco grocery shopping, and it's like, whatever's left, that's what's going to get us through." After contributing to his 401(k) and making their housing payment, Eddie says, "We don't have the cash at hand for the kids. I mean, if we have to do summer camp, it's four hundred bucks. We put it on the credit card or write a check out of the equity line or something to cover it. We're not dealing with [just] cash right now." Chelsea said that other things such as gas and paying for her stepson's car insurance also get put on the credit card. A year ago Eddie borrowed $15,000 from his 401(k) to buy a minivan. Like so many other Americans, the Jenners took on debt to cope with their shortfall.[1]

All told, the Jenners have close to $6,000 in debt on their credit card and $30,000 on the equity line of credit they took out to pay off two other credit cards and a Macy's card. Add in the loan from Eddie's 401(k) and the Jenners have around $50,000 in debt.

With money so tight, the Jenners are unable to save for their three children to go to college. Instead, the Jenners invest in building what Eddie describes as their children's "resumes." "We're crossing our fingers for the scholarship stuff," Eddie said when I asked him about college. "Right now, they're on a real good track . . . I think our investment in the camps and the church activities and the sports stuff is kind of like a college investment to us—kind of like building up a kid's resume, you know. So we're kind of banking on the [idea that the] path that we're giving them growing up is going to be the right one to lead them to college, and maybe they'll get partial scholarships that way or something." Eddie hopes that his children's good grades could open up scholarship possibilities. "Plus," Eddie added, "they've got 4.0s, so that helps."

COPING WITH INSECURITY

The Jenners are currently consolidating what they owe on several credit cards into their equity line of credit and are negotiating a lower interest rate on their one remaining credit card. Their longer-term plan is that when their youngest son, Keenan, goes to school full-time, Chelsea will increase her work hours. They'll use the extra income to pay off their debts. If necessary, they could sell one or both of their homes.

Unlike most of the other families in my study, in which one person took the helm in managing and paying the bills, the Jenners managed this task together. When I asked Chelsea about how their bills get paid, she said, "Actually, we both sit down and pay them. And originally either I would do it or he would do it, but I think both of us realized [that] we both really need to do it to know what is left . . . at the end of the month . . . so that we're conscious of that while we're spending throughout the rest of the month." Eddie agrees:

> We sit down and stress out together when we do our bills. [He chuckles.] It's like, okay, that one we [paid]. Now we've got $800 that will last us for the rest of the month now . . . this is what we've got left . . . What are we going to do this month? Let's see, we want to go to Yosemite? Okay. A little bit of short-term planning and not so much long-term planning. More of a month-to-month thing. Let's put $200 less on our MasterCard this month 'cause Katrina has Girl Scout camp coming up. So kind of short-term-planning type of stuff.

But Chelsea and Eddie see things differently when I ask them about whether one of them worried more about the finances. Eddie says, "I think we're pretty even," but Chelsea says, "I think I do." To illustrate why, she says that, despite their tight budget, Eddie will just go ahead and buy things, and then, when she expresses concern about how they will pay for them, Eddie tells her not to worry about it. For example, when Corey decided to switch from soccer to roller hockey, Eddie readily agreed to buy him the new gloves he needed, despite all the money the Jenners had recently spent on soccer gear. Chelsea recalls, "Then I'll be thinking, 'Okay, I was going to go and do this, but now I'm not going to do that because he just took that money.' . . . And Eddie is just like, 'I'm not going to worry about it. It's going to all be taken care of. It's going to all work out.' And he'll say, 'Go and do what you were going to do. We're going to buy his gloves, and it'll all be okay.' And I'll be like, 'Well, show me how!'"

It annoys Chelsea that Eddie spends more freely than she does. But her feelings are tempered by her awareness that he is the primary breadwinner:

> He is bringing in the money. And I always feel like, if there are things that he wants to do, he should be able to do them. He shouldn't be denied. If he wanted to golf one day a month . . . he's working all these hours during the week . . . he should be able to golf that one day. And if he wants to buy his son gloves or if he wants to take his daughter to the movies or whatever, he should be able to do that.

Instead of feeling resentful toward Eddie for worrying less (as Gina Calafato does), Chelsea says, "What I feel more like is I need to be contributing [more]." Chelsea feels a deep unease with the fact that she contributes very little financially to the Jenners' security project: "I've always worked [until having children], so I feel like, if I was working, making more [money], that I could take maybe some of that burden off of him . . . So I'm feeling like my work path definitely needs some adjusting."

Perhaps this difference between Gina Calafato and Chelsea Jenner is linked to the fact that although Eddie may sometimes worry less than Chelsea, he does worry on a regular basis, such as when they sit down and pay the bills together. Indeed, when I asked Eddie what he worried about most on a day-to-day basis, he said, "Paying the bills, which I don't know why I worry about that, 'cause I've always paid them, but it's always in the back of my mind." In contrast, Sam Calafato told me, "I'm not the kind that really, you know, worries."

Of course, as the primary wage earner, Eddie can scarcely divorce himself from the Jenners' financial worries. By contrast, as second in command to his breadwinning wife, Sam Calafato *can* distance himself from his family's financial worries. This, too, may help to explain why Gina feels more resentment toward her husband than Chelsea does.

Although at times Eddie reminded me of Sam Calafato in the way that he coped with his family's insecurity, at other times he reminded me of Laura Delgado. Like Laura, Eddie minimizes the economic obstacles he faces by focusing on the here and now.

The future financial hurdles the Jenners face include paying for college for their three children, funding their retirement, and paying off their debt. "I don't think we worry long-term," Eddie said. "We just worry short term, how to get to the next day. [He chuckles.] . . . So we're kind of treating the big expenses as we'll deal with them when they come. [He chuckles.]" Though the Jenners are banking on Eddie's 401(k) and pension as well as their real estate equity, they have not crafted a detailed plan for their long-term financial future. "We'll deal with it then," Eddie says with a laugh. By kicking his worry down the road rather than obsessing over it the way Paul Mah does, Eddie reduces and lightens the psychological load he carries on his shoulders, batting away its seriousness with a laugh.

Eddie also deals with the Jenners' tight cash flow and their steadily increasing debt by cultivating an inner sense that things will work out. He tries to cultivate this same optimistic outlook in Chelsea, though he has had limited success. When Chelsea expressed her concern about the small amount of money her facial business was generating, Eddie told her, "If you're enjoying it, it'll work itself out. Just keep doing it." By embracing this positive perspective, Eddie refuses to make the Jenners' insecurity the center of his world.

Like the downscaling Laura Delgado, Eddie copes with his economic situation by working on his feelings. He suppresses his worries and instead relies on coping mechanisms that evoke his confidence about the state of the Jenner family's security project. But when downscaling doesn't provide enough relief, Eddie, like Kapo Faleau, will allow himself to dream of winning the lotto. "A lottery ticket every now and then kind of boosts morale," Eddie says. "What if? [He chuckles.] Every now and then I'll go in and buy a dollar Quick Pick, and that dollar is worth three or four days of conversation." That is, three or four days of imagining what it would be like to escape from their debts.

Curiously, whereas Eddie, and to a lesser extent Chelsea, downscaled to cope with the Jenners' economic insecurity and debt, he and Chelsea engage in something akin to upscaling to manage their worries about their children. Like the kids in the upper-class families I studied, the Jenner children are busy with schoolwork, school events, sports, and clubs, in part to make up for what their parents lacked as children, in part as a way to keep the children on the right track. Eddie says, "It's kind of a security to us that they're hanging around the right kids. If they're just picking and choosing what they do after school on their own—with all the gangs and the trouble and stuff going on around the area—it's kind of our way of watching out for them. And . . . we know the families. We know the kids that they're hanging out with all the time. They can go to camps and we know 40 percent of the people that are going." Chelsea agrees, saying, "One of the things Corey does now is he skis. And I was thinking when he goes to high school there's probably a ski club. That will give him another group of friends that have some kind of focus [so they won't just be] out there kind of walking the streets. That will give him some kind of focus that he can be a part of. And I think that about almost all of the things that they do."

Eddie and Chelsea also view their kids' activities as a possible ticket to higher education. An additional motivation, then, behind the activity-rich childhood the Jenner children had was to build their resumes in the hopes they would one day translate into big scholarships. Ironically, then, instead of saving money to pay for their children's higher educations, the Jenners take on debt in part to position their kids for scholarships.

This type of resume building is a central part of the upscaled security project I found among upper-class families. The Jenners' goal, however, is somewhat different than that of better-off families. Whereas upper-class families build their children's resumes in order to help them gain entrance into elite universities (regardless of their cost), the Jenners are aiming at scholarship aid. For them, any college will do. When I asked Chelsea whether she was okay with her children attending community college, she said, "Yeah. And that was one of the approaches we took with Nelson [Eddie's son from his first marriage], 'cause he had no concept. So it's like, 'Okay, go to a community college. Get all your stuff done there. That's perfectly fine. Apply yourself, get it done there; look around, see what's out there, and then start thinking about where it is you want to go.' So that would be fine with me."

For the Mahs, only elite colleges are even on their radar. Their children attending anything less would be a major disappointment, a sign that their kids are not reaching their full potential. As one upper-class father I interviewed said, "I think that community college would be an indication that [my children] were not achieving much in their lives, which would be a bigger disappointment . . . It really would be disappointing to me if that's the only educational venue they could qualify for."

Whereas Brooke and Paul Mah are very concerned about where their children will land in a globally competitive world, Eddie and Chelsea are simply concerned about sending their kids to college. When I asked the Jenners whether they thought about their children's futures in relation to globalization and the rise of countries such as China and India, Chelsea sighed and said, "No, I really haven't." Eddie shook his head no: "It's the same kind of thing [as the finances]—the month-to-month thing. It's like, 'Get through next month. Do well. Do well.' I really don't look that far out. I could just be blocking out all the negative stuff and don't want to think about it [he chuckles], and how it would affect them. I've played dumb to it all, I guess."

Of course, these two families occupy different social classes and are affected by different aspects of the larger economic and political story of recent decades. The Jenners' upscaling is a response to the exploding costs of getting an increasingly important college education—the middle-class squeeze. The Mahs' upscaling is a defense against the threats they believe their children face in a globalized world. Accordingly, results that make one family feel as if their children are on the right track (report cards with straight A's) can leave another family feeling as if their children are still not measuring up. And a prospect such as community college for their children symbolizes progress for one family (higher education for cheap) but failure for another (non-elite schooling is equated with poor preparation for career competition). Because the Jenners and the Mahs have different standards for security, they have different worries and concerns, carry different burdens, cope in different ways, and live in different worlds.

THE LUCKY ONES

> From where I came from . . . [where I've gotten]
> is kind of revenge on my past life, you know.
> [He laughs.] To prove I can do it.
> Eddie Jenner

In many respects Eddie Jenner has lived the American dream. Through hard work, determination, and force of will, Eddie climbed his way up from the bottom and has gotten close to the top. In a country in which only 6 percent of children born into families at the lowest income levels make it to the top of the income distribution, Eddie's story is all the more remarkable.[2]

Eddie attributes his upward climb to luck:

> I think it's every time you come to one of those Y's in the road, you've gotta take the right decision. I've hit four or five of those Y's and got lucky, you know, by raising my hand and saying, 'I'm interested in the grant' to go to get my design certificate, and by raising my hand, saying, 'Yeah, I'll try that job at Burcell for six months as a designer.' . . . So it seems like I've gotten lucky on my decisions, and I just kind of go on my instincts. If you hit one of those Y's the wrong way, it may set you back a few years.

Reflecting on the steady progress he's had in his career at Burcell, he says, "Yeah, that was like a path made in heaven. [He laughs.] I kinda just followed it and it worked. I mean, I was just lucky."

Eddie is lucky because, unlike most Americans, particularly those without a college degree, he found a job with an employer who wants to share risk with him, a company that still honors a robust social contract. Over the years Burcell has invested in Eddie, mentored him, protected him from life's ups and downs, and enabled him to amass financial assets. By doing so, Burcell created the context in which Eddie's hard work could lead to upward mobility. Burcell has been the stand-in for the interested, committed, involved, and financially supportive parent that Eddie never had. Without Burcell and the college degree Burcell enabled Eddie to earn, Eddie and Chelsea's lives could have looked a lot more like Vince and Laura Delgado's. In a more insecure context in which Chelsea would have needed to work full-time, and given Eddie's tendency to worry less than his wife, it is easy to imagine that Chelsea would have become the designated worrier for the Jenner family, much like Gina Calafato was for hers. However, because Burcell buffered the Jenners from many risks, they didn't have to lower the bar for what they needed in order to feel secure (or, in other words, alter their standards for security), as Laura did. In fact, Eddie's employer enabled him to raise his expectations. Because of Burcell, the Jenners live in a nice house, not a small, inhospitable apartment like the one in which Eddie grew up.

And yet the fact remains that Eddie's job doesn't cover the Jenners' monthly bills, which has resulted in the steadily growing debt burden the Jenners have assumed. To be sure, the high cost of living in Silicon Valley has squeezed the Jenner family. Raising children in a middle-class, opportunity-rich environment carries a high price tag, beginning with buying a home in a good school district.[3] The costs grow as the children enroll in their resume-building activities.[4] Indeed, as families like the Mahs spare no expense in their quest to position their children, their inflated norms and their willingness to spend ups the ante for everyone. Thus, to keep pace with the rising importance of higher education in the new economy, families that don't have the resources that the Mahs have are taking on serious debt.

However, the Jenners' debt is quite different from Laura Delgado's, which is due to basic security lapses—a lack of medical insurance, for example. Instead, their debt grows out of their unwillingness to lower the bar on their notion of security and their determination to maintain the progress they have achieved in their lives by providing their children with a middle-class life. By holding on in this way, they resembled Gina and Sam Calafato. But unlike Gina Calafato, who refuses to take on any debt, the Jenners accept debt as a safety valve that allows them to make it from one month to the next. And it was because of their debt that the Jenners seemed less burdened than Gina Calafato, who refused to take on any debt at all.

On a monthly basis, though, the Jenners have to manage a security shortfall. To do so, in practical terms, they max out their credit cards, they borrow against their house, and they borrow from Eddie's 401(k). Emotionally, Eddie copes by kicking worry down the road, by cultivating a sense that things are all right, and by trying to cultivate that same outlook in his wife. Chelsea, on the other hand, allows her concerns to come to the surface more frequently. During these moments she criticizes herself for not contributing more financially, only reluctantly allowing Eddie to convince her that all is right in their world.

The Jenner family's story illustrates the myriad forces generating insecurity that are bearing down on American families. It is not just the rise of precarious work, or the shift in risk, or the increase in the cost of living, particularly the costs associated with middle-class life. It is the combination of these forces that makes life difficult for millions of families. Eddie Jenner has been lucky. He has not been a victim of precarious work or the shift in risk. This has enabled him to provide his children with a life he never was able to have as a child, but he has been affected by the exploding price tag for maintaining a middle-class life. In such a context, even those with good jobs can have fragile security projects. The result is that the Jenners take on debt today to fuel their hopes for the future.

Conclusion

THE SOCIAL COST

It seems like the country would be stronger with a stronger
middle class, like I grew up with. There used to be all kinds
of support systems for families like mine . . . the G.I. bill and
really good public schools . . . The commons were still really
important to people back then, you know—the schools,
libraries, roads, all that stuff. I mean, my family had its own
worries from time to time, but in general it worked . . . But
then there was deregulation and a lot of boom/bust cycles
and now unbridled money in politics, which has only gotten
worse with Citizens United . . . union busting. I mean it just
goes on and on. The system is kind of a little broken.

Paul Mah

Paul Mah's account of the differences between the life he had growing up
and the one he now lives reflects the economic, employment, and political
changes that have occurred over the last several decades—the shift away
from shared responsibility for the risks involved in managing lives, taking
care of families, and securing futures, and a movement toward greater
self-provisioning. Today the federal government is no longer in the business of supplying soft landings to those in free fall; employers no longer
provide a social contract to their workers to cushion life's ups and downs.
Thus, the risks for which Americans are individually responsible have
grown steadily.

In response to these transformations, we increasingly must "do" our
own security—deal with layoffs, grapple with rising costs, manage our

retirement savings, find the money to pay for our children's educations, take on debt, and otherwise make our way in a world where the safety net seems increasingly frayed. On a daily basis families have to figure out how to fill the gap between what they earn and what they need, between what they have and what they hope for, between where they are and where they need or want to be. Families have always done security work, of course, but there is a historical specificity to the kinds of security work they do and the kinds of security projects they have. In our era, the task of managing insecurity has become harder and more unpredictable for a larger number of families.

At the same time, forces such as rising economic inequality are also reshaping how Americans go about building financial stability. Whereas in the postwar years the lives of many Americans improved thanks to widespread access to secure, high-paying jobs with good benefits, since the 1970s progress has been divided along educational and class lines. In the new economy the rewards have largely gone to those at the top who possess the credentials and technical skills needed to win high-paying jobs with good benefits. As a result, the top has experienced a more limited version of the shift in risk than those in the middle and working classes. While the top has moved ahead, almost everyone else has stagnated or moved backward. This layering of inequalities in income, assets, and risk, one atop the other, has created an inequality of security.

To manage in these insecure times, all the families in my study engaged in security projects of various kinds. When Laura Delgado negotiated with bill collectors, rooted for her children at their baseball games, and increased her work hours, she was engaged in a security project. So was Gina Calafato when she had to manage the household budget in the wake of her pay cut; so was Paul Mah when he arranged a trip for his son to go to China; and so was Laeta Faleau when she turned to her church to get the food and diapers she could not afford.

Yet depending on their skill sets, earnings, savings, benefits, and likelihood of keeping their jobs, families encounter different problems (unemployment, pay cuts, children losing interest in math), rely on different resources (credit cards, savings, business school networks, churches), worry about different issues (bills, globalization), and address their security concerns in different ways (positive thinking, increased expectations, prayer, financial planning, outsourcing worry to a more educated spouse). Like the patterns of advantage and disadvantage I observed among the families in my study, I also uncovered differences in how people do security.

THE SOCIAL CONSEQUENCES

Now that the security landscape Americans navigate has fundamentally changed, many have raised concerns about the consequences.[1] What happens when more families have to struggle just to make ends meet? What happens to social mobility and the goal of equal opportunity? Moreover, what happens when Americans pull apart economically? Do they pull apart socially as well? And what price do we pay for these divisions?

Security Fault Lines: The Stratification of Risk

As this study has shown, the vast economic and social differences underpinning the inequality of security mean that the way families do security—the problems and hurdles they face and the manner in which they respond—varies enormously. For example, families like the Delgados, the Calafatos, and the Faleaus deal with much more objective insecurity than families like the Mahs. This pattern held true for the other middle-class and working-class families in my study. They were laid off more frequently, endured more pay cuts, and received far fewer benefits, particularly healthcare benefits, than families at the top. Other studies confirm these patterns, revealing that risk is not randomly distributed.[2] Furthermore, given the large differences in human capital (education, skills, etc.), families arrive at this new world of risk with varying degrees of preparation for the tasks we all are now expected to handle, such as managing our 401(k)s, getting into college, and navigating uncertainty. These inequalities in options, information, and income mean that we are not all living in the same risk society equipped with the same resources. Rather, individuals live in different types of risk climates in which they are more or less vulnerable and more or less on their own.

Undoubtedly, these kinds of inequalities have always existed among us. Yet in a time of huge disparity, when people are increasingly supposed to amass security on their own, these inequalities become magnified and they lead to a cruel irony: those who face the least risk are best equipped to handle it, while those who face the most risk are least equipped to handle it. This division of our society into "risk society winners" and "risk society losers" means that increasingly we encounter different obstacles, carry different burdens, and live in different worlds.[3]

Emotional Fault Lines: The Stratification of Feeling

So how are Americans coping? In a world rife with inequality and instability, what emotional strategies make sense for managing security? Do different strategies make sense depending on where someone is located within the inequality of security? And what are the social consequences of how different families do security? The vast literature devoted to rising inequality and insecurity provides few answers to these questions. We don't know very much about how objective factors (such as measures of income and wealth) interact with and influence people's sense of security or insecurity.[4] Nor do we know much about how people subjectively interpret the real security conditions they encounter.[5] In other words, we know very little about people's feelings of security and insecurity or about what people do with their feelings.

Lacking knowledge, we make assumptions. We assume that our measures of economic insecurity—the risk of unemployment or the loss of health insurance, for example—accurately reflect other people's definitions. And we assume that objective classifications and subjective feelings move together: if people have medical coverage, they should feel secure; if not, they should feel insecure. We presuppose what both security and insecurity are and what the experience of them is like.

To be sure, as the stories in this book show, objective realities such as employment status and access to health insurance are key factors in people's economic stability. Studies find that unemployment and medical emergencies are strongly associated with bankruptcy.[6] And undoubtedly, objective factors and individual feelings often overlap in expected ways. A study found that people reported lower levels of subjective insecurity in countries that spend more on social services.[7] Another survey found that those with low incomes were more worried about losing their job and finding another one than those with middle and high incomes.[8] These findings are not surprising.

Yet reliance on assumptions can lead to misunderstandings. For example, the increase in the proportion of poor women having children out of wedlock has led many to assume that marriage no longer matters very much in the lives of the poor. But when sociologists Kathryn Edin and Maria Kefalas interviewed poor women, they discovered the exact opposite: the "poor avoid marriage not because they think too little of it, but because they revere it." In the social world of these poor women, divorce is seen as a desecration of marriage. Consequently, in their view "it is better to have children outside of marriage than to marry foolishly and risk divorce."[9]

What studies like Edin and Kefalas's remind us is that people are dynamic agents in their own lives. They are, as sociologist Alford Young notes in his study of poor black men's beliefs about mobility and opportunity, "creative and complex actors."[10] Economic conditions don't mold individuals in some uniform and obvious way. Instead, people interact with, shape, push back against, struggle to make sense of, and erect moral codes in response to, or even in spite of, their objective conditions. As University of Melbourne professors Julie McLeod and Katie Wright point out, people are not just "bearers of inequality." They are "actors, with sophisticated emotional resources."[11]

It would, therefore, be a mistake to believe that we know how people feel by how we would feel in their situation. Indeed, cracks and fissures repeatedly emerge between expectations and realities, between factual conditions and subjective experiences, creating a dissonance in need of explanation. For example, I found that the rich don't always feel rich and secure, and the poor don't always feel poor and insecure. And this is where things get interesting—when sociologists step inside these apparent inconsistencies and try to understand them.

I spent a lot of time trying to make sense of the dissonances I discovered among the families I came to know. Why is Laura Delgado so upbeat in the face of poverty? Why are Brooke and Paul Mah so anxious when they have so much? Why is Gina Calafato so desperate while her husband Sam is so relaxed? Why do the Faleaus feel "rich and blessed" even though their daughter often went to school hungry? What could explain these paradoxes?

What I came to see is that emotional strategies like downscaling, upscaling, holding on, and turning to God "make sense" in an unequal and insecure world. By redefining notions of security and suppressing anxiety, downscaling allows those with less to block out their worry and feel that things aren't so bad. By raising the bar on what it takes to be secure, by sending one's children to the best schools, by meticulously planning one's retirement, upscaling allows the affluent to feel they are maintaining and reproducing their class privilege in a volatile world. By turning a family's security project over to a more educated wife, families of moderate means feel they have a better chance at holding on, even if the work exacts a huge emotional price. And by believing that God provides, has a plan, and rewards the faithful with material blessings, those with less are able to get their basic needs met and find consolation in the arms of a caring deity and a church community. In an age that requires us all to become comfortable with risk and uncertainty, these emotional strategies—and the emotion work they require—help us do just that.

From this vantage point, the fact that one family says they need just a few bucks in their pocket while another needs $10 million in the bank to feel secure becomes comprehensible. Perhaps not to the economist, who might view such beliefs as foolish or irrational, or to the psychologist, who might see such beliefs as evidence of denial or grandiosity. But to the sociologist, these beliefs are consistent with the economic and political changes that have taken place in the United States over the past several decades. In the context of sky-high inequality and the shift in risk, it has become rational for some people to expect and ask for more and for others to expect and ask for less; it has become rational for some people to turn to God for help and for others to turn to a more educated spouse. Viewed from this angle, such strategies are neither laughable nor unwise; rather, they are remarkably resourceful. They are adaptive responses for dealing with a set of difficult circumstances in which most of us feel that there are few options.

This adaptive aspect of coping strategies is frequently overlooked. For example, since playing the lottery came up several times in interviews I did with the less well off in my study, I read the research on this subject. I found it filled with implicit or explicit criticism of poor people who spend money playing the lottery. One study, for example, described it as "inefficient behavior that prevents low income individuals from improving their financial situation."[12] Playing the lottery may be inefficient from an economic point of view, but from a psychological perspective, it is highly effective. It is a way of holding on to hope that things can be better. And in the time that passes between buying the lottery ticket and finding out if they have won, people can dream, mentally escaping from their economic hardship into a world of plenty. Although this may seem irrational, even delusional, to those with sufficient means, among those with insufficient resources, it could be viewed as a highly rational response to the financial difficulties they encounter—a logical strategy derived from a different kind of cost-benefit analysis.

Even though the emotional strategies I discovered in my study may be reasonable and inventive ways of coping with the present historical moment, they simultaneously engender our consent to it. When we talk ourselves into feeling secure despite hard times, we compensate for the very inequality that created the hardship we must endure. When we adopt the belief that $10 million is the price tag for real security, we accept the premise that we alone are responsible for our security. When we believe that God provides, it is easier to let go of beliefs about what we owe each other. When we get annoyed with our spouse during tough times, we feel let down by our loved one rather than let down by the system.

Sociologists have long been interested in how people consent to these sorts of unequal situations. In his classic account of life on the factory floor, Michael Burawoy discovered that one way that workers consented was through a piece-rate system that created the illusion that their labor was a game. Burawoy found that workers competed with one another to "make out," or to surpass their expected production quota by using certain strategies and tricks. Focused on the game of making out, the workers didn't see that management garnered big gains in productivity while they received minimal monetary rewards in return.[13]

I was reminded of Burawoy's account when I examined the emotional strategies that the families in my study adopted. When Laura Delgado and her family had to go without heat during the winter, she described how they coped as a game: "I'm trying to make a game out of it with the kids. We use candles at night, like we're camping . . . so we're doing our own earthquake drill. How we can handle it and how we can survive . . . It's all in how you look at things." At the other end of the class spectrum, challenges like getting kids into the right colleges and creating financial models to pinpoint the stock option price that will ensure a secure retirement can be viewed as games as well. These games and the emotional needs they fulfill divert our attention so that we perpetuate the very system that requires us to play these games in the first place rather than questioning or challenging it.

As we have seen in this study, one's emotional life is influenced by one's place in the power structure. And sociologists have observed that emotions are unevenly distributed among different groups in society.[14] However, scholars have not spent much time empirically studying these relationships. As a result, we don't have much insight into how people's emotions both reflect and reproduce larger social structures and cultural systems.[15] For example, most research on emotion management would leave one with the impression that emotion work is done only on the job, as employees align their feelings with organizational expectations and goals (as when they remain pleasant while being yelled at by a customer). Yet work isn't the only system in which people must manage their emotions to make them fit with the larger social and economic situations we encounter. Indeed, doing so is essential for establishing and maintaining an unequal social order. As the sociologist Michael Schwalbe and his colleagues have noted, for inequality to continue,

> there must be, if not feelings of satisfaction, then feelings of complacency or resignation; there must be fear of change or of being punished for protest; and there must not be too much sympathy for the oppressed or too much anger towards elites. Sustaining a system of inequality, one that generates destabilizing feelings of anger, resentment, sympathy, and despair, requires that emotions be managed.[16]

In other words, to keep inequality going, people adopt emotional strategies that serve to endorse the status quo. They must talk themselves through moments of anger and depression. They must tone down or turn up their anxiety as circumstances demand. They must accept the underlying logics of the economic system as legitimate. They must bring their feelings in line with American ideologies of individualism, meritocracy, the free market, and neoliberalism so as to prevent rebellion. They must keep playing the game.

Of course, Americans accept and even embrace particular ideologies and cultural beliefs.[17] However, we don't know much about how these beliefs are transformed into feelings or how feelings are managed and regulated in response to these ideologies.[18] Moreover, we are just beginning to understand how a person's place in the social structure—how their social class, race, and gender—influences the emotional strategies they adopt and the emotion work they do.[19]

The goal of this book is to shed light on these questions, to illustrate how stratification works at the microlevel, how it makes its way deep inside us, shaping not only our actions but also the way we feel, try to feel, and try not to feel. It's a dimension of inequality that many people hint at but sociologists have left unexplored. As cultural sociologist Eva Illouz notes, "Our understanding of the relationship between one's emotional life and social class remains to be examined."[20] Other scholars have pointed out the need for research that sheds light on patterns of class thinking and feeling, or what British sociologist Diane Reay calls the neglected "psychic landscape of class."[21] By focusing on the emotional strategies individuals use to deal with their place within the inequality of security, this study provides insights into affective aspects of class, or, as sociologist Beverley Skeggs puts it, how "class becomes internalized as an intimate form of subjectivity."[22]

If we want to understand how inequality works in people's everyday lives, more attention needs to be given to the psychic and subjective dimensions of social class. What we have now, I would argue, is a great deal of understanding about the engine of inequality—how socioeconomic status shapes things like health outcomes, educational attainment, and future earnings—but much less understanding of the oil in the engine of inequality, or why and how people come to possess the thoughts and feelings that keep this engine humming along.

As the sociologist Arlie Russell Hochschild points out, power doesn't work around feeling, it works through feelings, typically raising the expectations of the more powerful and lowering the expectations of the less powerful.[23] This *stratification of feeling* reflects the emotional distance, or a kind of emotional inequality, that separates those with more from those with less. To understand economic inequality, then, we must dig deeper into emotional inequalities, into the oil that courses through the engine and makes the system go. The sociology of emotions, as a way of seeing, can help us do just that. In this study it became a way to detect at the level of feeling how people are grappling with the seismic changes in inequality and in the nature of risk that have occurred in American life.

Gaining insight into these relationships between emotions and inequality, between the microlevel and the macrolevel, is important because these relationships don't simply reflect inequalities or illustrate our consent to inequality. When combined, these cultural logics, which orient thinking, feeling, and doing, also drive inequality. Chapter 4, which detailed the Mahs' security project, highlights how the feeling that under-girds their project—the need for more and more—orients behavior at the top toward accruing more economic gains despite already high levels of wealth. A survey of five hundred ultrawealthy individuals, whose net worth was at least $5 million each, found something similar, with 34 percent seeking to gain "significant" additional wealth.[24]

By contrast, the cultivation of the sense among those with fewer resources, like Laura Delgado, that one needs less orients behavior toward accepting less and orients security projects toward achieving less. Furthermore, Laura's ability to work on her feelings, to make them fit with her economic predicament, prevents her from taking a critical stance toward the predicament itself, such as linking her financial situation to her lack of health insurance instead of to her perceived personal failings. As Laura's example shows, rather than working on changing political or economic issues, people often work on themselves to accept them.

Laura's story sheds light on the emotions involved in this process—the self-management we perform to shore up and perpetuate the current state of affairs. Tellingly, the only people I spoke with who wondered why those with less were not more politically active or angry about these issues were the well off. As Jason Bauer, an upper-class father, observed, "I'm surprised there aren't a lot more riots in the streets, frankly."

Ultimately, it is this crystallization of inequality into people's feelings that becomes a legitimizing force because it provides an emotional rationale for an unequal situation. Through strategies like the upscaling and downscaling of security, we simultaneously rev up inequality and achieve an absence of the political will to stop it. Like material disparities, emotional processes have real consequences. The social price we pay for pulling apart is that economic inequality and economic insecurity become experienced as more about who we are or just how the world is and less as a social problem that needs to be solved.

The Ultimate Social Cost: The Decline of the American Dream

As a nation, we hold dear the idea that America is the land of opportunity, that anyone, regardless of where he or she comes from, can get ahead and reach the top with enough hard work. It is the belief that in America people can go from rags to riches—that any of us can achieve the American dream—that makes our country unique, so special, so much better than the rest. This sensibility defines our understanding of ourselves as a people and as a country. Indeed, only 19 percent of Americans believe that coming from a wealthy family is essential or very important to getting ahead.[25]

Yet the United States has much less economic mobility than our cultural stories would have us believe. A study that looked at intergenerational mobility in nine countries found that the United States ranked next to last in mobility, ahead of only the United Kingdom.[26] With about half of parental earnings advantages passed on to sons in the United States, as opposed to only 20 percent passed on in Canada, Norway, Finland, and Denmark, it would take six generations, on average, for family income advantage to disappear in the United States.[27] *Six generations.* In spite of our national self-perception, it may be easier for someone to achieve the American dream by going abroad than by trying to achieve it at home.

These numbers require us to take a hard look in the mirror, to ask ourselves where we have been and where we are going. This book is an attempt to do just that. By charting the economic, employment, and political changes that form the backdrop against which the families I studied do security, I have highlighted the historical transformation that has taken place between the individual and the society, the citizen and the state, and the employee and the employer. This shift away from a social ethic that valorizes standing together and sharing risk toward a social ethic that valorizes individuals creating security on their own has undermined the context in which working hard can translate into moving up. For at any moment, your hard work can be undone by the vicissitudes of life. This shift in risk interacts and combines with other social developments like growing economic inequality to exact a huge personal and societal cost—

the inability to dream. Indeed, we have reached a point where it seems as if the only way to raise your expectations for yourself and your children is to go into debt or to place your dreams in God's hands.

A country where good jobs are both hard to find and hard to hold on to, where getting the education required to get a better job sinks many into massive debt, where people raid their retirement accounts to pay for basic expenses, is a country where dreams for a better life wither away. It's a country that has lost its way.

Yet there are public solutions to what are often experienced as private problems. If public policies gave rise to this age of insecurity, then public policies can also be used to usher in a better age. Scholars and commentators have come up with a long list of policies that would aid such an endeavor, ranging from an increase in the minimum wage, to stronger social insurance benefits, to high-quality child care, to regulating Wall Street.[28] The Affordable Care Act is a big step in this direction, as it reduces the negative consequences of unemployment by enabling millions of Americans to maintain their health insurance without a direct tie to an employer. Yet debate about such policies and the philosophical approach they reflect (the central role of government in creating security) is fierce.

In the midst of this raging discussion, I would like to propose a different lens through which we can view the problem, and that is to ask: What are the emotional strategies for doing security that we would like the majority of people to adopt? What kinds of emotional strategies would create a prosperous society? Do we want only a minority of people to think continually about how they can strengthen their security and get ahead in the new economy, while the majority accepts less and lets go of their dreams? Or would we like it to be the other way around? And if we want the latter, what policies will help get us there? If we want a world of equal opportunity, how do we drain the oil out of the engine of inequality?

Debates about the costs and benefits of these changing relationships between individuals and our government and between workers and employers will be topics of discussion for some time, as they strike at the heart of our society. For what is at stake in these discussions about risk and inequality is the meaning and definition of security, and the meaning and definition of American society itself. Is security a personal endeavor, in which case we are only responsible for ourselves? Or is security a collective endeavor, in which case we are responsible for each other? Are individuals and families empowered by the freedom to choose their own forms of provision? Or are they disempowered by the limited choices and resources available to them? The ways we as a country answer these questions will have real consequences, shaping the contours of the inequality of security and the character of the United States in the twenty-first century.

Epilogue

THE DELGADOS

In the years since I completed my in-depth research with Laura Delgado, her life has continued to be difficult. About three years ago, she suffered a massive heart attack. Fortunately, she got to the hospital in time and made a full recovery. Last year, she got evicted from the apartment she shares with her two daughters, now in their early twenties, after getting in a disagreement with their landlord. Her younger daughter, Hayley, was able to find them another apartment quickly, but for Laura, the whole ordeal was "shameful." And her most recent bad break was her termination from her job at the big-box store where she had worked for the last decade.

Despite these events, Laura feels that she rode out the Great Recession unscathed because, in her words, she didn't have much further to fall. "The economic downturn stuff really didn't have all that much effect on me personally," she says. "I think it's because I was already poor, so I didn't really have anywhere to go down-wise. I was already kind of at the bottom."

Now in her early fifties, Laura is beginning to show her age. Her hair, which is longer now, has flecks of gray in it. The creases around her eyes are deeper. She has lost a tooth and a noticeable gap appears when she smiles. Despite these physical changes, Laura's life and the way she copes with it have remained much the same. During our most recent interview she was still upbeat in spite of the hard times she has experienced. "Struggling isn't really all that bad," she says. "It's not. It builds character. I've had so much horrible stuff happen that I can see that I'm really quite lucky . . . I'm just grateful that I have three kids who have no major issues. I think I'm the eternal optimist." All these years later, Laura is still cultivating a rosy view of her life that is at odds with the grim reality: she has no savings, is not fully employed, and is barely able to cover her bills.

When I ended my in-depth research with the Delgado family, Laura had hoped to get on the management track at the big-box store, with a larger goal of getting back into the psychology profession. But between her increasing work hours (which she gradually added as her children got older) and the continuing needs of her children, she didn't have the time or energy to focus on these goals, so Laura continued to work as a cashier. Eventually she also started working as a sales associate on the store floor and was employed full-time.

She enjoyed her job and the people she worked with. She was even able to get health insurance through her company. But then, after nine years of employment, a new store manager came on board. He implemented sales goals for the sales associates and encouraged them to push customers to buy whatever was on sale that week. Laura did not like this approach—"I'm just not that aggressive," she said—so her supervisor began to write her up for falling short of sales targets. After a few months of poor reviews, Laura was fired. She received all her outstanding pay accrued through unused sick leave and vacation time, but her health insurance was terminated immediately.

Getting fired underscored something Laura had been telling her kids for some time, which is that they need to be able to take care of themselves: "I've told them that they need to start planning now for being retired people. Don't make decisions the way your mother did, thinking that it was all gonna keep going and everything was gonna be fine because you're not guaranteed. Nobody is. And in this day and age, the way things are in the economy, and with the way employers are, you never know. And then my firing comes along and that just backed up what I've been saying." Abandoned first by her husband and then by her employer, Laura wants her children—particularly her daughters—not to share her fate. "My thing has just been that, especially with the girls, I want them to plan on having the capacity to take care of themselves," she said.

A secure future for the Delgado children is far from a sure thing. Now in their early twenties and late teens, none of them has attended a four-year university. Laura's eldest daughter, Megan, always struggled in school; she now works as a waitress at a chain restaurant. But Haley usually got decent grades, and Laura had always expected that she would attend college. When I asked Laura why Haley didn't even apply, she said, "I don't know. I think with her a lot of it was she wanted to work. And she knew that college was not going to be something that her parents could afford to pay for and she didn't want to spend the time looking into help. So I know help was probably out there. We just have to do the research on it." Fortunately, Haley has a well-paying job with a grocery store, has health benefits, and has been promoted into a management role.

Dylan, Laura's youngest child, currently attends a local community college, works part-time at an ice-cream store, and plays on various sports teams. He did apply to a college in Southern California, where a baseball coach had promised him a spot on the team. But something was wrong with his application—though Dylan refuses to tell Laura what the problem was—and so he was never considered for admission. He still dreams of becoming a professional athlete.

Vince, Laura's ex-husband, is helping Dylan pay his community college tuition, despite economic pressure from the Great Recession. Laura says that Vince was out of work for close to twelve months out of the past two years. Once again he came close to losing his health insurance due to the long period he was unemployed. Fortunately, he was able to return to work just in time to keep his benefits.

This turn of events became an unexpected boon for Laura. Although she didn't realize it at the time, Vince never filled out the paperwork informing his employer of their divorce. As a result, Laura remained covered by his medical insurance—a godsend when she began having palpitations and some pain in her chest and went to the emergency room. She stayed overnight in the hospital, racking up a bill of $17,000. Laura was overjoyed when, upon checking out of the hospital, she "came up insured."

She said, "I was like, 'Thank you, Vince, for being so slow to take care of things. This is the one time it's been great for me!' [She laughs.]" Now that she doesn't have health insurance through an employer, Vince has agreed to hold off on turning in the divorce paperwork as long as he can, a gesture that Laura feels makes up for the two years of spousal support Vince owes her.

Though much of Laura's life seems to me the same as when I first met her, she seems a bit more forthcoming about her fears and how she copes with them. For example, when I ask her about her definition of security, she is silent for a moment, then sighs and says, "I don't know that feeling secure is ever gonna happen for me. You know, just being like, 'Whew! Now I can just relax and let it all go.' I don't know that that's ever gonna happen. And now I've come to the point where if something's just really causing me super stress, I just try to let it go. I try not to be focused on that. I try to focus on whatever I can do that is positive." Laura says that she let go of needing to feel secure after her divorce, which shattered her hope that Vince's union job would guarantee her future. She feels that letting go of the need to feel secure has helped her cope over the years, "because if you can't be in control, for me, I cannot stress over it; it just makes it worse." When I ask her what she does if stress starts to creep into her mind, she says, "I guess I kind of bury my head in the sand . . . I just go onto something else and try to ignore that, which really isn't very healthy but . . ."

Laura does have fears about her future. In a low voice, she says, "I do worry to a degree in private moments about how I'm gonna survive, what's gonna happen next, and what am I gonna do when the kids are all grown up." Thanks to her well-paying job at the grocery store, Haley is able to cover about half of their rent, with Megan and Laura splitting the rest. Once her daughters move out, Laura will be on her own, both emotionally and economically.

Yet Laura remains optimistic. Recently she applied for a department store credit card. Despite her current debt of about $20,000 and her poor credit history, Laura's application was approved—to her surprise and delight. "This is the first credit card of my new life," she says, smiling broadly. "I just look at it like that. And after all I've been through, why shouldn't my new life be in a positive direction?"

After hearing upbeat pronouncements from Laura over the years, I decide to press her about it, saying, "I see you being really optimistic in a lot of circumstances that many other people would not." In response, Laura leans back in her chair and says,

> That may be true. I think it's maybe forced optimism . . . I just try to keep myself hopeful . . . If I lose hope, if I don't think that I can in some way survive my life and come out the other side, then I would just curl up in a ball and say "That's it, I'm done, I can't do this anymore." And there have been moments when I've kind of felt like that, not completely but a little bit, where I've just said, "I give up! I can't take any more!" . . . But for some reason I choose to keep going because I don't like the alternative.
>
> So I guess I'm an optimist by choice but also kind of by circumstance . . . My life is not perfect. Whose is? I don't have everything I need and some months are a little leaner than others and really at some points we've survived on the free food Haley brings home from the grocery store. It's gotten to that point where it's been that bad. But I'm still surviving. I'm functioning and I wasn't starving, you know.

I now recognized something I had been unsure about earlier. Laura's downscaling strategy is conscious and deliberate. Pointing to her training in psychology, Laura says, "Therapists teach their patients that you just can't look at the totality of your situation because sometimes it would just overwhelm you. Everything would shut down, and you would say, 'I just cannot do this.' So I think maybe I kinda look at it that way too. I get it that if I just looked at the whole thing as [she sighs], 'How am I gonna do this?,' then I just wouldn't." Instead of looking at the totality of her situation, Laura limits her gaze to what absolutely must be taken care of and just keeps trying to move forward. "I kind of ignore [stuff], I think, by just putting one foot in front of the other and saying, 'Okay, what's the next thing I gotta accomplish? What has to happen now?'"

Reflecting on all the setbacks that she has experienced over the years I have known her, Laura said, "My life must look really *nuts* from somebody looking at it, you know—all that I've done and that has happened." But by surviving in the face of these setbacks, Laura has discovered her strength. "Honestly, the biggest surprise to me in all of this is learning that I do have strength," she says, her voice breaking. "I didn't think I did," she adds, wiping a tear from her cheek.

Laura went on to explain that what has really helped her endure is the example of her grandmother, a single mother who survived the Great Depression while successfully raising children. Laura said,

> I had a good role model to learn that kind of strength from . . . If you have a picture in your life where you can see what could happen, then it's easier to survive what's bad because you know that there are people in your life that have come out on the other side and been okay. So I think probably that's what sustains me the most is knowing that it's possible. Because sometimes even if I feel like it might not be possible, it could be. So maybe that's what keeps me so optimistic, too. I know that there are other people that have done it—so why can't I?

Laura's resiliency, her ability to hang on in hard times, is in many ways a heroic accomplishment.

THE MAHS

When I drove up to the Mahs' house in 2012, everything looked the same as when I had last seen it. The front garden was in perfect order, without a weed in sight. Brooke's running shoes were in the same spot, tucked away behind a large flowerpot. The inside of the house was the same as well. Brooke had decided against adding an office off the kitchen so she could better observe what Jacob and Alec were doing online. After researching the costs involved, she said that it would have been too expensive. "I decided to just have them use their computers at the kitchen table," she said.

In the last few years, the Mahs have been forced to pay more attention to costs. Just before the financial crisis of 2008, Paul decided to part ways with the small technology company where he served as the vice president of marketing, since he and the CEO had begun to disagree about almost everything. Soon thereafter the stock market crashed, which made finding a new job difficult. Paul began consulting as a stopgap measure; he ended up doing it for almost three years. Under pressure from Paul's reduced income, the Mahs ate out less, Paul washed his own shirts instead of taking them to the dry cleaners, and they were forced to draw from their savings. To help bring in more income, Brooke returned to work on a part-time basis two years ago, doing special projects in the marketing group of a nonprofit. She only works fifteen hours a week, so Paul remains the primary breadwinner. Describing this period, Paul says, "Of course it was stressful, but we were fortunate enough to have enough in the bank that I wasn't too worried about it. We sort of muddled through for a while . . . I wasn't at the point where I was panicked, saying I have to find a job right away kind of thing."

Eventually his network of business colleagues connected him with a good opportunity at a technology company. After working as a consultant for six months, he was hired full-time to run the marketing team. Paul's skill set remains a valuable commodity. "My skills are in very high demand still at my advanced age," Paul said with a chuckle. Currently he is earning around $250,000 annually, about twenty thousand more than he did when I first met the Mahs. Once again, the Mahs' multiple buffers (savings, business connections, and in-demand skills) provided them with great stability even during a terrible economic storm.

When I reconnected with the Mahs, Paul had not looked at the spreadsheet that mapped his family's economic security project for about six months. Now he needed to reevaluate it in light of recent developments. Brooke's mother had recently passed away, and the Mahs had decided to invite her elderly father to come live with them. Their older son, Jacob, had just been accepted to his top college choice, an Ivy League university. The Mahs had always planned to pay for Jacob and Alec's educations. As Brooke said, "From the beginning our gift to our kids [is paying for college]. Because it's very difficult to graduate with debt." Paul's parents were going to contribute some funds, but in the fall there would be a large tuition payment due. With a $50,000 tuition bill looming, Paul says that he still doesn't "feel rich." His security benchmark remains $10 million—that's "still reasonable," he says.

When I sat down to talk with the Mahs, they were reveling in the recent news that Jacob had been admitted to a top-ranked university. "It worked out in the end," Brooke told me, "but it was a ton of work—for both of us. It just took an enormous amount of time." Paul agreed, telling me, "Jacob was just working all the time. I mean, he definitely gave up his social life." Having heard from other parents about how difficult the college application process was, Paul wasn't surprised by the enormity of the endeavor. "Well, I guess we knew it was coming," he told me. "It was sort of [like] an oncoming train."

When Brooke applied to college, it was "easy," she says, but times have changed. "The college process now is significantly different than what it was decades ago," Brooke says. A college admissions consultant advised Brooke, "If you are a strong student—an academically competitive student—that wants to go to a school that is difficult to get into, because it's so competitive, you need to apply to ten of those schools just to have a chance of getting into one. They get flooded with such qualified [applicants] that it's just the odds. So it's a lot of work."

Brooke felt her role in Jacob's application process was to provide him with research and advice, especially since most children in the Mahs' city receive this sort of help from their parents. Brooke said, "When you're in a community where everyone else is advising their children, then you feel that it's really important that your child have the benefit of all that advice, right?" Whereas Paul took the lead on managing the family's finances during the downturn, Brooke took the lead on Jacob's college applications. To improve Jacob's chances, Brooke hired the consultant to read through Jacob's essays, provide feedback, and answer other questions that came up. But from Brooke's view, what mattered most was that Jacob identify a university that was a good fit for him rather than making his choice on reputation alone. "If you are not at the right place," Brooke says, "it wouldn't be satisfying for you . . . You wouldn't do your best work because you wouldn't feel connected." So the summer before Jacob's senior year, Brooke compiled information on about fifty schools for Jacob to peruse for "summer reading."

After narrowing down the list of schools, Jacob and Brooke went on two trips to visit various colleges and universities. It became clear to Brooke that what really mattered to Jacob was being in a welcoming environment. He wanted to be in a place where people were embracing and warm and accessible . . . and where people would support him in his studies." After deciding that he wanted to spend his college years on the East Coast and touring many schools there, Jacob settled on the school he really wanted to attend. He worked diligently on his application, and the family waited with bated breath to hear the results.

Brooke thinks she was more worried about Jacob getting into college than other parents were, "just because I read a lot," she said, "so I had a lot more information to worry about than most." Despite knowing that Jacob would likely get into a good school, Brooke found herself weighed down by the "frightening headlines" about students who didn't get into a single school they applied to. But since Jacob had applied to fourteen schools, including a few "safety schools," the odds of that happening were low.

Brooke was with Jacob when he received the email notifying him of his acceptance to his first choice. "I watched Jacob pull the email up and read it, and scream and yell and cry." "I shed a few tears, too," Brooke says. When Paul heard the news, he was delighted. "I was really proud," Paul says, "amazed."

At the time I was doing in-depth research with the Mahs, Jacob's shyness and reserved nature had been a big concern. But just as they had hoped, he blossomed at the small private middle school he attended. By the time he was ready to go to high school, he was a "new person," Brooke said, adding, he's a "completely different kid than he was when he was little."

When it came time for Jacob to go to high school, the Mahs looked at many schools, both public and private. Ultimately they decided he should go to a new charter public high school because it was very strong in math and science. This was important, Brooke said, because "the experts are saying the job opportunities are going to be [in math and science]. Right?" So we wanted to "pick a school that was strong in math and science, so that you would at least be in that flow . . . I do want to make sure my kids are set up for that." The Mahs also liked the school because they sensed that the families whose children went there were, like them, "grounded in education as a primary value in their families."

Jacob thrived at the school socially and academically. During his freshman year he formed a great group of friends and maintained those friendships all four years. He also poured himself into his studies, got on well with his teachers, and got good grades.

When it was time for Jacob's brother, Alec, to choose where he wanted to go for high school, the Mahs were happy that Alec settled on the same charter high school that Jacob had attended. He wanted to be at a "school that would challenge him the most," Brooke said, "with the kind of people who . . . value education first, doing well in school first. He could see the differences between the schools and that was number one to him."

Brooke and Paul had long sought to teach their children the value and the importance of education. At this stage it was clear that Jacob and Alec had internalized the message. Indeed, the family no longer worried about making sure that their children were sufficiently focused on their academics and doing well in school. Now the chief issue appeared to be getting them to understand the constraints of having only twenty-four hours in a day. As Brooke explains, "How do you pick when you want to do everything? There's a lot of talking about—you can't do it all, you can't do it all." After Brooke and Paul had modeled upscaling for so many years, it seemed that their children had adopted their approach.

In Alec's case, he wants to focus on both athletics and academics. Years ago the Mahs had worried a great deal about Alec losing interest in academics, particularly math and science, but that issue was resolved when Alec started attending a private middle school. The school provided him with a very challenging curriculum and he rediscovered his passion for math and science. With his interest in those subjects rekindled, the Mahs became less concerned about his continuing passion for baseball and other team sports. But taking honors classes and playing on sports teams year round is hard to balance. "There's tons of opportunities [at Alec's school], but they conflict," Brooke explains. "I tell Alec that you need to be realistic. Like, two months from now, when these tests come in, can you study for these tests and be on the baseball team and the flag football team? The conflicts just stack up."

Jacob had experienced similar conflicts. During his senior year of high school, his parents had worried that the four AP classes he was taking would be too many. Sure enough, Jacob was upset that he had to miss out on social events to keep up with his studies. "It caused a lot of consternation," Brooke said, adding that Jacob wondered if he had made the right decision. Referring to the personal sacrifices Jacob was making and the angst this was causing him, Brooke said, "Everyone goes through it . . . It's a rite of passage—sadly—for kids who are pushing themselves."

At the end of the school year Brooke and Paul asked Jacob why he had decided to carry such a full load, because "it wasn't that we said you have to do this," Paul said. Jacob attributed it to his friends. Brooke explained, "Everyone is proud to be learning a lot—that is the culture at the school," especially among the group of kids Jacob was friends with. "He was proud to be in that group," Brooke told me. "He liked being in that group. He was capable of learning it all. But it was purely peer-driven."

Even though Brooke didn't think that she and Paul played a role in Jacob's decision, in light of their long-standing emphasis on the importance of education, Jacob's decision is hardly surprising. Indeed, they had encouraged Jacob to go to his high school precisely because the school and its community valued education so highly. Brooke and Paul also encouraged Jacob to do well in his studies. Explaining the message they communicated to Jacob when he was preparing for the SATs, Brooke said that they told him, "Do the best work you can do. We were just encouraging him to work as hard as he could so he had as many options as he could, so he had choices." They didn't want Jacob to "underperform and kick [himself], saying, 'Well, I knew I could have done better but I didn't.'" His parents may not have demanded that Jacob take so many AP classes; they may even have advised him against it. But through countless behaviors over the years, they had certainly created the context in which Jacob had internalized an important lesson: always do more instead of doing less. When it came time for Jacob to make a decision on his own, he chose to increase his options.

Paul Mah viewed Jacob's decision through an even broader lens, connecting his desire to take more AP classes with an increase in competition across the board. Today's world, he says, "just is more competitive . . . It's kind of a global marketplace for talent now and so they have to really compete . . . I think the kids sense some of that. It's almost like a pride thing."

When I interviewed Brooke this time, she seemed much more at ease. She explained, "I think a big, big, big part is that we're in a school that is meeting most of their needs. Almost all their needs." Brooke no longer felt as if her children were being "shortchanged." Basking in the glow of Jacob getting into a top university, Brooke was actually savoring the people her children had become. "I'm more than proud," Brooke said, "I'm just extraordinarily pleased at the richness of my children's lives." With Alec engaged in science and math and Jacob a social person who now "pushed himself, and didn't just watch other people do that," Brooke seemed content.

However, Brooke still has a few worries. She is concerned about the uncertainty surrounding employment, noting how much things have changed since she graduated from business school. When she got her first job, Brooke thought, "This is the job for life. That was the expectation . . . And the whole world changed in front of me during that time." But people frequently change jobs nowadays. Brooke said. "I do worry about what that means for kids graduating now. Because if they're happy at their job, what happens to their career path? Do you have to be moving from job to job in order to kind of keep advancing? Will you be superfluous to the organization if you don't move and keep changing?"

Brooke also worries about the need to continually update one's skills. They keep saying that "the job you're going to have hasn't even been defined yet," Brooke told me. How does that work? [She laughs.] How do people develop those skills? Do you get hired to learn those skills? Are you somehow at night, after work, having to be online and figure it out? And I worry kind of what that means to family security, to personal happiness."

As for how these changes relate to Jacob and Alec, Brooke said, "You hope that they learned the concepts and the habits of mind that will allow them to be whatever that 'flexible' is that they need to be. I don't know how anyone would know if you succeeded with that. Right?" Brooke is concerned about Jacob and Alec's ability to be sufficiently flexible in a volatile employment environment.

If Brooke worries how the demand for flexibility will affect her children's futures, Paul Mah is also concerned about the bigger picture. "In terms of economic security and just world stability, there are big things to worry about," he says. Paul worries about climate change and how that may create food insecurity. But also problematic, he says, are economic issues. "Don't get me started on economic justice," he says, waving his hand. "The minimum wage hasn't increased. It's still like $7.25 an hour, which is insane. They're cutting social services . . . I mean, it's just, the government is not working for the average person."

Paul says he thinks our country would be better off if we had a stronger middle class: "If the country really does keep going [this way], then it's going to be like walled enclaves of rich people and then there's kinda like the great unwashed." Shaking his head with disapproval, Paul says he fears that the divide between the rich and everyone else is "going to destroy the American dream."

As for how such a development may impact Jacob and Alec, Paul says, "I'm assuming they won't, like, fall off the curve . . . so I guess my kids would be in the walled enclaves or something." To ride something like this out, Paul told me that Jacob and Alec will "need the [right] skills."

THE CALAFATOS

When I had last talked with the Calafatos, Gina was unemployed. "At some points it was desperate," Gina says, describing her spell of jobless-ness. "For me it was like, 'Oh my God!' It was only six months, but it seemed like the longest six months ever to be out of work." Between Gina's unemployment benefits and money they got from selling some of their stock investments, the Calafatos were able to squeak by. But, on the heels of being overworked for so many years, the insecurity took a real toll on Gina. "It was just a deep, deep, dark hole," she says. Consumed by anxiety and depression, Gina began to believe that she was alone and that she didn't have any friends. She even worried that her marriage might fail. Looking back, she now finds these thoughts ridiculous, but they indicate how bad things were for her at the time.

By networking with friends and business colleagues, Gina finally found a job with a company that sells office management software for small busi-nesses. She worked as a trainer, helping customers who purchased the software learn how to use it. Gina worked on contract, earning close to $70,000 a year but no benefits. (Luckily, she received health benefits through Sam's job.) However, her position ended after about two years when the economic downturn of 2008 hit. "It was really hard to find something that would pay the same," Gina recalls, so when the opportu-nity to manage customer relations for an office supply company came up, she took it, even though it meant she would earn about $20,000 less annually. "This is not what I should be making," Gina thought to herself, "but I have kids about to go to college and I need to have an income."

For the past three years Gina has earned around $50,000 annually, which is about the same as what Sam makes. "I don't even think we hit a hundred K together last year," Gina told me. No longer being the main breadwinner has been a blow to Gina: "I was the breadwinner for so long and all of a sudden I wasn't. It doesn't help your psyche very much." With their current income even lower than it was when I first met them, the difficulties that I observed the Calafatos grappling with many years ago, after Gina's salary first took a hit, ended up being not just a short-term bump in the road. Instead, it turned into a long-term structural adjustment.

Dealing with this adjustment is still primarily handled by Gina. "Sometimes I would have to say to everybody in the family, 'Okay, this is the paycheck where we have to pay the mortgage, so, you know, no dining out, no this, no having friends over for dinner.' I mean, it was tight." She has spent a lot of time with the spreadsheet she uses to monitor their budget, trying to figure out where they can spend less in order to keep it all going.

At one point, when things were really difficult during her unemployment, she again asked Sam to relieve her by managing the bills—and once again Gina felt he wasn't quite up to the task. "He's not good at it," she says. "We did try [having Sam do the bills], but then I would be, like, managing on the side, and that's kinda frustrating, too, because you're still kind of involved in it. And then I would find things that I didn't think were the right choices, and then that was like, 'Oh, forget it, I'm just gonna do it.'"

With Gina consumed by worry, Sam's lack of concern continued to cause marital friction. "I'm a type A personality and he is not," Gina said. "He does not worry as much as me. He's very optimistic. He just doesn't let it get to him." Gina said that she and Sam would get into fights about which stores had the lowest prices and about how they didn't have the money for the gym membership that Sam wanted. Though Gina was a bit irritated with Sam, in contrast, Sam is very appreciative of Gina's efforts over the years to keep the family afloat. "I'm lucky, Gina does all the finances. She keeps track of everything. I don't do any of that. She stresses, I don't stress; I just trust her," he says with a laugh.

Sam also did not stress about the college application process Mindy and Trevor went through. "I wasn't stressed from it because Gina did it. [He laughs.] She's a great wife. [He laughs.] She did the [financial aid] stuff and all that crap." Because Gina had personal experience applying to college and Sam did not, Sam left her in charge of shepherding their children through all the academic, financial, logistical, and emotional aspects of applying for college. It was something she worked on daily. "I was the one doing all the work to help the kids get to their college thing. So it was a huge amount of stress on me," Gina said.

Sam's hands-off attitude frustrated Gina. "It's a little bit annoying just because if you don't know how to work the system, it's not like you can't learn to do it." But Gina felt there was an upside to this, too, since the kids could go to Sam and complain about their mom or about the process, and Gina, too, could turn to Sam to complain about the kids. "He probably got an earful," Gina said with a laugh.

If the work that Gina put into the application process was considerable, the financial aspects of sending their children to college were even more daunting. The Calafatos had opened college savings accounts when their children were young, but they were unable to save as much as they wanted, and during the economic downturn their overall investments had fallen in value by almost $60,000. By the time Mindy was a senior in high school, Gina and Sam had only $5,000 set aside to pay for her education, which meant that financial aid would be a crucial factor in their decision about where she would go.

Mindy applied to several public universities in California as well as a few small private schools on the West Coast. Mindy was planning to major in journalism, and one of her teachers suggested she also apply to New York University (NYU) because of their strong program. If she got in, this would be a great opportunity for her.

The Calafatos were thrilled when Mindy was accepted by NYU. "It was just a *huge* big deal that she was selected to be in the program at NYU," Gina says. Gina wanted to take Mindy to visit to the school. The family didn't have the cash necessary for the trip, so Gina borrowed money from her parents to take Mindy to New York. When they got there, they loved the city, the people, and especially the school. The only thing they didn't love was the paltry financial aid package, which would provide Mindy with only $5,000 per year. With tuition at $50,000 a year, and living expenses on top of that, the grant was a drop in the bucket. "I don't know many families who can afford to spend a quarter million dollars on college," Gina says. "That's crazy."

After they got back from New York, Gina talked with Mindy frequently about the opportunity, but the Calafatos could not realistically afford for her to attend NYU. Gina tried to explain to Mindy that borrowing that much money herself would place too much of a burden on her in the future, but she felt Mindy was too young really to understand. "Mindy thought we could figure it out somehow," Gina says. Gina and Mindy talked about it until the last possible moment. "It was at the eleventh hour," Gina recalls, "when Mindy had to let them know online whether or not she was coming. I'll never forget the day when she came in and she goes, 'Well, what am I doing? What do I get to do?' And I think she kind of knew all along, but I said [her voice breaks], 'You can't go, Mindy. We can't swing it.' [She wipes tears from her cheeks.] And Mindy just turned around and walked away."

For Gina, a parent who had always been on the lookout for opportunities for her children, the inability to give this one to Mindy was extremely hard. "I was sad," Gina says. "I would cry. I couldn't sleep. I would wake up and think, like, you know, she's not gonna be happy where she ends up going to school. It was devastating for me." Worse still, Gina felt as if she were to blame. She thought, "Mindy has gotten into one of the top schools in the United States and we are not in a position to pay for that opportunity for her. Like, we weren't good at saving. Like, we should have been saving religiously, no matter what." When I ask her whether such thoughts are really accurate or if she is being too hard on herself, she replied, "I think it's partially true, but, I mean, you have to have groceries."

When I ask Sam about Mindy's college decision, his recollections are different. "I think her first choice was New York University or USC, one of those. But she didn't get accepted there. Or did she? You know, I can't remember now." In contrast to Gina's piercing, lingering pain over not being able to send Mindy to NYU, Sam is nonchalant, unable to recall the exact details.

Sam's detached response is likely shaped by his sense that he and Gina are providing their children with a major opportunity simply by sending them to a four-year university, even if that school isn't their first choice. As Sam notes, many parents say to their kids, "'You know what? We can't afford for you to go to college. You have to go to a junior college for two years.' We didn't tell them that. We never said, 'Hey, you know what? We can't afford it,' which realistically we couldn't because we had to borrow the money . . . But they wanted the four-year college experience, and you try to do what is best for your kids. We try to make it work out." Since paying the $250,000 price tag for NYU was simply not achievable, Sam moved on to more practical options.

To Gina's great relief, Mindy ended up getting into a small private college in Oregon, which provided her with a great financial aid package that covered almost half the cost of attending. Mindy was excited about the school and Gina felt that, even though it wasn't NYU, her daughter would get a good education. Mindy has enjoyed her classes and learned a lot, but she has been unhappy in Oregon and has never felt as if she belongs at the school. She is currently considering transferring to another university.

Trevor also attends a small private university now. He was recruited to play soccer for the school and receives a scholarship covering about half of the tuition. Trevor was matched with the university through a private recruiting service that the Calafatos paid $1,500 to use. "It was worth every single penny," Gina says when describing how happy she is that Trevor is now living his dream of playing soccer at the collegiate level.

Despite the financial aid their children receive, the Calafatos still are on the hook for close to $30,000 a year for their children's educations. Mindy and Trevor have each taken out some loans to cover about $5,000 each year, but the bulk of the money comes out of the Calafatos' resources—specifically, the equity in their house. As Sam tells me, "We live paycheck to paycheck, 'cause, like, I think last year we spent $25,000 more than we made." Fortunately, the Calafatos' house, which they bought almost twenty years ago for about $325,000, is now worth around $850,000. So last year they refinanced and took out an equity line of credit to help pay for future educational expenses. Sam's mother recently passed away and Sam received an inheritance of close to $30,000, which will help to finance this year's tuition bills and give them a bit of a cushion.

The enormous costs involved in sending their children to college finally led Sam to conclude that he could no longer purchase season tickets for his beloved 49ers. "I had to make some sacrifices," he says with a laugh. "I don't go to as many Giants games, don't go to sporting events. I don't spend that kind of money." After being a season ticket holder for almost thirty years, Sam let the tickets go.

Sam has also let go of other plans. For example, he had always hoped to be able to stay in their house for the rest of his life. However, it has become clear to him that they will eventually have to sell the house to pay back what they owe for their children's educations and to help fund their retirement.

Acknowledging this reality, Sam said, "I think our only hope is maybe one day selling the house to retire." If Sam now seems a bit more tuned into the Calafatos' financial situation, Gina seems to be a bit more tuned out—or at least she is trying to be.

The last time I interviewed Gina she was doing really well. When I asked her how things were going, she began by telling me that, after years of feeling anxious and depressed, she has tried acupuncture, yoga, and meditation and has started to educate herself about nutrition and eating naturally. For the first time in a decade, she is sleeping well, she is happy, and she is envisioning a future career in health and wellness. "The depression's gone, the anxiety's gone. I have a better way about me."

As she explains it, this "better way" means trying not to approach things with "dread." Previously, when an issue came up, it was "like a big mountain," she says. Now, "I just kinda take life day by day . . . I'm not going to get myself into the emotional and physical unhealthiness of it all."

Despite this new approach, which sounds reminiscent of Laura Delgado's, Gina hasn't ignored her security project. She says she is "still constantly planning and watching what we spend. I still do that. I still keep a spreadsheet with every single penny—it drives Sam crazy—but I'm just doing that to keep an eye on things, not to make it like, 'Oh my God! How am I gonna get this with that?'" After years of being pulled under by the tides of insecurity, Gina is trying to let go and float where the currents take her.

Gina's new approach has made her relationship with Sam better. "I don't know if you remember me saying this," Gina says, "but sometimes I would get mad at Sam because he was so optimistic. 'Can't you just be down one day?'" She laughs. "How stupid is that?" Gina has come to believe that Sam copes with stress better than she does. "He has such a different personality," she says when describing how Sam reacted to her six months of unemployment and the subsequent decline in her earnings. "He was stressed . . . Not that he was under the same amount of pressure that I was, but I think he is [more] adept in dealing with things than me." She even thinks his ability to cope is what kept their marriage going when she was so depressed: "Thank God he is who he is because, any other marriage, I don't know if it would have survived."

For Sam, what has been stressful about the insecurity the Calafatos have experienced is not the insecurity itself, but rather what the insecurity has done to Gina. "It was more stressful because I don't like seeing her that way," Sam tells me. "Obviously I want her to be happy. That's why it's great that, with the [yoga and everything], she's happier now than she's been in a long time."

Sam and Gina seem more at peace now than when I was doing my in-depth research with them. Gina has a new take on life and feels more purpose. She is even hopeful that she can turn her interest in health and well-being into a career that will bring in a higher income than what she is earning now. Sam is grateful that Gina is happier than she used to be. Gina is grateful that Sam hung in there, even through her darkest moments.

They still have worries, especially about their children's futures. They are concerned that it will be hard for Mindy and Trevor to get good jobs. As Sam says, "Just 'cause you go to college and you get a degree doesn't guarantee you a job." And Gina notes that her nephews who have already graduated from college have had difficulty landing decent entry-level positions. They are also concerned about accumulating enough money to retire. Sam had hoped to be able to retire at fifty-five, but now it looks as if he will have to work ten years longer to pay off their debts and build a nest egg. Right now their investments are in aggressive funds, since they are trying to make up for what they lost when the stock market crashed. "Hopefully the economy will turn up and we can catch that wave," Gina says with a smile.

THE FALEAUS

When I caught up with the Faleaus, life was easier for them than it had been when I had gotten to know them years earlier. "It's better now," Kapo says. "Not everything, but it make a difference." The difference Kapo is referring to is that the Faleaus now have only one child, their youngest daughter, Nonni, living at home. Describing how he has fewer worries than he used to, Kapo told me that he sleeps more easily now. He said, "Before I would lay down, not sleep, thinking [about money], not be sleep [until] after twelve o'clock. [He laughs.]" With fewer financial worries, Kapo now feels that he and Laeta worry equally about their finances. Now their fights are usually about how much to give when friends and family ask for help. Laeta is very open to giving, while Kapo would like to give a bit less so they can try to save more.

Peter and Beth, the Faleaus' two older children, are now in their mid- to late twenties. Peter lives in Arizona with his wife and their baby daughter; Beth finished her degree, got married, and lives with her husband in Utah.

David and Rebecca, the Faleaus' two middle children, are in college. Currently Rebecca is in Chile serving on a mission. David, who completed his mission in Mexico about a year ago, should graduate from college in the next year.

Nonni has recently started high school. She attends the same college prep charter school that David and Rebecca attended.

With only one child at home, the Faleaus' expenses have decreased substantially. Kapo estimates that their food bill has gone down by as much as 60 percent since I first met them. Recalling how difficult it was to feed the children when they all lived at home, Kapo explained how he used to wake up early to drive to San Francisco to shop at a warehouse market: "I had to leave at five o'clock in the morning, sometimes four o'clock. You could buy forty pounds of tomatoes for ten dollars, thirty pounds of potatoes for eight dollars. Good deals. Better than Safeway. But sometimes we see our money and it only twenty dollars. If I drive to city, it will be ten dollars for the gas, not much left for food. It was very stressful." Touching his temples, he laughs, saying, "See, that's why I have more gray hair." (In fact, Laeta tells me with a broad smile, people often think he is Nonni's grandfather.) "Because it's very stressful," Kapo continues, "you know, it's very stressful. I don't know how I go through that. Like I said, we blessed." Referring to their continued ability to get by, Kapo said, "The Lord has continued to show us what to do."

Once Beth, their first American-born child, turned twenty-one, the Faleaus applied for their green cards, and a few years later they became citizens. Not having to deal with work visas and lapses in their employment eligibility has been a huge relief. "Now we like a normal people," Kapo says. "We free. It's like we free, free people."

With their citizenship in hand and with only Nonni at home to take care of, Kapo has been able to work more. Three days a week, after dropping Nonni at school and Laeta at work, he goes to a private elementary school where he works as a custodian and handyman. Working part-time allows him to pick up Nonni from school in the afternoons and drive her to her various activities. Laeta continues to work as a caretaker. After the elderly man she took care of for about four years passed away, she found a job through a friend caring for another elderly man. At this point Laeta earns about $45,000 annually and Kapo earns close to $15,000, so the Faleaus' joint income is about $20,000 more than it was when I first met them.

Even though the Faleaus earn significantly more money than they used to, their monthly rent is much higher now. The apartment complex they live in was sold a few years ago, and the new manager decided to maintain it himself, so the great deal Kapo had—getting cheap rent in return for doing maintenance—was gone. Now their rent is $1,100 per month, which makes money tight for the Faleaus, "but we still survive," Kapo says. Fortunately, the family of the elderly man Laeta cares for has not been impacted by the economic downturn, so her job has remained secure. The recession "doesn't affect us. It's the same thing . . . For us, it's just, we go by weekly," Laeta says.

The Faleaus continue to feel that it is their church and their faith that have gotten them through the hard times. "We came to this country with nothing," Kapo says, "but we never sleep hungry." Explaining how they have managed to eke out an existence despite the tough odds they faced as a poor immigrant family, Kapo says, "We believe if we do the right things the Lord's gonna bless." Clarifying, he says, "The money is coming from God. Nobody is going to come and say, 'Hey, here's a million dollars for your needs,' But there's a way . . . the Lord have a plan." Laeta still believes that God is looking out for her and her family. "He just like a father . . . I feel like the Lord is helping my family somehow in different ways." When she is concerned about something, she says, "I tell myself things will be okay. There will always be a way."

Kapo describes the scholarships his children have received as proof that God rewards the faithful: "And how many kids in this country go to school for free? That's what I'm thinking about—if we don't have faith, I don't know what [would have] happened to the children, because I cannot afford to send them to college." From Kapo's perspective, his children received the opportunity to go to college because "we believe and [have] faith."

When they look at their lives, Laeta and Kapo feel blessed. Referring to how the two older children have married and Peter has a beautiful baby,

Kapo says, "For me and my wife, sometimes we think we blessed." Laeta, too, talks about how grateful she is for all that they have and the opportunities her children have been given. She says, "We are so lucky and blessed. We don't have [much] money, but we're not poor-poor, you know. I just feel like, 'Man, how lucky we are.'"

As chapter 6 explained, Peter and Beth both received college scholarships from their church. Peter's scholarship, however, was not extended after he decided not to go on a mission, and he has not returned to complete his degree. Similarly, David and Rebecca received church scholarships for the first two years of their college educations. After that, they applied to the schools they attend for financial aid. Combining the funding they received with part-time jobs and some extra help from their older siblings, they should be able to get by.

Having his children earn college degrees is tightly linked with Kapo's own sense of security, since he sees his future and his children's futures as intimately connected. "If my children graduate from college, I think it's secure," he says, "because they can find a job. But it's hard to find a job if you not graduate from college . . . If they [don't graduate], it's not secure . . . You cannot [have] success in this country without education."

Now Kapo and Laeta are starting to think more about getting older. After telling me about Peter and Beth getting married, Kapo asked rhetorically, "What's gonna happen to me? [He chuckles.]" And later, remarking on how a college education will enable his children to get good jobs, he said, "If they do their best to work, [they] might afford some bread for us to eat."

In Samoan culture it is common for a daughter, often the youngest one, to care for her aging parents. The Faleaus are hopeful that this will happen in their family. Laeta even talks to Nonni about it, telling her, "That's why you need to study hard. You have to take care of us. It's not an option, Nonni." Laeta laughs. "Let's hope maybe her husband will accept that. Because if not, then it's a different story, and maybe we will go back then to the island."

The Faleaus have always been concerned about how their children's marriages will affect their situation, especially should they marry white Americans. Kapo and Laeta have long encouraged their children to marry fellow Mormons so that their spouses would share similar values. They even suggested that their children attend universities with large populations of Mormon students, which would make it more likely that they would find a Mormon mate. However, they seem to be just as concerned about their children marrying people who will understand the Samoan way of life. Now that two of their children have married—Peter to Rachel, a white American Mormon, and Beth to Joshua, a half-Samoan, half-white Mormon—things are looking a bit unsure.

Laeta complains to me that Peter's wife, Rachel, gets annoyed because Peter often helps out his younger brother, David, who is attending a university near Peter's home in Arizona—for example, picking up David when he was stranded without a ride. Even worse in Laeta's eyes, Rachel refused to spend money for her and Peter to fly home and visit the Faleaus this past Christmas. Laeta said that Beth's husband has a different attitude: "He part Samoan, so he understand." But Kapo and Laeta are unsure whether they can count on their children to hold on to the Samoan ethic of caring for one's whole family, not just one's nuclear family. Indeed, Kapo says that he has seen children—even those with plenty of money—refuse to care for their own parents in order to avoid a rift with a spouse: "This country is different, especially they married to the foreigner [non-Samoan]. I witness how that happen and that's what I'm worried about. I'm old. My children [have said they will help], but now they have wife or husband, it's no guarantee they gonna take care of us. So maybe we can lean on them, but they not [take care of us] 100 percent." If their children are unable to care for them, the Faleaus may have to return to Samoa, where both of their families still own land and they could build a house.

With that stage of life still a ways off, the Faleaus continue to survive by turning to their church and their family and friends when they need help. "If we need help, the church is always there," Laeta says. "The church and the people over there is so helpful if you ask for the help." A few years ago, when the Faleaus' rent shot up and their car broke down, their church gave them the $600 they needed to cover the rent. When the Faleaus needed help to hold a reception for Beth's wedding, friends and family pitched in and provided them with the food, the flowers, and some extra cash to pull it off.

The Faleaus are planning to move from the Bay Area within the next year or two. Their daughter Beth, who has graduated from college, now works in marketing for a hotel chain in Utah. With Beth firmly established in Utah, Kapo and Laeta think it is best for the family to relocate to a suburb outside Salt Lake City. "Utah is so cheap," Kapo says. Though their ward will be sad to see them go, church members have already told Kapo and Laeta that when the time comes, they will try to help them find new jobs by tracking down job leads from family and friends living in Salt Lake City. Once again, the church is providing the Faleaus with a leg up—and possibly entry into a better life.

THE JENNERS

When I caught up with the Jenners, their lives seemed just as busy as they were when I interviewed them six years earlier. At almost fifty years old, Chelsea Jenner is now back to full-time work. After several years of working part-time as a cosmetologist and just breaking even, Chelsea decided to switch careers and now works in an administrative role for the local public school district. "I've always volunteered so much at the schools, and so I was like, 'I'm just gonna apply for a job here,'" Chelsea says with a chuckle. In addition, she has returned to her studies. "It's something I've wanted to do for a long time," she says about her desire to earn a college degree.

With Chelsea and Eddie both working full-time and Chelsea back at school, juggling their children's many activities—and paying for them—remains a challenge, although the Jenners' income is now almost $60,000 higher than it was when I last spoke with them. (Eddie now earns about $125,000 per year in systems design, while Chelsea contributes another $25,000.) Yet things still feel tight. "It's paycheck to paycheck," Eddie Jenner, now in his early fifties, says. "We know what it's like to have to wait four more days until we can go grocery shopping. I think we're just out of that, but it's close enough that we could fall back into it . . . I mean, if something major happens to one of our cars, what are we gonna do? I'd have to pull out a credit card, which we don't want to do . . . but that's our backup."

Nonetheless, the Jenners' increased income has made it easier for them to cover their monthly bills. "We've used the higher pay to get more comfortable and be less stressed out . . . It's not as complicated now," Eddie says. Previously, Chelsea and Eddie were always behind, always trying to figure out which bills had to be paid in full so something would not get turned off, which bills they could just pay the minimum on, and which bills they could let slide. Now bill paying requires less strategizing.

As a result, the way they manage their finances has changed. When I first interviewed them, Chelsea and Eddie used to pay the bills together, a tag-team approach that ensured "we each knew where we were at," as Eddie says. But once Chelsea starting working and they had more resources, they didn't have to strategize as much about how to pay their bills. This development, combined with Chelsea having less time because she was going to school, ushered in a change. Now Eddie pays the bills by himself.

Even though Eddie is now in charge of paying the bills, Chelsea still feels as if she worries more about their financial situation than he does, while Eddie thinks they worry about the same amount. "I'm really frugal in my spending," Chelsea says. "And Eddie is the one that's more free-wheeling with the money." Eddie's tendency to say yes to whatever their children want, whether it's going out to eat, signing up for a trip, or playing a new sport, continues to be a source of tension between Chelsea and Eddie. "A lot of times I'm like, 'But look at the cost,'" Chelsea says, "and Eddie's like, 'Oh, we'll figure it out.' That's kind of his philosophy."

Chelsea feels ambivalent about being less involved in managing the family budget. On the one hand, with her job, her family, and her studies, she doesn't have the time to keep up with all the financial details. However, she feels anxious about not being on top of everything. On a few occasions she was annoyed to learn about big budget decisions only after they were made—their daughter joining a traveling softball team or their son going on a school trip to the East Coast, for example. Her feelings about this shift in power reflect her ambivalence. "I think, subconsciously," Chelsea says, "since he's making the majority of the money, if that's a decision he wants to make, I have to be okay with that. Even though in reality, when I think about it, I don't [have to be okay with it]." She laughs at her contradictory assertions.

It seems Chelsea is right to be concerned about the cost of all those activities for their children. Eddie reports spending almost $4,000 in the last six months for Katrina's out-of-state softball tournaments, which is the kind of expense that makes it hard for the family to get ahead. "We're kind of slowly going uphill, trying to stay afloat," Eddie explains. With the higher income, "now at least we've leveled it off. The stressful part is—here's our normal bills, and all of a sudden they need $300 for Katrina's tournament. Okay, so there's a spike in the norm." To "get us through those spikes," the Jenners pull out their credit card.

Despite their higher income, the Jenners still rely on credit to buy the things they need. Rather than pass up opportunities for themselves and their children, they borrow with the hope of bettering their family's future. Consequently, their debt situation remains very much the same as when I first met them. They carry a balance of about $1,500 on their credit card, they owe $40,000 on their equity line of credit, and they owe $20,000 on a school loan that Eddie took out to finance a master's degree he earned two years ago.

Getting the degree was a "personal goal" for Eddie, an achievement he thought would give him more "stability" as well as additional career credibility. Also lurking in the back of Eddie's mind were the continual rumors that his company, Burcell, might move out of the Bay Area altogether after years of layoffs. Over the decades that Eddie has worked at Burcell, the company has gone from three thousand employees to about seven hundred as parts of the company have been sold off or moved to cheaper parts of the United States. "I might as well build up my resume a little bit," Eddie explains, so that if Burcell closes, "at least I can walk out with something." Just as when Eddie earned his undergraduate degree, Burcell paid for 75 percent of the cost upfront and then reimbursed Eddie for the remaining 25 percent when he graduated after two years of night classes. But the Jenners needed about "half the money to pay off other things," so Eddie took out a student loan for $20,000.

The Jenners have a plan to pay down their debt by refinancing their house at the current low mortgage rates and using the proceeds to pay off their equity line of credit. Fortunately, although their house has lost about a hundred thousand dollars from its value at the height of the housing bubble, it's still worth about two hundred thousand more than when they bought it. So they can use the equity in their house to help them take care of the debt—"just in time for whatever other college fees the kids are gonna come to us with," jokes Eddie.

Eddie and Chelsea both know how hard it is to earn a degree while raising a family and working full-time, so they're very concerned that their two oldest children, Nelson and Corey, have not gone the college route.

They've taken a few classes at a local community college, but they're struggling to figure out what they want to do with their futures. Nelson, Eddie's son from a previous marriage, has worked as a waiter and bartender since graduating from high school. Corey, who graduated from high school a year ago, is beginning to think about becoming a coach.

Compared with the Mah family, the Jenners approached the college application process in a very laid-back fashion. Nelson didn't apply at all because his grades were too low. Corey applied to a few graphic design programs with Eddie's help, and he was even accepted by one. Yet Eddie and Chelsea were concerned about spending a lot of money when Corey was not "academically inclined" and was more of a social person. Chelsea says, "I had hesitation in sending him there because it's $40,000 a year. And how do I know the effort [he's] gonna put into it? I was not willing to just sign on because they kept calling us, 'Are you gonna sign the papers and send them back?' And it's like, 'No, I'm not going be in debt to you for $160,000 dollars.'" Chelsea laughs, saying, "I'm not gonna do it." Until Corey showed more passion and commitment to a specific goal, Eddie and Chelsea felt that he should live at home, take some courses at a local community college, and figure out what he wants to do.

But the fact that neither Nelson nor Corey is making much progress in figuring out his next steps is worrisome. In fact, Chelsea told me that the biggest worry in her life is that Corey is not going to finish his education. Chelsea worries about Corey because, "as times goes by, without a degree it's gonna be much more difficult . . . I think at a minimum [my children] need to have at least a bachelor's degree, at a very minimum. Because there are so many people out there who have that and are still unemployed." Chelsea is also worried about what Nelson will do next year when he is no longer eligible to be covered by Eddie's health insurance.

Eddie is concerned, too, but he thinks Corey will figure things out soon enough. As for Nelson, Eddie thinks that it's time he learns to stand on his own: "We've given him opportunities, we've helped him with his vehicles, we've helped him take courses in school, and he just keeps falling back to his job [at the restaurant] . . . So we've basically said, 'We have three other kids to consider. You're twenty-five. We've invested as much as we can.' He's fine with it. He's independent so . . . independently struggling," Eddie concludes with a laugh.

By contrast, their daughter, Katrina, is academically driven, takes advanced placement classes, and has good grades and high test scores. Currently a senior in high school, she is setting her sights on applying to a four-year school. For a while Stanford University was Katrina's first choice, but because of Stanford's high cost, Eddie is relieved that Katrina has recently become interested in other options. "Thank goodness she's not looking at Stanford [now]," Eddie says, explaining that because Katrina wants to become a paramedic, there are state schools that have "more of what she wants to do" and cost significantly less.

Paying for college for any of the four Jenner children—or Chelsea—will be difficult. Besides Eddie's 401(k), which now has about $385,000 in it, and college savings accounts Eddie's parents set up for the children, which have about $6,000 each, the Jenners have no savings. "We don't even have a savings account," Eddie told me. "We really haven't planned how we're gonna do it, so we'll see what happens," Eddie explains. Chelsea and Eddie hope that Katrina will get some sort of financial aid, but if no assistance arises, then "we will fall back on loans," Eddie says.

Consequently, the Jenners will need to keep working much longer than they would like. Just like Sam Calafato, Eddie has realized that he will not be able to retire as soon as he had hoped. Eddie says, "We have a little computer thing at work—you can calculate your retirement. I've put in five years from now and then ten years from now, and it's like, 'Oh, I better wait till then . . . I think we've got a good ten to fifteen years [of work] before we can consider doing something for ourselves," he says with a rueful laugh.

Yet Eddie is thankful for the good pension he still has. Over the years his company has made significant changes to their retirement program, but Eddie and the other veterans have been "grandfathered in." "I feel bad," he confesses, "because . . . for the new employees it's slowly slipping away and not being offered."

After watching decades of benefit cuts, layoffs, and employee transfers, Eddie sometimes worries that his good deal at Burcell may go bust. "Well, we've been what they call rightsizing or downsizing for twenty years now. I survived the big hits . . . So I'm at a point now where if . . . 90 percent of the people are [gone], they're probably just gonna close the doors and leave the janitors to clean up the mess, you know." Recent events have made this possibility seem more likely. The sequestration legislation of 2013 significantly limited the amount of government funding available for medical research. With fewer government contracts available, the higher-ups at Burcell are concerned about controlling costs, "so we're kind of just nickel and diming it, trying to survive through the next couple years," Eddie says, "until this all washes over, hopefully."

But Eddie tries not to worry about his employment. "It's not worth it. I'd be dead if I stressed over my job security over all those years . . . I just put it out somewhere else and don't think about it. It's a worry, but I just try not to—I try to block it out of my mind . . . It's out of my control." Eddie also tries not to worry about their day-to-day financial stresses. "I'm not very stressed over it," Eddie says, noting that he knows they could always sell their house and move to a less expensive area if necessary. "It's a little bit of an insurance policy," Eddie says. Although Eddie might have concerns about how they are going to pay for long-term expenses such as college and their retirement, "in the short term," he says, "I'm just winging it day to day."

As for Chelsea, she vacillates between worrying a lot and trying not to worry, especially when she realizes that "worrying is not going to make a difference." Worrying for "a sustained amount of time is really difficult," Chelsea says. Eventually, however, the worry always begins to creep back in. How will they pay for her studies? When will Corey return to school? "If I don't worry about it, no one else will," Chelsea says, "and someone's got to worry about it . . . I have to worry about it because I realize it's not even on Eddie's radar."

It is this difference between Chelsea and Eddie that undermines Chelsea's sense of security. To feel secure, "Eddie and I [need] to be in sync," Chelsea says. "I think that's probably the biggest thing, maybe even more so than financially." When she and Eddie are in sync, Chelsea explains, "Then it's like, okay, I can come and talk to him about whatever and we are going along this path together as opposed to me feeling like I'm going it alone."

Lately, however, now that she is back in school, Eddie has not managed things on the home front as well as Chelsea would like. When Chelsea's classes started, she told Eddie, "Okay, now it's your turn to make sure that you're turning [their] stuff in on time. You have to look at all their homework. You have to be, like, on them . . . And so we went to my young-est son's parent-teacher conference. And they were like, 'Oh, he missed all this homework.' And I was just livid."

Eddie is doing a better job now, but he is still not on top of things the way Chelsea would like. "It drives me crazy," Chelsea says with a laugh, but for the time being she has decided to "just let it go." "If I don't [go back to school] now, I'm never going to do it," Chelsea explains. "I'm gonna be seventy years old getting my degree, and what good is that going to do me then?"

The Jenners hope that in the years to come they will continue to inch closer to their dreams. Chelsea hopes to graduate from college within the next five years and become a speech therapist. Eddie hopes to retire sooner rather than later and then get a job that he is more passionate about, per-haps working with children. Though the Jenners have come through the Great Recession ahead of where they were when the downturn began, it's hard to know what the future holds for them, given their high debts and the uncertainty surrounding Eddie's job. If the Jenners' security project is a bit precarious even when Eddie has a good job, what will happen if he loses it?

One thing they are not concerned about is the growing gap between the haves and the have-nots in American society. When I ask Chelsea about it, she says, "You hear, like, about the 99 percent. And the gap widening. I don't really think about that that much, though, 'cause I figure they're in their space and I just need to worry about my space and what's going on with my kids." Eddie echoes her sentiment: "I just accept it as the way it is. Yeah, I do."

Notes

PREFACE

1. Kevin Mayhood, "Robber Gets Wish: 3 Years in Prison," *Columbus Dispatch*, October 12, 2006.

2. John Schwartz, "A Financial Plan That Comes with Mug Shots," *New York Times*, January 7, 2007.

3. Jonathan Rosen, "The Genius of Timothy J. Bowers," *Huffington Post*, October 18, 2006.

INTRODUCTION

1. All names and identifying characteristics have been changed to maintain the confidentiality of the participants in this study.

2. California Budget Project, "Making Ends Meet: How Much Does It Cost to Raise a Family in California?" (2007).

3. Between 1970 and 2007 the percentage of married women who were more educated than their husbands increased from 20 to 28 percent. This trend is likely to continue, given that women are attaining higher levels of education than are men, especially among those at the bottom half of the socioeconomic status distribution. See Richard Fry and D'Vera Cohn, "Women, Men and the New Economics of Marriage," Pew Research Center (January 2010); and Claudia Goldin,

Lawrence F. Katz, and Ilyana Kuziemko, "The Homecoming of American College Women: The Reversal of the College Gender Gap," *Journal of Economic Perspectives* 20, no. 4 (2006): 133–56.

4. Jacob Hacker, *The Great Risk Shift: The Assault on American Jobs, Families, Health Care, and Retirement and How You Can Fight Back* (New York: Oxford University Press, 2006), ix.

5. For a detailed review and explanation of economic inequality in the United States, see Rebecca M. Blank, *Changing Inequality* (Berkeley: University of California Press, 2011).

6. Edward N. Wolff, "Recent Trends in Household Wealth in the United States: Rising Debt and the Middle-Class Squeeze—An Update to 2007" (June 2010), Levy Economics Institute of Bard College, Working Paper No. 589.

7. Edward N. Wolff, "The Asset Price Meltdown and the Wealth of the Middle Class" (November 2012), National Bureau of Economic Research, Working Paper No. 18559.

8. For a review of the distribution of economic risk, see Bruce Western et al., "Economic Insecurity and Social Structure," *Annual Review of Sociology* 38 (2012): 341–59.

9. Neil Fligstein and Taek-Jin Shin, "The Shareholder Value Society: A Review of Changes in Working Conditions and Inequality in the United States," in *Social Inequality*, ed. Kathryn M. Neckerman (New York: Russell Sage Foundation, 2004), 401–32.

10. Ibid., 402–3.

11. Laura McCloud and Rachel Dwyer, "The Fragile American: Hardship and Financial Troubles in the 21st Century," *Sociological Quarterly* 52, no. 1 (2011): 13–35; Jacob S. Hacker et al., "Economic Security at Risk: Findings from the Economic Security Index" (July 2010), The Rockefeller Foundation.

12. For a review of how analyses of the risk society fail to take social class and educational differences into consideration, see Marianne Cooper, "The Inequality of Security: Winners and Losers in the Risk Society," *Human Relations* 61, no. 9 (2008): 1229–58.

13. For scholarship that focuses on economic struggles and economic provisioning, see Katherine Porter, ed., *Broke: How Debt Bankrupts the Middle Class* (Stanford, CA: Stanford University Press, 2012); Hacker, *The Great Risk Shift;* Elizabeth Warren and Amelia Warren Tyagi, *The Two-Income Trap: Why Middle-Class Parents Are Going Broke* (New York: Basic Books, 2003); Teresa A. Sullivan, Elizabeth Warren, and Jay Lawrence Westbrook, *The Fragile Middle Class: Americans in Debt* (New Haven, CT: Yale University Press, 2000); Margaret K. Nelson and Joan Smith, *Working Hard and Making Do: Surviving in Small Town America* (Berkeley: University of California Press, 1999).

14. Richard Wilkinson and Kate Pickett, *The Spirit Level: Why Greater Equality Makes Societies Stronger* (New York: Bloomsbury Press, 2010).

15. Arlie Russell Hochschild, *The Managed Heart* (Berkeley: University of California Press, 1983), 85.

16. Candace West and Don Zimmerman, "Doing Gender," *Gender & Society* 1, no. 2 (1987): 125-51; and Judith Butler, *Gender Trouble: Feminism and the Subversion of Identity* (New York: Routledge, 1990).

17. Arlie Russell Hochschild, "Emotion Work, Feeling Rules, and Social Structure," *American Journal of Sociology* 85, no. 3 (1979): 551-75.

18. Hochschild, *The Managed Heart*.

1. FROM SHARED PROSPERITY TO THE AGE OF INSECURITY

1. Sanford M. Jacoby, *Employing Bureaucracy: Managers, Unions, and the Transformation of Work in the 20th Century* (New York: Columbia University Press, 1985).

2. It is important not to overstate the level of public support that existed in the 1930s for New Deal policies. In their book *Who Cares? Public Ambivalence and Government Activism from the New Deal to the Second Gilded Age* (Princeton, NJ: Princeton University Press, 2010), Katherine S. Newman and Elisabeth Jacobs illustrate that Americans were divided in their support for the New Deal. Moreover, Newman and Jacobs's analysis of American public policy since the New Deal sets forth a nuanced historical story in which Americans have often held more mixed political views than the politicians they have elected.

3. Franklin D. Roosevelt, "Statement on Signing the Social Security Act," August 14, 1935.

4. For more on the history of America's hybrid public/private welfare system, see Jennifer Klein, *For All These Rights: Business, Labor, and the Shaping of America's Public-Private Welfare State* (Princeton, NJ: Princeton University Press, 2003).

5. For more on this three-way power-sharing arrangement, see David Harvey, *The Condition of Postmodernity: An Enquiry into the Origins of Cultural Change* (Oxford: Blackwell, 1989); and Robert B. Reich, *The Work of Nations: Preparing Ourselves for 21st Century Capitalism* (New York: A.A. Knopf, 1991).

6. Sheldon Danziger and Peter Gottschalk, *America Unequal* (New York: Russell Sage Foundation, 1995).

7. Frank Levy, *The New Dollars and Dreams: American Incomes and Economic Change* (New York: Russell Sage Foundation, 1998), 35.

8. Erik Olin Wright and Rachel E. Dwyer, "The Patterns of Job Expansions in the USA: A Comparison of the 1960s and 1990s," *Socio-Economic Review* 1, no. 3 (2003): 289-325.

9. Arthur F. Jones Jr. and Daniel H. Weinberg, "The Changing Shape of the Nation's Income Distribution, 1947–1998," U.S Census Bureau, Current Population Reports, P60-204 (Washington, DC: U.S. Government Printing Office, 2000).

10. Jacob S. Hacker, *The Divided Welfare State: The Battle over Public and Private Social Benefits in the United States* (New York: Cambridge University Press, 2002), especially pp. 79, 262.

11. Klein, *For All These Rights*, 5.

12. Levy, *The New Dollars and Dreams*, 29.

13. Tamara Draut, "The Growing College Gap," in *Inequality Matters: The Growing Economic Divide in America and Its Poisonous Consequences*, ed. James Lardner and David A. Smith (New York: New Press, 2005), 91–92.

14. John F. Kennedy, "Remarks Made in Heber Springs, Arkansas, at the Dedication of Greers Ferry Dam," October 6, 1963.

15. For more information about the economic conditions after World War II, see Reich, *The Work of Nations*; Levy, *The New Dollars and Dreams*; and Charles R. Morris, *Apart at the Seams: The Collapse of Private Pension and Health Care Protections* (New York: Century Foundation Press, 2006), especially chapter 2.

16. Martina Morris and Bruce Western, "Inequality in Earnings at the Close of the Twentieth Century," *Annual Review of Sociology* 25 (1999): 623–57, especially p. 626.

17. Michael Greenstone and Adam Looney, *Trends: Reduced Earnings for Men in America* (June 2011), The Hamilton Project.

18. Michael Greenstone and Adam Looney, *Women in the Workforce: Is Wage Stagnation Catching Up to Them Too?* (April 2011), The Hamilton Project.

19. Michael Greenstone and Adam Looney, *The Great Recession May Be Over, but American Families Are Working Harder Than Ever* (July 2011), The Hamilton Project.

20. Hacker, *The Great Risk Shift*, 89.

21. U.S. Census Bureau, Table F-7, "Type of Family (All Races) by Median and Mean Income: 1947 to 2011, Current Population Survey, Annual Social and Economic Supplements."

22. Lawrence Mishel, Jared Bernstein, and Sylvia Allegretto, *The State of Working America 2006/2007* (Ithaca, NY: IRL Press, 2007), 45.

23. Heather Boushey and Joshua Holland, "If This Is Such a Rich Country, Why Are We Getting Squeezed?," July 18, 2007.

24. The lowest-earning workers are workers at the tenth percentile of the income distribution; the highest-earning workers are workers at the ninety-fifth percentile. Heather Boushey and Christian E. Weller, "What the Numbers Tell Us," in *Inequality Matters: The Growing Economic Divide in America and Its Poisonous Consequences*, ed. James Lardner and David A. Smith (New York: New Press, 2005), 30–31.

25. David H. Autor, Lawrence F. Katz, and Melissa S. Kearney, "Trends in U.S Wage Inequality: Revising the Revisionists," *Review of Economics and Statistics* 90, no. 2 (2008): 300–323.

26. Gary Burtless, "Comments on 'Has U.S Income Inequality Really Increased,'" The Brookings Institution, January 11, 2007.

27. Jared Bernstein, "Updated CBO Data Reveal Unprecedented Increase in Inequality," Economic Policy Institute Issue, Brief No. 239, December 13, 2007.

28. For a review of wage inequality, see Thomas Lemieux, "The Changing Nature of Wage Inequality," *Journal of Population Economics* 21, no. 1 (2008): 21–48.

29. Mishel, Bernstein, and Allegretto, *The State of Working America 2006/2007*, 251.

30. Edward N. Wolff, "Recent Trends in Household Wealth in the United States: Rising Debt and the Middle-Class Squeeze" (June 2007), Levy Economics Institute at Bard College, Working Paper No. 502.

31. Edward N. Wolff, "The Asset Price Meltdown and the Wealth of the Middle Class" (November 2012), National Bureau of Economic Research, Working Paper No. 18559.

32. Thomas Piketty and Emmanuel Saez, "Income Inequality in the United States, 1913–1998," *Quarterly Journal of Economics* 118, no. 1 (2003): 1–39.

33. Linda Levine, *The U.S. Income Distribution and Mobility: Trends and International Comparisons* (November 2012), Congressional Research Service.

34. Matissa Hollister, "Employment Stability in the U.S. Labor Market: Rhetoric versus Reality," *Annual Review of Sociology* 37 (2011): 305–24.

35. Women's tenure in the private sector has actually increased, from 8.9 years in the 1970s to 9.7 years in the early 2000s, but this is largely due to women's greater attachment to the labor market over time. Henry S. Farber, "Job Loss and the Decline in Job Security in the United States" (December 7, 2009), Princeton University Industrial Relations Section, Working Paper No. 520.

36. Henry S. Farber, "The Incidence and Costs of Job Loss: 1982–91," Brookings Papers on Economic Activity: Microeconomics (1993): 73–119; Henry S. Farber, "The Changing Face of Job Loss in the United States, 1981–1995," Brookings Papers on Economic Activity: Microeconomics (1997): 55–128; Kenneth A. Couch and Dana W. Placzek, "Earnings Losses of Displaced Workers Revisited," *American Economic Review* 100, no. 1 (2010): 572–89.

37. Mark Szeltner, Carl Van Horn, and Cliff Zukin, *Diminished Lives and Futures: A Portrait of America in the Great-Recession Era* (February 2013), John J. Heldrich Center for Workforce Development, Edward J. Bloustein School of Planning and Public Policy, Rutgers University.

38. Hacker, *The Great Risk Shift*, 27. For a summary of several studies on the rise in income volatility, see Karen Dynan, "The Income Rollercoaster: Rising Income Volatility and Its Implications," *Pathways*, Spring 2010, 3.

39. Jacob S. Hacker et al., "Economic Insecurity and the Great Recession: Findings from the Economic Security Index" (November 2011), The Rockefeller Foundation.

40. Hacker, *The Great Risk Shift*, 31.

41. Jacob S. Hacker et al., "Economic Security at Risk: Findings from the Economic Security Index" (July 2010), The Rockefeller Foundation.

42. Bankrate.com, "Financial Security Index: Americans Neutral" (2012).

43. Teresa A. Sullivan, Elizabeth Warren, and Jay Lawrence Westbrook, "Less Stigma or More Financial Distress: An Empirical Analysis of the Extraordinary Increase in Bankruptcy Filings," *Stanford Law Review* 59, no. 2 (2006): 215; ConsumerAffairs.org, "Bankruptcy Filings Set Record in 2005," January 11, 2006.

44. United States Courts, U.S. Bankruptcy Courts, Table F2, "Business and Nonbusiness Cases Commenced, by Chapter of the Bankruptcy Code, During the 12-Month Period Ending December 31, 2012"; United States Courts, "Bankruptcy Filings Down in Fiscal Year 2012," November 7, 2012; United States Courts, "Judicial Facts and Figures 2010, U.S. Bankruptcy Courts, Business and Non-business Cases Filed by Chapter of the Bankruptcy Code."

45. Christine Dugas, "Only a Fraction of Those in Need File for Bankruptcy," *USA Today*, June 9, 2010.

46. Elizabeth Warren and Amelia Warren Tyagi, *The Two-Income Trap: Why Middle-Class Parents Are Going Broke* (New York: Basic Books, 2003), 7.

47. Daron Blomquist, "2012 Foreclosure Market Outlook," RealtyTrac, February 12, 2012.

48. Center for Responsible Lending, "California Foreclosure Statistics: The Crisis Is Not Over" (April 2012).

49. The Century Foundation, "Life and Debt: Why American Families Are Borrowing to the Hilt" (2004), The Century Foundation.

50. Kevin B. Moore and Michael G. Palumbo, "The Finances of American Households in the Past Three Recessions: Evidence from the Survey of Consumer Finances," 2010, The Federal Reserve, Finance and Economics Discussion Series. For the middle class, the ratio of debt to net worth grew from 37 percent in 1983 to 46 percent in 2001, then surged to 61 percent in 2007 and surged again to 72 percent in 2010 due to a big contraction in net worth as housing values plunged. Similarly, the debt-to-income ratio among the middle class rose from 67 percent in 1983 to 100 percent in 2001, then shot up to 157 percent in 2007 before declining to 135 percent as families sought to pay down their debts in a shaky economy, access to credit became more restrictive, and large numbers of Americans defaulted on their debts. See Edward N. Wolff, "Recent Trends in Household Wealth in the United States: Rising Debt and the Middle-Class Squeeze—An Update to 2007" (June 2010), Levy Economics Institute of Bard College, Working Paper No. 589; Edward N. Wolff, "The Asset Price Meltdown

and the Wealth of the Middle Class" (November 2012), National Bureau of Economic Research, Working Paper No. 18559. In these studies the middle class is comprised of the middle three income and wealth quintiles.

51. New America Foundation, "Debt in American Households: A Collection of Facts and Statistics" (May 2009).

52. Moore and Palumbo, "The Finances of American Households in the Past Three Recessions."

53. Brian K. Bucks et al., "Changes in U.S. Family Finances from 2004 to 2007: Evidence from the Survey of Consumer Finances," 2009, The Federal Reserve, Federal Reserve Bulletin; Jesse Bricker et al., "Changes in U.S. Family Finances from 2007 to 2010: Evidence from the Survey of Consumer Finances," Federal Reserve Bulletin 98, no. 2 (2012).

54. Bricker et al., "Changes in U.S. Family Finances from 2007 to 2010."

55. Karen Dynan, "Changing Household Financial Opportunities and Economic Security," *Journal of Economic Perspectives* 23, no. 4 (Fall 2009): 49–68.

56. Warren and Tyagi, *The Two-Income Trap*, 133 and 202 (note 63).

57. Families USA, "Too Great a Burden: America's Families at Risk" (December 2007), Publication No. 07-113.

58. Gary Claxton et al., "Health Benefits in 2012: Moderate Premium Increase for Employer-Sponsored Pans; Young Adults Gained Coverage under ACA," *Health Affairs* 31, no. 10 (2012): 2324-33.

59. College Board, "Trends in College Pricing" (2003); College Board, "2007–2008 College Costs."

60. The Project on Student Debt, "Quick Facts about Student Debt" (January 2010).

61. Pew Research Center, "A Record One-in-Five Households Now Owe Student Loan Debt" (September 2012).

62. ChildCare Aware of America, "Parents and the High Cost of Child Care" (2012).

63. Arne L. Kalleberg, "Precarious Work, Insecure Workers: Employment Relations in Transition," *American Sociological Review* 74, no. 1 (2009): 2.

64. Robert Perrucci and Carolyn C. Perrucci, *America at Risk: The Crisis of Hope, Trust, and Caring* (Lanham, MD: Rowman and Littlefield, 2009).

65. Stephen Herzenberg, John A. Alic, and Howard Wial, *New Rules for a New Economy: Employment and Opportunity in Postindustrial America* (Ithaca, NY: IRL Press, 1998).

66. Saskia Sassen, *The Global City: New York, London, Tokyo* (Princeton, NJ: Princeton University Press, 1991); Manuel Castells, *The Rise of the Network Society* (Malden, MA: Blackwell, 1996); Wright and Dwyer, "The Patterns of Job Expansions in the USA"; Lawrence F. Katz and Kevin M. Murphy, "Changes in Relative Wages, 1963–1987: Supply and Demand Factors," *Quarterly Journal of*

Economics 107, no. 1 (1992): 35–44; Frank Levy and Richard J. Murnane, "U.S. Earnings Levels and Earnings Inequality: A Review of Recent Trends and Proposed Explanations," *Journal of Economic Literature* 30, no. 3 (1992): 1333–81; Alan B. Krueger, "How Computers Have Changed the Wage Structure: Evidence from Microdata, 1984–1989," *Quarterly Journal of Economics* 108, no. 3 (1993): 28–33; Richard B. Freeman and Lawrence F. Katz, *Differences and Changes in Wage Structures* (Chicago: University of Chicago Press, 1995); Timothy Bresnahan, Eric Brynjofsson, and Lorin Hitt, "Technology, Organization, and the Demand for Skilled Labor," in *The New Relationship: Human Capital in the American Corporation*, ed. Margaret M. Blair and Thomas A. Kochan (Washington, DC: The Brookings Institution, 2000), 145–93.

67. Kalleberg, "Precarious Work, Insecure Workers."

68. David M. Gordon, *Fat and Mean: The Corporate Squeeze of Working Americans and the Myth of the Managerial "Downsizing"* (New York: The Free Press, 1996); Paul Osterman, *Securing Prosperity: The American Labor Market: How It Has Changed and What to Do About It* (Princeton, NJ: Princeton University Press, 1999); Chris Benner, *Work in the New Economy: Flexible Labor Markets in Silicon Valley* (Oxford: Blackwell, 2002).

69. Gerald Mayer, "Union Membership Trends in the United States" (2004), Congressional Research Service.

70. Bureau of Labor Statistics, "Union Members—2012" (January 2013).

71. Richard B. Freeman, *When Earnings Diverge: Causes, Consequences, and Cures for the New Inequality in the U.S.* (Washington, DC: National Policy Association, 1997); David Card, "The Effect of Unions on Wage Inequality in the U.S. Labor Market," *Industrial and Labor Relations Review* 54, no. 2 (2001): 296–315.

72. Bruce Western and Jake Rosenfeld, "Unions, Norms, and the Rise in U.S. Wage Inequality," *American Sociological Review* 76, no. 4 (2011): 513–37.

73. Louis Uchitelle, *The Disposable American: Layoffs and Their Consequences* (New York: Knopf, 2006).

74. Christopher J. Goodman and Steven M. Mance, "Employment Loss and the 2007–09 Recession: An Overview," *Monthly Labor Review*, April 2011.

75. Hacker et al., *Economic Insecurity and the Great Recession*.

76. Hacker, *The Great Risk Shift*; Pat O'Malley, *Risk, Uncertainty and Government* (London: Glass House Press, 2004).

77. Center for Retirement Research, "Private Workers with Pension Coverage, by Pension Type, 1980, 1992, and 2004" (August 2006).

78. Lawrence Mishel, Jared Bernstein, and Sylvia Allegretto, *The State of Working America 2006/2007*, executive summary.

79. Elise Gould, "A Decade of Declines in Employer-Sponsored Health Insurance Coverage" (February 2012), Economic Policy Institute, Briefing Paper No. 337.

80. Employee Benefit Research Institute and Mathew Greenwald and Associates, "How Rising Health Care Costs Affect Household Finances" (November 2005).

81. Congressional Budget Office, "Estimates for the Insurance Coverage Provisions of the Affordable Care Act Updated for the Recent Supreme Court Decision" (July 2012).

82. The Commonwealth Fund, *State Participation in the Affordable Care Act's Expansion of Medicaid Eligibility* (August 2013).

83. KPMG, "Lack of Medicaid Expansion Could Leave 5.3 Million without Coverage under Affordable Care Act," February 23, 2013.

84. Annie-Rose Strasser, "Governors for 7 of the 10 Least-Insured Cities Have Refused to Expand Medicaid," *ThinkProgress*, September 27, 2012.

85. College Board, "Trends in Student Aid 2012" (2012), College Board Advocacy and Policy Center.

86. Ibid.; Lawrence E. Gladieux, "Low-Income Students and the Affordability of Higher Education," in *America's Untapped Resource: Low-Income Student in Higher Education*, ed. Richard D. Kahlenberg (New York: Century Foundation Press, 2004), 29; The Institute for College Access and Inclusion, "Pell Grants Help Keep College Affordable for Millions of Americans" (February 2012).

87. Advisory Committee on Student Financial Assistance, "The Rising Price of Inequality: How Inadequate Aid Limits College Access and Persistence," Report to Congress and the Secretary of Education (June 2010).

88. Martha J. Bailey and Susan M. Dynarski, "Gains and Gaps: Changing Inequality in U.S. College Entry and Completion" (December 2011), National Bureau of Economic Research, Working Paper No. 17633.

89. Jacob S. Hacker, Philipp Rehm, and Mark Schlesinger, "Standing on Shaky Ground: Americans' Experiences with Economic Insecurity" (December 2010), The Rockefeller Foundation.

90. Richard Curtin, "What Recession? What Recovery? The Arrival of the 21st Century Consumer," *Business Economics* 38, no. 2 (2003): 25–32.

91. Richard Curtin, "Economic Discontent: Causes and Consequences" (November 2008), University of Michigan Survey of Consumers.

92. Ibid., 3.

93. Elizabeth Jacobs and Katherine S. Newman, "Rising Angst? Change and Stability in Perceptions of Economic Insecurity," in *Laid Off, Laid Low: Political and Economic Consequences of Employment Insecurity*, ed. Katherine S. Newman (New York: Columbia University Press, 2008), 74–101.

94. Hacker, Rehm, and Schlesinger, *Standing on Shaky Ground*.

95. Pew Charitable Trusts, "Economic Mobility and the American Dream: Where Do We Stand in the Wake of the Great Recession?" (May 2011), Economic Mobility Project.

96. Emily Alpert, "Amid Slow Economic Recovery, More Americans Identify as 'Lower Class,'" *Los Angeles Times*, September 15, 2013.

97. Amy Sullivan, "The American Dream, Downsized," *National Journal*, April 26, 2013.

98. Pew Charitable Trusts, "Economic Mobility and the American Dream."

99. MetLife, "The MetLife Study of the American Dream: Against the Backdrop of the Financial Burden Shift" (January 2007).

100. Christine DiGangi, "Does Debt Define the New American Dream," *Credit.com Blog*, September 5, 2013.

101. Sullivan, "The American Dream, Downsized."

102. Ibid.

103. Ulrich Beck, *Risk Society: Towards a New Modernity* (London: Sage, 1992).

104. Jared Bernstein, *All Together Now: Common Sense for a New Economy* (San Francisco: Barrett-Koehler, 2006).

2. FORGING SECURITY IN AN INSECURE AGE

1. Among upper-class families, both parents worked full-time in three families. In five of the families, the father worked full-time and the mother worked part-time. In seven of the families, the fathers worked full-time and the mothers were stay-at-home parents. And in one family, their net worth was so high that neither of the parents worked for pay at the time I interviewed them.

Among the eighteen middle-income families, both parents worked full-time in half of the families. However, in one of these families the father was out of work at the time I interviewed him and in another family the mother was out of work. In five of the middle-class families, the father worked full-time and the mother worked part-time. In two families the father worked full-time and the mother was a stay-at-home parent. In one family the mother worked full-time and the father was retired. In one family the father worked full-time and the mother was in school.

Among the eight working-class families, both parents worked full-time in four families. In two families, the fathers worked full-time and the mothers worked part-time. In one family, the mother worked full-time and the father worked part-time. In one family, the father worked full-time and the mother was a stay-at-home parent.

2. These income and educational levels are derived from self-reported data given by the research subjects.

3. California Budget Project, "Making Ends Meet: How Much Does It Cost to Raise a Family in California?" (2007).

4. California Budget Project, "Making Ends Meet: How Much Does It Cost to Raise a Family in California" (June 2010).

5. Judith Stacey, *Brave New Families: Stories of Domestic Upheaval in Late-Twentieth-Century America* (New York: Basic Books, 1990).

6. Louise Auerhahn et al., *Life in the Valley Economy: Saving the Middle Class: Lessons from Silicon Valley—2012* (October 2012), Working Partnerships USA.

7. Ibid.

8. The interviews usually lasted between ninety minutes and two hours for adults and thirty to sixty minutes for teenagers. All interviews were recorded and transcribed.

9. I employed grounded theory techniques for the data analysis. This involved coding themes from the interviews and field notes and using the qualitative software program Atlas.ti to help establish patterns, write analytic memos, and make connections among related categories of analysis.

10. See Arlie Russell Hochschild, *The Second Shift* (New York: Avon, 1989); and Annette Lareau, *Unequal Childhoods: Class, Race, and Family Life, Second Edition with an Update a Decade Later* (Berkeley: University of California Press, 2011).

11. For more on how qualitative researchers are like detectives, see Allison Pugh, "What Good Are Interviews for Thinking About Culture? Demystifying Interpretive Analysis," *American Journal of Cultural Sociology* 1, no. 1 (2013): 42–68.

12. For more on my findings regarding social, economic, and cultural capital differences among the families in this study, see my "The Inequality of Security: Winners and Losers in the Risk Society," *Human Relations* 61, no. 9: 1229–58.

3. DOWNSCALING FOR SURVIVAL

1. For studies on these issues, see Katherine S. Newman, *Falling from Grace: The Experience of Downward Mobility in the American Middle Class* (Berkeley: University of California Press, 1988); Rand D. Conger et al., "Linking Economic Hardship to Marital Quality and Instability," *Journal of Marriage and Family* 52, no. 3 (1990): 643–56; Lillian B. Rubin, *Families on the Fault Line: America's Working Class Speaks About the Family, the Economy, Race, and Ethnicity* (New York: HarperCollins, 1994); Rand D. Conger, Martha A. Rueter, and Glen H. Elder, "Couple Resilience to Economic Pressure," *Journal of Personality and Social Psychology* 76, no. 1 (1999): 54–71; Jeffrey Dew, "Two Sides of the Same Coin? The Differing Roles of Assets and Consumer Debt in Marriage," *Journal of Family and Economic Issues* 28, no. 1 (2007): 89–104.

2. Rubin, *Families on the Fault Line.*

3. For research on the achievement of masculinity, see David Collinson, *Managing the Shopfloor: Subjectivity, Masculinity, and Workplace Culture* (New

York: W. de Gruyter, 1992); Raewyn Connell, *Masculinities* (Berkeley: University of California Press, 1995); Marianne Cooper, "Being the 'Go-To Guy': Fatherhood, Masculinity, and the Organization of Work in Silicon Valley," *Qualitative Sociology* 23, no. 4 (2000): 379–405; Nicholas Townsend, *The Package Deal: Marriage, Work and Fatherhood in Men's Lives* (Philadelphia: Temple University Press, 2002). C. J. Pascoe, *Dude You're a Fag: Masculinity and Sexuality in High School* (Berkeley: University of California Press, 2007).

4. Arlie Russell Hochschild, *The Commercialization of Intimate Life: Notes from Home and Work* (Berkeley: University of California Press, 2003), 86.

5. Richard R. Peterson, "A Re-Evaluation of the Economic Consequences of Divorce," *American Sociological Review* 61, no. 3 (1996): 528–36. For another review, see Karen D. Holden and Pamela J. Smock, "The Economic Costs of Marital Dissolution: Why Do Women Bear a Disproportionate Cost?," *Annual Review of Sociology* 17 (1991): 528–536. For a qualitative analysis of these financial issues, see Demie Kurz, *For Richer, For Poorer: Mothers Confront Divorce* (New York: Routledge, 1995).

6. Arlie Russell Hochschild, "Emotion Work, Feeling Rules, and Social Structure," *American Journal of Sociology* 85, no. 3 (1979): 551–75; Arlie Russell Hochschild, *The Managed Heart: Commercialization of Human Feeling* (Berkeley: University of California Press, 1983).

7. For research on changing embarrassment to anger, see Robert Sutton, "Maintaining Norms about Expressed Emotion: The Case of Bill Collectors," *Administrative Science Quarterly* 36 (1991): 245–68. For research on changing contentment to happiness, see Jennifer Pierce, *Gender Trials: Emotional Lives in Contemporary Law Firms* (Berkeley: University of California Press, 1995). For research on changing shame to pride, see Lory Britt and David Heise, "From Shame to Pride in Identity Politics," in *Self, Identity, and Social Movements*, ed. Sheldon Stryker, Timothy J. Owens, and Robert W. White (Minneapolis: University of Minnesota Press, 2000), 252–70. For research on changing guilt to innocence, see Sandra E. Godwin, "Managing Guilt: The Personal Responsibility Rhetoric among Parents of 'Troubled' Teens," *Sociological Quarterly* 45, no. 3 (2004): 575–96.

8. Kathryn J. Lively and David R. Heise, "Sociological Realms of Emotional Experience," *American Journal of Sociology* 109, no. 5 (2004): 1109–36.

9. Interestingly, Katherine S. Newman (1988) found a similar type of antimaterialism among women raised in the 1970s who were dealing with downward mobility as a result of divorce. She found that the downward mobility these women experienced after their divorces caused them to emphasize the value of relationships with friends, education, and autonomy over the value of material things. Raised in the 1970s, Laura seems to hold a similar type of logic.

10. Eric Rosenbaum, "Six Feet Under as Retirement Plan?" CNBN.com, October 22, 2013.

11. Alicia H. Munnell, Anthony Webb, and Francesca Golub-Sass, "The National Retirement Risk Index: An Update" (October 2012), Center for Retirement Research at Boston College.

12. Barbara Ehrenreich, *Bright-Sided: How Positive Thinking Is Undermining America* (New York: Picador, 2009).

13. For research on how income scarcity and income instability shape consumption in low-income families, see Allison Pugh, "Windfall Child Rearing: Low-Income Care and Consumption," *Journal of Consumer Culture* 4, no. 2 (2004): 229–49.

4. THE UPSCALING OF SECURITY AT THE TOP

1. For a cross-class analysis that explores the rise of anxiety among parents, see Margaret K. Nelson, *Parenting Out of Control: Anxious Parents in Uncertain Times* (New York: New York University Press, 2010).

2. Richard B. Freeman, *When Earnings Diverge: Causes, Consequences, and Cures for the New Inequality in the U.S.* (Washington, DC: National Policy Association, 1997); Lawrence Katz and David Autor, "Changes in the Wage Structure and Earnings Inequality," in *Handbook of Labor Economics,* ed. Orley Ashenfelter and David E. Card (New York: North Holland, 1999), 1463–1555.

3. Neil Fligstein and Taek-Jin Shin, "The Shareholder Value Society: A Review of Changes in Working Conditions and Inequality in the United States," in *Social Inequality,* ed. Kathryn M. Neckerman (New York: Russell Sage, 2004), 402.

4. Annette Lareau, *Unequal Childhoods: Class, Race, and Family Life, Second Edition with an Update a Decade Later* (Berkeley: University of California Press, 2011).

5. Carol Vincent and Stephen J. Ball, "'Making Up' the Middle-Class Child: Families, Activities and Class Dispositions," *Sociology* 41, no. 6 (2007): 1061–77; Lareau, *Unequal Childhoods.*

6. Max Weber, *The Protestant Ethic and the Spirit of Capitalism* (New York: Scribner, 1958).

7. Thomas L. Friedman, *The World Is Flat: A Brief History of the Twenty-First Century* (New York: Farrar, Straus and Giroux, 2005).

8. Ellen Gamerman, "Drilling Kids in Chinese," *Wall Street Journal*, March 17, 2007.

9. Sharon Hays, *The Cultural Contradictions of Motherhood* (New Haven, CT: Yale University Press, 1996); Stephen J. Ball, *Class Strategies and the Education Market: The Middle Classes and Social Advantage* (London: RoutledgeFalmer, 2003), 77.

10. NYU sociologist Kathleen Gerson also uses the term "neo-traditional" to refer to the approach young men take in regard to work and family. They prefer

to prioritize their career when faced with family and work conflict and problems establishing egalitarian relationships. See Kathleen Gerson, *The Unfinished Revolution: How a New Generation Is Reshaping Family, Work, and Gender in America* (Oxford: Oxford University Press, 2010).

11. Gary Rivlin, "In Silicon Valley, Millionaires Who Don't Feel Rich," *New York Times,* August 5, 2007.

12. Barclays Wealth, "The True Value of Wealth" (December 2007).

13. Ibid., 7.

14. Ibid.

15. PNC Advisors, "Many Wealthy Americans Have Done Nothing to Protect Assets and Are Worried About Financial Security, Family Values, According to Largest Study of Its Kind Released Today," January 10, 2005.

16. Barclays Wealth, "The True Value of Wealth," 7.

17. For more about the types of packages fathers feel they owe their families, see Nicholas Townsend, *The Package Deal: Marriage, Work, and Fatherhood in Men's Lives* (Philadelphia: Temple University Press, 2002).

18. Raewyn Connell, *Masculinities* (Berkeley: University of California Press, 1995).

19. Douglas S. Massey, "The Age of Extremes: Concentrated Affluence and Poverty in the Twenty-First Century," *Demography* 33, no. 4 (1996): 395–412.

20. Ibid., 409.

5. HOLDING ON AT THE MIDDLE

1. Joanna Dreby, "Honor and Virtue: Mexican Parenting in the Transnational Context," *Gender & Society* 20, no. 1 (2006): 32–59.

2. "Studied Sleep," in *India Today Woman,* January 2008, 10.

3. In the survey, 78.4 percent of wives and 61 percent of husbands said there were "very likely" to lie awake at night worrying about finances. Men were more than twice as likely as the women to say that they lost no sleep at all. See Deborah Thorne, "Women's Work, Women's Worry?" in *Broke: How Debt Bankrupts the Middle Class,* ed. Katherine Porter (Stanford, CA: Stanford University Press, 2012), 136–53.

4. Elizabeth Warren and Amelia Warren Tyagi, *The Two-Income Trap: Why Middle-Class Parents Are Going Broke* (New York: Basic Books, 2003); Thorne, "Women's Work, Women's Worry?"

5. Bureau of Labor Statistics, "The Change in Real Earnings Since 1979 Has Been More Favorable for Woman Than for Men at All Levels of Education," Chart 5–9.

6. Ibid.

7. Ibid.

8. Catherine E. Freeman, *Trends in Educational Equity of Girls and Women: 2004* (Washington, DC: U.S. Government Printing Office, 2004), National Center for Education Statistics; Claudia Goldin, Lawrence F. Katz, and Ilyana Kuziemko, "The Homecoming of American College Women: The Reversal of the College Gender Gap," *Journal of Economic Perspectives* 20, no. 4 (2006): 133-56.

9. Andrew Sum et al., *The Growing Gender Gap in College Enrollment and Degree Attainment in the U.S. and Their Potential Economic and Social Consequences* (2003), Center for Labor Market Studies, Prepared for The Business Roundtable.

10. National Center for Education Statistics, Table 283, "Degrees Conferred by Degree Granting Institutions, by Level of Degree and Sex of Student: Selected Years, 1869-70 through 2020-21," in *Digest of Education Statistics* (2012).

11. Andrea Livingston and John Wirt, "The Condition of Education 2003 in Brief" (June 2003), National Center for Education Statistics; Sum et al., "The Growing Gender Gap in College Enrollment and Degree Attainment."

12. Pew Research Center, "Breadwinner Moms" (May 2013).

13. Census Bureau, "Married-Couple Families with Wives Earnings Greater Than Husband's Earnings, 1981 to 2005 (selected years)," Table F-22, Historical Income Tables.

14. Bureau of Labor Statistics, "Wives Who Earn More Than Their Husbands," 1987-2011 and 1988-2012, Annual Social and Economic Supplements to the Current Population Survey.

15. Sarah Jane Glynn, "The New Breadwinners: 2010 Update" (April 2012), Center for American Progress.

16. Mirra Komarovsky, *Blue-Collar Marriage* (New York: Random House, 1962); Lillian Rubin, *Worlds of Pain: Life in the Working-Class Family* (New York: Basic Books, 1976); Lydia D. Morris, "Redundancy and Patterns of Household Finance," *Sociological Review* 32, no. 3 (1984): 492-523; Jan Pahl, "Household Spending, Personal Spending and the Control of Money in Marriage," *Sociology* 24, no. 1 (1990): 119-38; Carolyn Vogler and Jan Pahl, "Money, Power and Inequality within Marriage," *Sociological Review* 42, no. 2 (1994): 263-88; Deborah Thorne, "Extreme Financial Strain: Emergent Chores, Gender Inequality and Emotional Distress," *Journal of Family and Economic Issues* 31, no. 2 (2010): 185-97.

17. Rubin, *Worlds of Pain.*

18. For more on the relationship between economic change and changing definitions of masculinity, see Jennifer Sherman, *Those Who Work, Those Who Don't: Poverty, Morality, and Family in Rural America* (Minneapolis: University of Minnesota Press, 2009.

19. Thorne, "Extreme Financial Strain."

20. MacArthur Foundation Research Network, "Earnings by Education for Young Workers, 1975-2000" (November 2004), Networks on Transitions to Adulthood.

6. WHEN RELIGION FILLS THE GAP

1. Susan Burke Crawford Sullivan, "Faith and Poverty: Personal Religiosity and Organized Religion in the Lives of Low-Income Urban Mothers," *Dissertation Abstracts International* 66, no. 5 (2005): 1978A–1979A.

2. Ram A. Cnaan, Robert J. Wineburg, Stephanie C. Boddie, *The Newer Deal: Social Work and Religion in Partnership* (New York: Columbia University Press, 1999).

3. Mark Chaves and William Tsitsos, "Congregations and Social Services: What They Do, How They Do It, and with Whom," *Nonprofit and Voluntary Sector Quarterly* 30, no. 4 (2001): 660–83.

4. David A. Reingold, Maureen Pirog, and David Brady, "Empirical Evidence on Faith-Based Organizations in an Era of Welfare Reform," *Social Service Review* 81, no. 2 (2007): 245–83.

5. Robert J. Wineburg et al., "Leveling the Playing Field: Epitomizing Devolution through Faith-Based Organizations," *Journal of Sociology and Social Welfare* 35, no. 1 (2008): 17–42.

6. Reingold, Pirog, and Brady, "Empirical Evidence on Faith-Based Organizations," 247; Robert J. Wineburg et al., "Leveling the Playing Field," 33.

7. Robert P. Weiss, "Charitable Choice as Neoliberal Social Welfare Strategy," *Social Justice* 28, no. 1 (2001): 35–53; Wineburg et al., "Leveling the Playing Field."

8. Reingold, Pirog, and Brady, "Empirical Evidence on Faith-Based Organizations"; Wineburg et al., "Leveling the Playing Field," 33.

9. Josh Good, "Assessing Four Years of Obama's Faith-Based Initiatives," *National Review Online*, February 13, 2013.

10. Wineburg et al., "Leveling the Playing Field," 38.

11. Marvin Olasky, *The Tragedy of American Compassion* (Washington, DC: Regnery Gateway, 1992); Amy L. Sherman, "Cross Purposes: Will Conservative Welfare Reform Corrupt Religious Charities?," *Policy Review* 74 (Fall 1995): 58–63; Stanley L. Carlson-Thies, "'Don't Look to Us': The Negative Responses of the Churches to Welfare Reform," *Notre Dame Journal of Law, Ethics, and Public Policy* 11, no. 2 (1997): 667–89.

12. Weiss, "Charitable Choice as Neoliberal Social Welfare Strategy," 36.

13. Some research has found that religious organizations do not provide the type of holistic and personal services that charitable choice advocates claim; that they generally address only immediate needs for food or shelter, not long-term needs; that they perform less well than traditional social service agencies; and that FBOs are, in any case, too few in number to enhance government welfare programs. However, other studies indicate that FBOs can offer service recipients a better experience than nonreligious providers and that clients consider FBOs to be more trustworthy. Despite this growing body of research, it is impossible to draw

firm conclusions about the scope and efficacy of religious organizations' work in social services. For research testing the belief that FBOs are better equipped to deal with the needy, see Chaves and Tsitsos, "Congregations and Social Services"; Susan Suess Kennedy and Wolfgang Bielefeld, *Charitable Choice: First Results from Three States* (Indianapolis: Center for Urban Policy and the Environment, 2003); Mark Chaves, "Religious Congregations and Welfare Reform," *Society* 38 (2001): 21–27; Laura A. Reese, "A Matter of Faith: Urban Congregations and Economic Development," *Economic Development Quarterly* 18, no. 1 (2004): 50–66. For research highlighting the positive aspects of FBO social service programs, see John Bartkowski et al., "Comparative Case Studies of Faith-Based and Secular Service Agencies," Roundtable on Religion and Social Welfare Policy; Robert Wuthnow, Conrad Heckett, and Becky Yang Hsu, "The Effectiveness and Trustworthiness of Faith-Based and Other Service Organizations: A Study of Recipients' Perceptions," *Journal for the Scientific Study of Religion* 43, no. 1 (2004): 1–17.

14. Charlene C. McGrew and Ram A. Cnaan, "Finding Congregations: Developing Conceptual Clarity in the Study of Faith-Based Social Services," *Journal of Religion and Spirituality in Social Work* 25, nos. 3–4 (2006): 19–37.

15. John McCarthy and Jim Castelli, "Religion-Sponsored Social Service Providers: The Not-So-Independent Sector" (1998), Aspen Institute, Nonprofit Sector Research Fund.

16. Chaves, "Religious Congregations and Welfare Reform." Ironically, although conservatives have generally supported the expansion of religion into social services while liberals tend to oppose it, at the congregational level, conservative churches are generally leery of government funding (largely due to fears of governmental interference) while liberal churches are more likely to want it. One study found that only 28 percent of congregations in conservative or evangelical denominations said they would be willing to apply for government funds, while 41 percent of congregations in the liberal/moderate Protestant denominations and 40 percent of Catholic congregations would be interested. See ibid.

17. Ram A. Cnaan and Stephanie C. Boddie, *The Invisible Caring Hand: American Congregations and the Provision of Welfare* (New York: New York University Press, 2002).

18. Chaves and Tsitsos, "Congregations and Social Services."

19. Garth L. Mangum, "Welfare Services," Light Planet.

20. Ibid.

21. John P. Bartkowski et al., "Religion, Job Readiness, and Employment Outcomes: The Case of Latter-Day Saint Employment Resource Services," *Research on Social Work Practice* 17, no. 2 (2007): 188–98.

22. Ibid.

23. Ibid.

24. Richard N. Ostling and Joan K. Ostling, *Mormon America: The Power and the Promise* (San Francisco: HarperCollins, 1999).

25. Paul H. Thompson, "Lay Participation and Leadership," Light Planet.

26. Val Dan MacMurray, "Self-Sufficiency," Light Planet.

27. Gordon Bitner Hinckley, *The Teachings of Gordon B. Hinckley* (Salt Lake City, UT: Deseret, 1997), 172.

28. Mangum, "Welfare Services."

29. MacMurray, "Self-Sufficiency."

30. Michael W. Foley and Dean R. Hoge, *Religion and the New Immigrants: How Faith Communities Form Our Newest Citizens* (Oxford: Oxford University Press, 2007).

31. Kenneth I. Pargament, *The Psychology of Religion and Coping: Theory, Research, Practice* (New York: Guilford Press, 1997).

32. Ian Urbina, "In Hard Times, the Truck Stop Offers a Place to Pray," *New York Times,* June 18, 2008.

33. Ingela C. Thune-Boyle et al., "Do Religious/Spiritual Coping Strategies Affect Illness Adjustment in Patients with Cancer? A Systematic Review of the Literature," *Social Science and Medicine* 63, no. 1 (2006): 151–64; Scott T. Michael et al., "Widowhood and Spirituality: Coping Responses to Bereavement," *Journal of Women and Aging* 15, nos. 2–3 (2003): 145–65; Erin E. Emery and Kenneth I. Pargament, "The Many Faces of Religious Coping in Late Life: Conceptualization, Measurement, and Links to Well-Being, *Ageing International* 29, no. 1 (2004): 3–27; Tameka L. Gillum, Cris M. Sullivan, and Deborah L. Bybee, "The Importance of Spirituality in the Lives of Domestic Violence Survivors," *Violence against Women* 12, no. 3 (2006): 240–50.

34. Susan Crawford Sullivan, "The Work-Faith Connection for Low-Income Mothers: A Research Note," *Sociology of Religion* 67, no. 1 (2006) 99–108.

35. For more on the "prosperity gospel" movement, see Laurie Goodstein, "Believers Invest in the Gospel of Getting Rich," *New York Times,* August 15, 2009.

36. Kenneth I. Pargament and Crystal L. Park, "Merely a Defense? The Variety of Religious Means and Ends," *Journal of Social Issues* 51, no. 2 (1995): 13–32.

37. Ibid.

38. William K. Tabb, "Wage Stagnation, Growing Inequality, and the Future of the U.S. Working Class," *Monthly Review* 59, no. 2 (2007): 28.

39. For research on socioeconomic status and feeling connected to God, see Neal Krause, "Church-Based Social Support and Health in Old Age: Exploring Variations by Race," *Journal of Gerontology: Social Sciences* 57B, no. 6 (2002): S332–47. For research on socioeconomic status and divine control, see Scott Schieman et al., "The Sense of Divine Control and Psychological Distress: Variations by Race and Socioeconomic Status," *Journal for the Scientific Study of Religion* 45, no. 4 (2006): 529–49.

40. Garrick Blalock, David R. Just, and Daniel H. Simon, "Hitting the Jackpot or Hitting the Skids: Entertainment, Poverty, and the Demand for State

Lotteries," *American Journal of Economics and Sociology* 66, no. 3 (2007): 545-70.

41. Wineburg et al., "Leveling the Playing Field," 39.

42. Weiss, "Charitable Choice as Neoliberal Social Welfare Strategy," 43.

43. Chaves and Tsitsos, "Congregations and Social Services."

44. Reingold et al., "Empirical Evidence on Faith-Based Organizations."

45. Rodney Stark and Reid L. Nelson, *The Rise of Mormonism* (New York: Columbia University Press, 2005), 140.

46. Association of Statisticians of American Religious Bodies, "2010 U.S. Religion Census: Religious Congregations & Membership Study" (May 2012).

47. Pew Research Center, "A Portrait of Mormons in the U.S," July 24, 2009.

48. Tabb, "Wage Stagnation, Growing Inequality, and the Future of the U.S. Working Class," 28.

7. DEBT AND HOPE

1. Josh Bivens, *Failure by Design: The Story behind America's Broken Economy* (Ithaca, NY: IRL Press, 2011).

2. Julia B. Isaacs, Isabel V. Sawhill, and Ron Haskins, "Getting Ahead or Losing Ground: Economic Mobility in America" (2008), The Brookings Institution, Pew Charitable Trusts.

3. Elizabeth Warren and Amelia Warren Tyagi discuss the rising costs of houses located in good school districts in their book *The Two-Income Trap: Why Middle-Class Parents Are Going Broke* (New York: Basic Books, 2003), 28-32.

4. Annette Lareau discusses the high costs involved in middle-class children's extracurricular activities, which range from entry fees to special clothing and sports equipment to having to eat meals at restaurants due to hectic schedules, in her book *Unequal Childhoods: Class, Race, and Family Life, Second Edition with an Update a Decade Later* (Berkeley: University of California Press, 2011).

CONCLUSION

1. Saskia Sassen, *The Global City: New York, London, Tokyo* (Princeton, NJ: Princeton University Press, 1991); Erik Olin Wright and Rachel E. Dwyer, "The Patterns of Job Expansions in the USA: A Comparison of the 1960s and 1990s," *Socio-Economic Review* 1, no. 3 (2003): 289-325; Michael Hout "Money and Morale: What Growing Inequality is Doing to Americans' Views of Themselves and Others" (January 2003), Survey Research Center, U.C. Berkeley, Working Paper.

2. See Neil Fligstein and Taek-Jin Shin, "The Shareholder Value Society: A Review of Changes in Working Conditions and Inequality in the United States,"

in *Social Inequality,* ed. Kathryn M. Neckerman (New York: Russell Sage, 2004), 401–32; Teresa A. Sullivan, Elizabeth Warren, and Jay Lawrence Westbrook, *The Fragile Middle Class: Americans in Debt* (New Haven, CT: Yale University Press, 2000).

3. For more on winners and losers, see my "The Inequality of Security: Winners and Losers in the Risk Society," *Human Relations* 61, no. 9 (2008): 1229–58.

4. Elizabeth Jacobs and Katherine S. Newman, "Rising Angst? Change and Stability in Perceptions of Economic Insecurity," in *Laid Off, Laid Low: Political and Economic Consequences of Employment Insecurity,* ed. Katherine S. Newman (New York: Columbia University Press, 2008), 74–101; Steffan Mau, Jan Mewes, and Nadine M. Schöneck, "What Determines Subjective Socio-Economic Insecurity? Context and Class in Comparative Perspective," *Socio-Economic Review* 10, no. 4 (2012): 655–82.

5. For insight into the experiential side of low-wage work, see Katherine Newman, *No Shame in My Game: The Working Poor in the Inner City* (New York: Russell Sage Foundation, 1999); and Katherine S. Newman, *Chutes and Ladders: Navigating the Low-Wage Labor Market* (New York: Russell Sage Foundation, 2006).

6. Katherine Porter, ed., *Broke: How Debt Bankrupts the Middle Class* (Stanford, CA: Stanford University Press, 2012).

7. Mau, Mewes, and Schöneck, "What Determines Subjective Socio-Economic Insecurity?"

8. Jacob S. Hacker, Philipp Rehm, and Mark Schlesinger, "The Insecure American: Economic Experiences, Financial Worries, and Policy Attitudes," *Perspectives on Politics* 11 (2013): 23–49.

9. Kathryn Edin and Maria Kefalas, *Promises I Can Keep: Why Poor Women Put Motherhood before Marriage* (Berkeley: University of California Press, 2007).

10. Alford A. Young Jr., *The Minds of Marginalized Black Men: Making Sense of Mobility, Opportunity, and Future Life Chances* (Princeton, NJ: Princeton University Press, 2004).

11. Julie McLeod and Katie Wright, "The Talking Cure in Everyday Life: Gender, Generations and Friendship," *Sociology* 43, no. 1 (2009): 122–39.

12. Emily, Haisley, Romel Mostafa, and George Loewenstein, "Subjective Relative Income and Lottery Ticket Purchases," *Journal of Behavioral Decision Making* 21, no. 3: 284.

13. Michael Burawoy, *Manufacturing Consent: Changes in the Labor Process under Monopoly Capitalism* (Chicago: University of Chicago Press, 1979).

14. Cecilia L. Ridgeway, "Expectation States Theory and Emotion," in *Handbook of the Sociology of Emotions,* ed. Jan E. Stets and Jonathan H. Turner (New York: Springer, 2006), 347–67; Andrew Sayer, *The Moral Significance of Class* (Cambridge: Cambridge University Press, 2005); J. M. Barbalet, *Emotion, Social*

Theory, and Social Structure (Cambridge: Cambridge University Press, 2001); Richard Sennett and Jonathan Cobb, *The Hidden Injuries of Class* (New York: Knopf, 1972).

15. Jan E. Stets, "Current Emotion Research in Sociology: Advances in the Discipline," *Emotion Review* 4, no. 3 (2012): 332; Jessica L. Collett and Omar Lizardo, "Occupational Status and the Experience of Anger," *Social Forces* 88, no. 5 (2010): 2079–2104.

16. Michael Schwalbe et al., "Generic Processes in the Reproduction of Inequality: An Interactionist Analysis," *Social Forces* 79, no. 2 (2000): 419–52.

17. For a recent analysis of how laid-off high-tech workers embrace neoliberalism, see Carrie M. Lane, *A Company of One: Insecurity, Independence, and the New World of White-Collar Unemployment* (Ithaca, NY: Cornell University Press, 2011).

18. Research into this question will contribute to a deeper understanding of system justification theory, which argues that people have a need to view the world around them as orderly and in control. As a result they rationalize the fairness of the system to maintain its integrity. Research related to this theory has also found that people will rationalize changes to the social system if those changes appear likely to occur. Solak et al. argue that more insight into how emotions are managed and regulated in this rationalization process and how such things differ by social status is needed. See Nevin Solak et al., "Rage Against the Machine: The Case for System-Level Emotions," *Social and Personality Psychology Compass* 6, no. 9 (2012): 674–90. For more on system justification theory, see John T. Jost, Mahzarin R. Banaji, and Brian A. Nosek, "A Decade of System Justification Theory: Accumulated Evidence of Conscious and Unconscious Bolstering of the Status Quo," *Political Psychology* 25, no. 6 (2004): 881–919; Danielle Gaucher, Aaron C. Kay, and Kristin Laurin, "The Power of the Status Quo: Consequences for Maintaining and Perpetuating Inequality," in *The Psychology of Justice and Legitimacy,* ed. Ramona Bobocel et al. (Philadelphia: Psychology Press, 2010).

19. For a review of research in the sociology of emotions that addresses social structure, see Stets, "Current Emotion Research in Sociology," 332. Also see Amy Wilkins, "'Not Out to Start a Revolution': Race, Gender, and Emotional Restraint among Black University Men," *Journal of Contemporary Ethnography* 41, no. 1 (2012): 34–65.

20. Eva Illouz, *Cold Intimacies: The Making of Emotional Capitalism* (Cambridge: Polity Press, 2007).

21. Diane Reay, "Beyond Consciousness? The Psychic Landscape of Social Class," *Sociology* 39, no. 5 (2005): 911–28.

22. For research on social class and subjectivity, see Carolyn Steedman, *Landscape for a Good Woman: A Story of Two Lives* (New Brunswick, NJ: Rutgers University Press, 1987); Helen Lucey and Diane Reay, "Social Class and the

Psyche," *Soundings* 15 (2000): 139–54; Michael Savage, *Class Analysis and Social Transformations* (Philadelphia: Open University, 2000); Beverley Skeggs, *Formations of Class and Gender* (London: Sage, 1997); Beverley Skeggs, *Class, Self, Culture* (London: Routledge, 2004). The quotation is from Skeggs, *Formations of Class and Gender*, 86.

23. Arlie Russell Hochschild, *The Commercialization of Intimate Life: Notes from Home and Work* (Berkeley: University of California Press, 2003).

24. "The Status of Wealth in America: A Survey of Wealth," *Worth Magazine*, November 1, 2005.

25. Julia B. Isaacs, "International Comparisons of Economic Mobility," The Brookings Institution, 2008.

26. Miles Corak, "Do Poor Children Become Poor Adults? Lessons from a Cross Country Comparison of Generational Earnings Mobility," IZA Discussion Paper No. 1993 (Bonn: Institute for the Study of Labor, 2006).

27. Isaacs, "International Comparisons of Economic Mobility."

28. For more on specific public policies, see Timothy Noah, *The Great Divergence: America's Growing Inequality Crisis and What We Can Do About It* (New York: Bloomsbury Press, 2012); Arne L. Kalleberg, "Precarious Work, Insecure Workers: Employment Relations in Transition," *American Sociological Review* 74, no. 1 (2009): 1–22.

References

Advisory Committee on Student Financial Assistance. 2010. "The Rising Price of Inequality: How Inadequate Aid Limits College Access and Persistence." June. Report to Congress and the Secretary of Education.

Alpert, Emily. 2013. "Amid Slow Economic Recovery, More Americans Identify as 'Lower Class.'" *Los Angeles Times*, September 15.

Arrington, Leonard J. 1958. *Great Basin Kingdom: An Economic History of the Latter-Day Saints, 1830–1900.* Cambridge, MA: Harvard University Press.

Association of Statisticians of American Religious Bodies. 2012. "2010 U.S. Religion Census: Religious Congregations and Membership Study." May.

Auerhahn, Louise, Bob Brownstein, Cindy Chavez, and Esha Menon. 2012. "Life in the Valley Economy: Saving the Middle Class: Lessons from Silicon Valley—2012." October. Working Partnerships USA.

Autor, David, Lawrence Katz, and Mellisa Kearney. 2008. "Trends in U.S Wage Inequality: Revising the Revisionists." *Review of Economics and Statistics* 90, no. 2: 300–323.

Bailey, Martha J., and Susan M. Dynarski. 2011. "Gains and Gaps: Changing Inequality in U.S. College Entry and Completion." December. National Bureau of Economic Research, Working Paper No. 17633.

Ball, Stephen J. 2003. *Class Strategies and the Education Market: The Middle Classes and Social Advantage.* London: RoutledgeFalmer.

Bankrate.com. 2012. "Financial Security Index: Americans Neutral."

Barbalet, J. M. 2001. *Emotion, Social Theory, and Social Structure.* Cambridge: Cambridge University Press.

Barclays Wealth. 2007. "The True Value of Wealth." December.

Bartkowski, John P., Vaughn R. A. Call, Tim B. Heaton, and Renata Forste. 2007. "Religion, Job Readiness, and Employment Outcomes: The Case of Latter-Day Saint Employment Resource Services." *Research on Social Work Practice* 17, no. 2: 188–98.

Bartkowski, John, Susan Grettengerger, Leda Hall, and Steven Rathgeb Smith. 2003. "Comparative Case Studies of Faith-Based and Secular Service Agencies." Roundtable on Religion and Social Welfare Policy.

Beck, Ulrich. 1992. *Risk Society: Towards a New Modernity.* London: Sage.

Benner, Chris. 2002. *Work in the New Economy: Flexible Labor Markets in Silicon Valley.* Oxford: Blackwell.

Bernstein, Jared. 2006. *All Together Now: Common Sense for a New Economy.* San Francisco: Barrett-Koehler.

———. 2007. "Updated CBO Data Reveal Unprecedented Increase in Inequality." Economic Policy Institute.

Bertrand, Marianne, Claudia Goldin, and Lawrence F. Katz. 2010. "Dynamics of the Gender Gap for Young Professionals in the Financial and Corporate Sectors." *American Economic Journal: Applied Economics* 2, no. 3: 228–55.

Bivens, Josh. 2011. *Failure by Design: The Story behind America's Broken Economy.* Ithaca, NY: IRL Press.

Blalock, Garrick, David R. Just, and Daniel H. Simon. 2007. "Hitting the Jackpot or Hitting the Skids: Entertainment, Poverty, and the Demand for State Lotteries." *American Journal of Economics and Sociology* 66, no. 3: 545–70.

Blank, Rebecca M. 2011. *Changing Inequality.* Berkeley: University of California Press.

Blomquist, Daron. 2012. "2012 Foreclosure Market Outlook." RealtyTrac, February 12.

Boushey, Heather, and Joshua Holland. 2007. "If This Is Such a Rich Country, Why Are We Getting Squeezed." July 18.

Boushey, Heather, and Christine E. Weller. 2005. "What the Numbers Tell Us." In *Inequality Matters: The Growing Economic Divide in America and Its Poisonous Consequences,* edited by James Lardner and David A. Smith, 27–40. New York: New Press.

Bresnahan, Timothy, Eric Brynjofsson, and Lorin Hitt. 2000. "Technology, Organization, and the Demand for Skilled Labor." In *The New Relationship: Human Capital in the American Corporation,* edited by Margaret M. Blair and Thomas A. Kochan. Washington, DC: Brookings Institution.

Bricker, Jesse, Arthur B. Kennickell, Kevin B. Moore, and John Sabelhaus. 2012. "Changes in U.S. Family Finances from 2007 to 2010: Evidence from the Survey of Consumer Finances." Federal Reserve Bulletin 98, no. 2.

Britt, Lory, and David Heise. 2000. "From Shame to Pride in Identity Politics." In *Self, Identity, and Social Movements*, edited by Sheldon Stryker, Timothy J. Owens, and Robert W. White, 252–70. Minneapolis: University of Minnesota Press.

Bucks, Brian K., Arthur B. Kennickell, Traci L. Mach, and Kevin B. Moore. 2009. "Changes in U.S. Family Finances from 2004 to 2007: Evidence from the Survey of Consumer Finances." The Federal Reserve, Federal Reserve Bulletin.

Burawoy, Michael. 1979. *Manufacturing Consent: Changes in the Labor Process under Monopoly Capitalism*. Chicago: Univeristy of Chicago Press.

Bureau of Labor Statistics. 2006. "The Change in Real Earnings since 1979 Has Been More Favorable for Woman Than for Men at All Levels of Education," Chart 5-9.

———. 2012. "Wives Who Earn More Than Their Husbands," 1987–2011 and 1988–2012. Annual Social and Economic Supplements to the Current Population Survey.

———. 2013. "Union Members—2012." January. USDL-13-0105.

Burtless, Gary. 2007. "Comments on 'Has U.S. Income Inequality Really Increased.'" The Brookings Institution.

Butler, Judith. 1990. *Gender Trouble: Feminism and the Subversion of Identity*. New York: Routledge.

California Budget Project. 2007. "Making Ends Meet: How Much Does It Cost to Raise a Family in California?"

———. 2010. "Making Ends Meet: How Much Does It Cost to Raise a Family in California?" June.

Card, David. 2001. "The Effect of Unions on Wage Inequality in the U.S. Labor Market." *Industrial and Labor Relations Review* 54, no. 2: 296–315.

Carlson-Thies, Stanley. 1997. "'Don't Look to Us': The Negative Responses of the Churches to Welfare Reform." *Notre Dame Journal of Law, Ethics, and Public Policy* 11, no. 2: 667–89.

Castells, Manuel. 1996. *The Rise of the Network Society*. Malden, MA: Blackwell.

Census Bureau. "Married-Couple Families with Wives Earnings Greater Than Husband's Earnings, 1981 to 2005 (selected years)," Table F-22, Historical Income Tables.

Center for Responsible Lending. 2012. "California Foreclosure Statistics: The Crisis Is Not Over." April.

Center for Retirement Research. 2006. "Private Workers with Pension Coverage, by Pension Type, 1980, 1992, and 2004." August.

The Century Foundation. 2004. "Life and Debt: Why American Families Are Borrowing to the Hilt." The Century Foundation.

Chaves, Mark. 2001. "Religious Congregations and Welfare Reform." *Society* 38: 21–27.

Chaves, Mark, and William Tsitsos. 2001. "Congregations and Social Services: What They Do, How They Do It, and with Whom." *Nonprofit and Voluntary Sector Quarterly* 30, no. 4: 660–83.

ChildCare Aware of America. 2012. "Parents and the High Cost of Child Care."

Claxton, Gary, Matthew Rae, Nirmita Panchal, Anthony Damico, Heidi Whitmore, Kevin Kenward, and Aso Osei-Anto. 2012. "Health Benefits in 2012: Moderate Premium Increases for Employer-Sponsored Plans; Young Adults Gained Coverage under ACA." *Health Affairs* 31, no. 10: 2324–33.

Cnaan, Ram A., and Stephanie C. Boddie. 2002. *The Invisible Caring Hand: American Congregations and the Provision of Welfare.* New York: New York University Press.

Cnaan, Ram A., Robert J. Wineburg, and Stephanie C. Boddie. 1999. *The Newer Deal: Social Work and Religion in Partnership.* New York: Columbia University Press.

The College Board. 2003. "Trends in College Pricing."

———. 2007. "2007–2008 College Costs."

———. 2012. "Trends in Student Aid 2012." College Board Advocacy and Policy Center.

Collett, Jessica L., and Omar Lizardo. 2010. "Occupational Status and the Experience of Anger." *Social Forces* 88, no. 5: 2079–2104.

Collinson, David. 1992. *Managing the Shopfloor: Subjectivity, Masculinity, and Workplace Culture.* New York: W. de Gruyter.

The Commonwealth Fund. 2103. "State Participation in the Affordable Care Act's Expansion of Medicaid Eligibility." August.

Conger, Rand D., Glen H. Elder Jr., Frederick O. Lorenz, Katherine J. Conger, Ronald L. Simons, Les B. Whitbeck, Shirley Huck, and Janet N. Melby. 1990. "Linking Economic Hardship to Marital Quality and Instability." *Journal of Marriage and the Family* 52, no. 3: 643–56.

Conger, Rand D., Martha A. Rueter, and Glen H. Elder. 1999. "Couple Resilience to Economic Pressure." *Journal of Personality and Social Psychology* 76, no. 1: 54–71.

Congressional Budget Office. 2012. "Estimates for the Insurance Coverage Provisions of the Affordable Care Act Updated for the Recent Supreme Court Decision." July.

Connell, Raewyn. 1995. *Masculinities.* Berkeley: University of California Press.

ConsumerAffairs.org. 2006. "Bankruptcy Filings Set Record in 2005." January 11.

Cooper, Marianne. 2000. "Being the 'Go-To Guy': Fatherhood, Masculinity, and the Organization of Work in Silicon Valley." *Qualitative Sociology* 23, no. 4: 379–405.

———. 2008. "The Inequality of Security: Winners and Losers in the Risk Society." *Human Relations* 61, no. 9: 1229–58.

Corak, Miles. 2006. "Do Poor Children Become Poor Adults? Lessons from a Cross Country Comparison of Generational Earnings Mobility." IZA Discussion Paper No. 1993. Bonn, The Institute for the Study of Labor.

Couch, Kenneth A., and Dana W. Placzek. 2010. "Earnings Losses of Displaced Workers Revisited." *American Economic Review* 100, no. 1: 572–89.

Curtin, Richard. 2003. "What Recession? What Recovery? The Arrival of the 21st Century Consumer." *Business Economics* 38, no. 2: 25–32.

———. 2008. "Economic Discontent: Causes and Consequences." November. University of Michigan Survey of Consumers.

Danziger, Sheldon, and Peter Gottschalk. 1995. *America Unequal*. Cambridge, MA: Harvard University Press.

Dew, Jeffrey. 2007. "Two Sides of the Same Coin? The Differing Roles of Assets and Consumer Debt in Marriage." *Journal of Family and Economic Issues* 28, no. 1: 89–104.

DiGangi, Christine. 2013. "Does Debt Define the New American Dream?" Credit.com blog, September 5.

Draut, Tamara. 2005. "The Growing College Gap." In *Inequality Matters: The Growing Economic Divide in America and Its Poisonous Consequences*, edited by James Lardner and David A. Smith, 88–101. New York: New Press.

Dreby, Joanna. 2006. "Honor and Virtue: Mexican Parenting in the Transnational Context." *Gender & Society* 20, no. 1: 32–59.

Dugas, Christine. 2010. "Only a Fraction of Those in Need File for Bankruptcy." *USA Today*, June 9.

Dynan, Karen. 2009. "Changing Household Financial Opportunities and Economic Security." *Journal of Economic Perspectives* 23, no. 4 (Fall): 49–68.

———. 2010. "The Income Rollercoaster: Rising Income Volatility and Its Implications." *Pathways*, Spring.

Edin, Kathryn, and Maria Kefalas. 2007. *Promises I Can Keep: Why Poor Women Put Motherhood before Marriage*. Berkeley: University of California Press.

Emery, Erin E., and Kenneth I. Pargament. 2004. "The Many Faces of Religious Coping in Late Life: Conceptualization, Measurement, and Links to Well-Being." *Ageing International* 29, no. 1: 3–27.

Employee Benefit Research Institute, and Mathew Greenwald and Associates. 2005. "How Rising Health Care Costs Affect Household Finances." November.

Families USA. 2007. "Too Great a Burden: America's Families at Risk." December. Publication No. 07–113.

Farber, Henry S. 1993. "The Incidence and Costs of Job Loss: 1982–91." In Brookings Papers on Economic Activity: Microeconomics.

———. 1997. "The Changing Face of Job Loss in the United States, 1981–1995." Brookings Papers on Economic Activity: Microeconomics.

————. 2009. "Job Loss and the Decline in Job Security in the United States." December 7. Princeton University Industrial Relations Section, Working Paper No. 520.

Fligstein, Neil, and Taek-Jin Shin. 2004. "The Shareholder Value Society: A Review of the Changes in Working Conditions and Inequality in the United States." In *Social Inequality*, edited by Kathryn M. Neckerman, 401–32. New York: Russell Sage.

Foley, Michael W., and Dean R. Hoge. 2007. *Religion and the New Immigrants: How Faith Communities Form Our Newest Citizens*. Oxford: Oxford University Press.

Freeman, Catherine E. 2004. *Trends in Educational Equity of Girls and Women: 2004*. Washington, DC: U.S. Government Printing Office. National Center for Education Statistics.

Freeman, Richard B. 1997. *When Earnings Diverge: Causes, Consequences, and Cures for the New Inequality in the U.S.* Washington, DC: National Policy Association.

Freeman, Richard B., and Lawrence F. Katz. 1995. *Differences and Changes in Wage Structures*. Chicago: University of Chicago Press.

Friedman, Thomas L. 2005. *The World Is Flat: A Brief History of the Twenty-First Century*. New York: Farrar, Straus and Giroux.

Fry, Richard, and D'Vera Cohn. 2010. "Women, Men and the New Economics of Marriage." January. Pew Research Center.

Gamerman, Ellen. 2007. "Drilling Kids in Chinese." *Wall Street Journal*, March 17.

Gaucher, Danielle, Aaron C. Kay, and Kristin Laurin. 2010. "The Power of the Status Quo: Consequences for Maintaining and Perpetuating Inequality." In *The Psychology of Justice and Legitimacy*, edited by Ramona Bobocel, Aaron C. Kay, Mark P. Zanna, and James M. Olson. Philadelphia: Psychology Press.

Gerson, Kathleen. 2010. *The Unfinished Revolution: How a New Generation Is Reshaping Family, Work, and Gender in America*. Oxford: Oxford University Press.

Gillum, Tameka L., Cris M. Sullivan, and Deborah L. Bybee. 2006. "The Importance of Spirituality in the Lives of Domestic Violence Survivors." *Violence against Women* 12, no. 3: 240–50.

Gladieux, Lawrence E. 2004. "Low-Income Students and the Affordability of Higher Education." In *America's Uuntapped Resource: Low-Income Students in Higher Education*, edited by Richard D. Kahlenberg, 17–58. New York: Century Foundation Press.

Glynn, Sarah Jane. 2012. "The New Breadwinners: 2010 Update." April. Center for American Progress.

Godwin, Sandra E. 2004. "Managing Guilt: The Personal Responsibility Rhetoric among Parents of 'Troubled' Teens." *Sociological Quarterly* 45, no. 3: 575–96.

Goldin, Claudia, Lawrence F. Katz, and Ilyana Kuziemko. 2006. "The Homecoming of American College Women: The Reversal of the College Gender Gap." *Journal of Economic Perspectives* 20, no. 4: 133–56.

Good, Josh. 2013. "Assessing Four Years of Obama's Faith-Based Initiatives." *National Review Online*, February 13.

Goodman, Christopher J., and Steven M. Mance. 2011. "Employment Loss and the 2007–09 Recession: An Overview." *Monthly Labor Review*, April.

Goodstein, Laurie. 2009. "Believers Invest in the Gospel of Getting Rich." *New York Times*, August 15.

Gordon, David M. 1996. *Fat and Mean: The Corporate Squeeze of Working Americans and the Myth of Managerial "Downsizing."* New York: The Free Press.

Gould, Elise. 2012. "A Decade of Declines in Employer-Sponsored Health Insurance Coverage." February. Economic Policy Institute, Briefing Paper No. 337.

Greenstone, Michael, and Adam Looney. 2011a. "The Great Recession May Be Over, but American Families Are Working Harder Than Ever." July. The Hamilton Project.

———. 2011b. "Trends: Reduced Earnings for Men in America." June. The Hamilton Project.

———. 2011c. "Women in the Workforce: Is Wage Stagnation Catching Up to Them Too?" April. The Hamilton Project.

Hacker, Jacob S. 2002. *The Divided Welfare State: The Battle over Public and Private Social Benefits in the United States.* New York: Cambridge University Press.

———. 2006. *The Great Risk Shift: The Assault on American Jobs, Families, Health Care, and Retirement and How You Can Fight Back.* New York: Oxford University Press.

Hacker, Jacob S., Gregory A. Huber, Austin Nichols, Philipp Rehm, and Stuart Craig. 2011. "Economic Insecurity and the Great Recession: Findings from the Economic Security Index." November. The Rockefeller Foundation.

Hacker, Jacob S., Gregory A. Huber, Philipp Rehm, Mark Schlesinger, and Rob Valletta. 2010. "Economic Security at Risk: Findings from the Economic Security Index." July. The Rockefeller Foundation.

Hacker, Jacob S., Philipp Rehm, and Mark Schlesinger. 2010. "Standing on Shaky Ground: Americans' Experiences with Economic Insecurity." December. The Rockefeller Foundation.

———. 2013. "The Insecure American: Economic Experiences, Financial Worries, and Policy Attitudes." *Perspectives on Politics* 11: 23–49.

Haisley, Emily, Romel Mostafa, and George Loewenstein. 2008. "Subjective Relative Income and Lottery Ticket Purchases." *Journal of Behavioral Decision Making* 21, no. 3: 283–295.

Harvey, David. 1989. *The Condition of Postmodernity: An Enquiry into the Origins of Cultural Change*. Oxford: Blackwell.

Hays, Sharon. 1996. *The Cultural Contradictions of Motherhood*. New Haven, CT: Yale University Press.

Herzenberg, Stephen, John A. Alic, and Howard Wial. 1998. *New Rules for a New Economy: Employment and Opportunity in Postindustrial America*. Ithaca, NY: ILR Press.

Hinckley, Gordon Bitner. 1997. *The Teachings of Gordon B. Hinckley*. Salt Lake City, UT: Deseret.

Hochschild, Arlie Russell. 1979. "Emotion Work, Feeling Rules, and Social Structure." *American Journal of Sociology* 85, no. 3: 551–75.

———. 1983. *The Managed Heart: Commercialization of Human Feeling*. Berkeley: University of California Press.

———. 1989. *The Second Shift*. New York: Avon.

———. 2003. *The Commercialization of Intimate Life: Notes from Home and Work*. Berkeley: University of California Press.

Holden, Karen C., and Pamela J. Smock. 1991. "The Economic Costs of Marital Dissolution: Why Do Women Bear a Disproportionate Cost?" *Annual Review of Sociology* 17: 528–36.

Hollister, Matissa. 2011. "Employment Stability in the U.S. Labor Market: Rhetoric versus Reality." *Annual Review of Sociology* 37: 305–24.

Hout, Michael. 2003. "Money and Morale: What Growing Inequality Is Doing to Americans' Views of Themselves and Others." January. Survey Research Center, U.C. Berkeley, Working Paper.

Illouz, Eva. 2007. *Cold Intimacies: The Making of Emotional Capitalism*. Cambridge: Polity Press.

The Institute for College Access and Inclusion. 2012. "Pell Grants Help Keep College Affordable for Millions of Americans." February.

Isaacs, Julia B. 2008. "International Comparisons of Economic Mobility." The Brookings Institution.

Isaacs, Julia B., Isabel V. Sawhill, and Ron Haskins. 2008. *Getting Ahead or Losing Ground: Economic Mobility in America*. The Brookings Institution. Pew Charitable Trusts.

Jacobs, Elizabeth, and Katherine S. Newman. 2008. "Rising Angst? Change and Stability in Perceptions of Economic Insecurity." In *Laid Off, Laid Low: Political and Economic Consequences of Employment Insecurity*, edited by Katherine S. Newman, 74–101. New York: Columbia Univeristy Press.

Jacoby, Sanford M. 1985. *Employing Bureaucracy: Managers, Unions, and the Transformation of Work in the 20th Century*. New York: Columbia University Press.

Jones, Arthur F., Jr., and Daniel H. Weinberg. 2000. "The Changing Shape of the Nation's Income Distribution, 1947–1998." U.S. Census Bureau, Current

Population Reports, P60–204. Washington, DC: U.S. Government Printing Office.

Jost, John T., Mahzarin R. Banaji, and Brian A. Nosek. 2004. "A Decade of System Justification Theory: Accumulated Evidence of Conscious and Unconscious Bolstering of the Status Quo." *Political Psychology* 25, no. 6: 881–919.

Kalleberg, Arne L. 2009. "Precarious Work, Insecure Workers: Employment Relations in Transition." *American Sociological Review* 74, no. 1: 1–22.

Katz, Lawrence, and David Autor. 1999. "Changes in the Wage Structure and Earnings Inequality." In *Handbook of Labor Economics*, edited by Orley Ashenfelter and David E. Card, 1463–1555. New York: North Holland.

Katz, Lawrence F., and Kevin M. Murphy. 1992. "Changes in Relative Wages, 1963–1987: Supply and Demand Factors." *Quarterly Journal of Economics* 107, no. 1: 35–44.

Kennedy, Sheila Suess, and Wolfgang Bielefeld. 2003. *Charitable Choice: First Results from Three States*. Indianapolis: Center for Urban Policy and the Environment.

Klein, Jennifer. 2006. *For All These Rights: Business, Labor, and the Shaping of America's Public-Private Welfare State*. Princeton, NJ: Princeton University Press.

Komarovsky, Mirra. 1962. *Blue-Collar Marriage*. New York: Random House.

KPMG. 2013. "Lack of Medicaid Expansion Could Leave 5.3M without Coverage under Affordable Care Act." February 28.

Krause, Neal. 2002. "Church-Based Social Support and Health in Old Age: Exploring Variations by Race." *Journal of Gerontology: Social Sciences* 57B, no. 6: S332–S47.

Krueger, Alan B. 1993. "How Computers Have Changed the Wage Structure: Evidence from Microdata, 1984–1989." *Quarterly Journal of Economics* 108, no. 1: 28–33.

Kurz, Demie. 1995. *For Richer, For Poorer: Mothers Confront Divorce*. New York: Routledge.

Lane, M. Carrie. 2011. *A Company of One: Insecurity, Independence, and the New World of White-Collar Unemployment*. Ithaca, NY: Cornell University Press.

Lareau, Annette. 2003. *Unequal Childhoods: Class, Race, and Family Life*. Berkeley: University of California Press.

Lemieux, Thomas. 2008. "The Changing Nature of Wage Inequality." *Journal of Population Economics* 21, no. 1: 21–48.

Levine, Linda. 2012. *The U.S. Income Distribution and Mobility: Trends and International Comparisons*. November. Congressional Research Service.

Levy, Frank. 1998. *The New Dollars and Dreams: American Incomes and Economic Change*. New York: Russell Sage Foundation.

Levy, Frank, Richard J. Murnane. 1992. "U.S. Earnings Levels and Earnings Inequality: A Review of Recent Trends and Proposed Explanations." *Journal of Economic Literature* 30, no. 3: 1333–81.

Lively, Kathryn J., and David R. Heise. 2004. "Sociological Realms of Emotional Experience." *American Journal of Sociology* 109, no. 5: 1109–36.

Livingston, Andrea, and John Wirt. 2003. "The Condition of Education 2003 in Brief." June. National Center for Education Statistics.

Lucey, Helen, and Diane Reay. 2000. "Social Class and the Psyche." *Soundings* 15: 139–54.

MacArthur Foundation Research Network. 2004. "Earnings by Education for Young Workers, 1975–2000." November. Networks on Transitions to Adulthood.

Massey, Douglas S. 1996. "The Age of Extremes: Concentrated Affluence and Poverty in the Twenty-First Century." *Demography* 33, no. 4: 395–412.

Mau, Steffan, Jan Mewes, and Nadine M. Schöneck. 2012. "What Determines Subjective Socio-Economic Insecurity? Context and Class in Comparative Perspective." *Socio-Economic Review* 10, no. 4: 655–82.

Mayer, Gerald 2004. "Union Membership Trends in the United States." Congressional Research Service.

Mayhood, Kevin. 2006. "Robber Gets Wish: 3 Years in Prison." *Columbus Dispatch*, October 12.

McCarthy, John, and Jim Castelli. 1998. "Religion-Sponsored Social Service Providers: The Not-So-Independent Sector." Aspen Institute, Nonprofit Sector Research Fund.

McCloud, Laura, and Rachel Dwyer. 2011. "The Fragile American: Hardship and Financial Troubles in the 21st Century." *Sociological Quarterly* 52, no. 1: 13–35.

McGrew, Charlene C., and Ram A. Cnaan. 2006. "Finding Congregations: Developing Conceptual Clarity in the Study of Faith-Based Social Services." *Journal of Religion and Spirituality in Social Work* 25, nos. 3–4: 19–37.

McLeod, Julie, and Katie Wright. 2009. "The Talking Cure in Everyday Life: Gender, Generations and Friendship." *Sociology* 43, no. 1: 122–39.

MetLife. 2007. "The MetLife Study of the American Dream: Against the Backdrop of the Financial Burden Shift." January.

Metz, Christine. 2008. "Reliance on Credit Increasing: Rising Consumer Debt Strains Families." *Lawrence Journal-World,* March 16.

Michael, Scott T., Martha R. Crowther, Bettina Schmid, and Rebecca S. Allen. 2003. "Widowhood and Spirituality: Coping Responses to Bereavement." *Journal of Women and Aging* 15, nos. 2–3: 145–65.

Miller, G. Wayne. 2007. "Education Key to New Economy." *Providence Journal,* January 30.

Miller, Lisa. 2011. "How to Raise a Global Kid." *Daily Beast,* July 18.

Mishel, Lawrence R., Jared Bernstein, and Sylvia A. Allegretto. 2007. *The State of Working America 2006/2007.* Ithaca, NY: ILR Press.

Moore, Kevin B., and Michael G. Palumbo. 2010. "The Finances of American Households in the Past Three Recessions: Evidence from the Survey of Consumer Finances." The Federal Reserve, Finance and Economics Discussion Series.

Morley, Hugh R. 2003. "Laid Off and Left Out: As Old Jobs Die, New Ones Are Scarce and Not as Good." *Bergen Record,* September 14.

Morris, Charles R. 2006. *Apart at the Seams: The Collapse of Private Pension and Health Care Protections.* New York: Century Foundation Press.

Morris, Lydia D. 1984. "Redundancy and Patterns of Household Finance." *Sociological Review* 32, no. 3: 492–523.

Morris, Martina, and Bruce Western. 1999. "Inequality in Earnings at the Close of the Twentieth Century." *Annual Review of Sociology* 25: 623–57.

Munnell, Alicia H., Anthony Webb, and Francesca Golub-Sass. 2012. "The National Retirement Risk Index: An Update." October. Center for Retirement Research at Boston College.

National Center for Education Statistics. 2012. Table 283, "Degrees Conferred by Degree Granting Institutions, by Level of Degree and Sex of Student: Selected Years, 1869–70 through 2020–21." *Digest of Education Statistics.*

Nelson, Margaret K. 2010. *Parenting Out of Control: Anxious Parents in Uncertain Times.* New York: New York University Press.

Nelson, Margaret K., and Joan Smith. 1999. *Working Hard and Making Do: Surviving in Small Town America.* Berkeley: University of California Press.

New America Foundation. 2009. "Debt in American Households: A Collection of Facts and Statistics." May.

Newman, Katherine S. 1988. *Falling from Grace: Downward Mobility in the Age of Affluence.* Berkeley: University of California Press.

———. 1999. *No Shame in My Game: The Working Poor in the Inner City.* New York: Russell Sage Foundation, 1999.

———. 2006. *Chutes and Ladders: Navigating the Low-Wage Labor Market.* New York: Russell Sage Foundation, 2006.

Newman, Katherine S., and Elisabeth S. Jacobs. 2010. *Who Cares? Public Ambivalence and Government Activism from the New Deal to the Second Gilded Age.* Princeton, NJ: Princeton University Press.

Noah, Timothy. 2012. *The Great Divergence: America's Growing Inequality Crisis and What We Can Do About It.* New York: Bloomsbury Press.

Olasky, Marvin. 1992. *The Tragedy of American Compassion.* Washington, DC: Regnery Gateway.

O'Malley, Pat. 2004. *Risk, Uncertainty and Government.* London: Glass House Press.

Osterman, Paul. 1999. *Securing Prosperity: The American Labor Market: How It Has Changed and What to Do About It*. Princeton, NJ: Princeton University Press.

Ostling, Richard N., and Joan K. Ostling. 1999. *Mormon America: The Power and the Promise*. San Francisco: HarperCollins.

Pahl, Jan. 1990. "Household Spending, Personal Spending and the Control of Money in Marriage." *Sociology* 24, no. 1: 119–38.

Pappano, Laura. 2011. "The Master's as the New Bachelor's." *New York Times*, July 22.

Pargament, Kenneth I. 1997. *The Psychology of Religion and Coping: Theory, Research, Practice*. New York: Guilford Press.

Pargament, Kenneth I., and Crystal L. Park. 1995. "Merely a Defense? The Variety of Religious Means and Ends." *Journal of Social Issues* 51, no. 2: 13–32.

Pascoe, C.J. 2007. *Dude You're a Fag: Masculinity and Sexuality in High School*. Berkeley: University of California Press.

Perrucci, Robert, and Carolyn C. Perrucci. 2009. *America at Risk: The Crisis of Hope, Trust, and Caring*. Lanham, MD: Rowman and Littlefield.

Peterson, Richard R. 1996. "A Re-Evaluation of the Economic Consequences of Divorce." *American Sociological Review* 61, no. 3: 528–36.

Pew Charitable Trusts. 2011. "Economic Mobility and the American Dream: Where Do We Stand in the Wake of the Great Recession?" May. Economic Mobility Project.

Pew Research Center. 2009. "A Portrait of Mormons in the U.S." July 24.

———. 2012. "A Record One-in-Five Households Now Owe Student Loan Debt." September.

———. 2013. "Breadwinner Moms." May.

Pierce, Jennifer L. 1995. *Gender Trials: Emotional Lives in Contemporary Law Firms*. Berkeley: University of California Press.

Piketty, Thomas, and Emmanuel Saez. 2003. "Income Inequality in the United States, 1913–1998." *Quarterly Journal of Economics* 118, no. 1: 1–39.

PNC Advisors. 2005. "Many Wealthy Americans Have Done Nothing to Protect Assets and Are Worried About Financial Security, Family Values, According to Largest Study of Its Kind Released Today."

Porter, Katherine, ed. 2012. *Broke: How Debt Bankrupts the Middle Class*. Stanford, CA : Stanford University Press.

The Project on Student Debt. 2010. "Quick Facts About Student Debt." January.

Pugh, Allison. 2004. "Windfall Child Rearing: Low-Income Care and Consumption." *Journal of Consumer Culture* 4, no. 2: 229–49.

———. 2013. "What Good Are Interviews for Thinking About Culture? Demystifying Interpretive Analysis." *American Journal of Cultural Sociology* 1, no. 1: 42–68.

———. Forthcoming. *The Tumbleweed Society: Working and Caring in an Age of Insecurity*. New York: Oxford University Press.

Reay, Diane. 2005. "Beyond Consciousness? The Psychic Landscape of Social Class." *Sociology* 39, no. 5: 911–28.

Reese, Laura A. 2004. "A Matter of Faith: Urban Congregations and Economic Development." *Economic Development Quarterly* 18, no. 1: 50–66.

Reich, Robert B. 1991. *The Work of Nations: Preparing Ourselves for 21st Century Capitalism*. New York: A.A. Knopf.

Reingold, David A., Maureen Pirog, and David Brady. 2007. "Empirical Evidence on Faith-Based Organizations in an Era of Welfare Reform." *Social Service Review* 81, no. 2: 245–83.

Ridgeway, Cecilia L. 2006. "Expectation States Theory and Emotion." In *Handbook of the Sociology of Emotions*, edited by Jan E. Stets and Jonathan H. Turner, 347–67. New York: Springer.

Rivlin, Gary. 2007. "In Silicon Valley, Millionaires Who Don't Feel Rich." *New York Times*, August 5.

Rosen, Jonathan. 2006. "The Genius of Timothy J. Bowers." *Huffington Post*, October 18.

Rosenbaum, Eric. 2013. "Six Feet Under as Retirement Plan?" CNBC.com, October 22.

Rubin, Lillian B. 1976. *Worlds of Pain: Life in the Working-Class Family*. New York: Basic Books.

———. 1994. *Families on the Fault Line: America's Working Class Speaks About the Family, the Economy, Race, and Ethnicity*. New York: HarperCollins.

Sassen, Saskia. 1991. *The Global City: New York, London, Tokyo*. Princeton, NJ: Princeton University Press.

Savage, Michael. 2000. *Class Analysis and Social Transformation*. Philadelphia: Open University.

Sayer, Andrew. 2005. *The Moral Significance of Class*. Cambridge: Cambridge University Press.

Schieman, Scott, Tetyana Pudrovska, Leonard I. Pearlin, and Christopher G. Ellison. 2006. "The Sense of Divine Control and Psychological Distress: Variations by Race and Socioeconomic Status." *Journal for the Scientific Study of Religion* 45, no. 4: 529–49.

Schnurman, Mark. 2009. "There's No Corporate Ladder to Climb: You're on Your Own." *Star-Ledger*, May 24, 2009.

Schwalbe, Michael, Sandra Godwin, Daphne Holden, Douglas Schrock, Shealy Thompson, and Michele Wolkomir. 2000. "Generic Processes in the Reproduction of Inequality: An Interactionist Analysis." *Social Forces* 79, no. 2: 419–52.

Schwartz, John. 2007. "A Financial Plan That Comes with Mug Shots." *New York Times*, January 7.

Sennett, Richard, and Jonathan Cobb. 1972. *The Hidden Injuries of Class.* New York: Knopf.

Sherman, Amy L. 1995. "Cross Purposes: Will Conservative Welfare Reform Corrupt Religious Charities?" *Policy Review* 74 (Fall): 58–63.

Sherman, Jennifer. 2009. *Those Who Work, Those Who Don't: Poverty, Morality, and Family in Rural America.* Minneapolis: University of Minnesota Press.

Silva, Jennifer M. 2013. *Coming Up Short: Working-Class Adulthood in an Age of Uncertainty.* New York: Oxford University Press.

Skeggs, Beverly. 1997. *Formations of Class and Gender.* London: Sage.

———. 2004. *Class, Self, Culture.* London: Routledge.

Solak, Nevin, John T. Jost, Nebi Sumer, and Gerald L. Clore. 2012. "Rage Against the Machine: The Case for System-Level Emotions." *Social and Personality Psychology Compass* 6, no. 9: 674–90.

Stacey, Judith. 1990. *Brave New Families: Stories of Domestic Upheaval in Late-Twentieth-Century America.* New York: Basic Books.

Steedman, Carolyn. 1987. *Landscape for a Good Woman: A Story of Two Lives.* New Brunswick, NJ: Rutgers University Press.

Stets, Jan E. 2012. "Current Emotion Research in Sociology: Advances in the Discipline." *Emotion Review* 4, no. 3: 326–34.

Stiglitz, Joseph E. 2012. *The Price of Inequality.* New York: W. W. Norton and Co.

Strasser, Annie-Rose. 2012. "Governors for 7 of the 10 Least-Insured Cities Have Refused to Expand Medicaid." *ThinkProgress,* September 27.

"Studied Sleep." 2008. *India Today Woman,* January, 10.

Sullivan, Amy. 2013. "The American Dream, Downsized." *National Journal,* April 26.

Sullivan, Bob. 2007. "Life Is Harder Now, Experts Say: After Paying Bills, Middle-Class Pockets Are Emptier." MSNBC.com, October 16.

Sullivan, Susan Burke Crawford. 2005. "Faith and Poverty: Personal Religiosity and Organized Religion in the Lives of Low-Income Urban Mothers." *Dissertation Abstracts International* 66, no. 5: 1978A–1979A.

Sullivan, Susan Crawford. 2006. "The Work-Faith Connection for Low-Income Mothers: A Research Note." *Sociology of Religion* 67, no. 1: 99–108.

Sullivan, Teresa A., Elizabeth Warren, and Jay Lawrence Westbrook. 2000. *The Fragile Middle Class: Americans in Debt.* New Haven, CT: Yale University Press.

———. 2006. "Less Stigma or More Financial Distress: An Empirical Analysis of the Extraordinary Increase in Bankruptcy Filings." *Stanford Law Review* 59, no. 2: 213–56.

Sum, Andrew, Neeta Fog, and Paul Harrington. 2003. "The Growing Gender Gap in College Enrollment and Degree Attainment in the U.S. and Their

Potential Economic and Social Consequences." Center for Labor Market Studies, prepared for the Business Roundtable.

Sutton, Robert. 1991. "Maintaining Norms About Expressed Emotions: The Case of Bill Collectors." *Administrative Science Quarterly* 36: 245–68.

Szeltner, Mark, Carl Van Horn, and Cliff Zukin. 2013. *Diminished Lives and Futures: A Portrait of America in the Great Recession Era.* February. John J. Heldrich Center for Workforce Development, Edward J. Bloustein School of Planning and Public Policy, Rutgers University.

Tabb, William K. 2007. "Wage Stagnation, Growing Insecurity, and the Future of the U.S. Working Class." *Monthly Review* 59, no. 2: 20–30.

Thomson, Susan C. 2003. "Boys Lose Ground to Girls in Race to Finish College." *St. Louis Post-Dispatch,* August 10.

Thorne, Deborah. 2010. "Extreme Financial Strain: Emergent Chores, Gender Inequality and Emotional Distress." *Journal of Family and Economic Issues* 31, no. 2: 185–97.

———. 2012. "Women's Work, Women's Worry?" In *Broke: How Debt Bankrupts the Middle Class,* edited by Katherine Porter, 136–53. Stanford, CA: Stanford University Press.

Thune-Boyle, Ingela C., Jan A. Stygall, Mohammed R. Keshtgar, and Stanton P. Newman. 2006. "Do Religious/Spiritual Coping Strategies Affect Illness Adjustment in Patients with Cancer? A Systematic Review of the Literature." *Social Science and Medicine* 63, no. 1: 151–64.

Townsend, Nicholas. 2002. *The Package Deal: Marriage, Work and Fatherhood in Men's Lives.* Philadelphia: Temple University Press.

Uchitelle, Louis. 2006. *The Disposable American: Layoffs and Their Consequences.* New York: Knopf.

Urbina, Ian. 2008. "In Hard Times, the Truck Stop Offers a Place to Pray." *New York Times,* June 18.

Vincent, Carol and Stephen J. Ball. 2007. "'Making Up' the Middle-Class Child: Families, Activities and Class Dispositions." *Sociology* 41, no. 6: 1061–77.

Vogler, Carolyn, and Jan Pahl. 1994. "Money, Power and Inequality within Marriage." *Sociological Review* 42, no. 2: 263–88.

Warren, Elizabeth, Amelia Warren Tyagi. 2003. *The Two-Income Trap: Why Middle-Class Parents Are Going Broke.* New York: Basic Books.

Weber, Max. 1958. *The Protestant Ethic and the Spirit of Capitalism.* New York: Scribner.

Weiss, Robert P. 2001. "Charitable Choice as Neoliberal Social Welfare Strategy." *Social Justice* 28, no. 1: 35–53.

West, Candace, and Don Zimmerman. 1987. "Doing Gender." *Gender & Society* 1, no. 2: 125–51.

Western, Bruce, Deirdre Bloome, Benjamin Sosnaud, and Laura Tach. 2012. "Economic Insecurity and Social Structure." *Annual Review of Sociology* 38: 341–59.

Western, Bruce, and Jake Rosenfeld. 2011. "Unions, Norms, and the Rise in U.S. Wage Inequality." *American Sociological Review* 76, no. 4: 513–37.

Wilkins, Amy. 2012. "'Not Out to Start a Revolution': Race, Gender, and Emotional Restraint among Black University Men." *Journal of Contemporary Ethnography* 41, no. 1: 34–65.

Wilkinson, Richard, and Kate Pickett. 2010. *The Spirit Level: Why Greater Equality Makes Societies Stronger*. New York: Bloomsbury Press, 2010.

Wineburg, Robert J., Brian L. Coleman, Stephanie C. Boddie, and Ram A. Cnaan. 2008. "Leveling the Playing Field: Epitomizing Devolution through Faith-Based Organizations." *Journal of Sociology and Social Welfare* 35, no. 1: 17–42.

Wolff, Edward N. 2007. "Recent Trends in Household Wealth in the United States: Rising Debt and the Middle-Class Squeeze." June. Levy Economics Institute of Bard College, Working Paper No. 502.

———. 2010. "Recent Trends in Household Wealth in the United States: Rising Debt and the Middle-Class Squeeze—An Update to 2007." June. Levy Economics Institute of Bard College, Working Paper No. 589.

———. 2012. "The Asset Price Meltdown and the Wealth of the Middle Class." National Bureau of Economic Research, Working Paper No. 18559.

Wright, Erik Olin, and Rachel E. Dwyer. 2003. "The Patterns of Job Expansions in the USA: A Comparison of the 1960s and 1990s." *Socio-Economic Review* 1, no. 3: 289–325.

Wuthnow, Robert, Conrad Hackett, and Becky Yang Hsu. 2004. "The Effectiveness and Trustworthiness of Faith-Based and Other Service Organizations: A Study of Recipients' Perceptions." *Journal for the Scientific Study of Religion* 43, no. 1: 1–17.

Young, Alford A., Jr. 2004. *The Minds of Marginalized Black Men: Making Sense of Mobility, Opportunity, and Future Life Chances*. Princeton, NJ: Princeton University Press.

Index